LET THE FLOWERS GO: A LIFE OF MARY CHOLMONDELEY

GENDER AND GENRE

Series Editor: *Ann Heilmann*

FORTHCOMING TITLES

Mary Cholmondeley Reconsidered
Carolyn W. de la L. Oulton and SueAnn Schatz (eds)

Edith Wharton's The Custom of the Country: A Reassessment
Laura Rattray (ed.)

www.pickeringchatto.com/gender

LET THE FLOWERS GO: A LIFE OF MARY CHOLMONDELEY

BY

Carolyn W. de la L. Oulton

LONDON
PICKERING & CHATTO
2009

Published by Pickering & Chatto (Publishers) Limited
21 Bloomsbury Way, London WC1A 2TH

2252 Ridge Road, Brookfield, Vermont 05036-9704, USA

www.pickeringchatto.com

BRITISH LIBRARY CATALOGUING IN PUBLICATION DATA

Oulton, Carolyn, 1972–
Let the flowers go: a life of Mary Cholmondeley. – (Gender and genre)
1. Cholmondeley, Mary, 1859–1925. 2. Women novelists, English – 20th
century – Biography. 3. Novelists, English – 20th century – Biography.
I. Title II. Series
823.9'12-dc22

ISBN-13: 9781851966493
e: 9781851966646

This publication is printed on acid-free paper that conforms to the American
National Standard for the Permanence of Paper for Printed Library Materials.

Typeset by Pickering & Chatto (Publishers) Limited
Printed in Great Britain by the MPG Books Group, Bodmin and King's Lynn

CONTENTS

LIST OF FIGURES

ACKNOWLEDGEMENTS

My biggest debt is of course to the Cholmondeley family. I can still remember the excitement of that initial phone call one hot summer's day, and how I watched helplessly as my daughter made off with my best pen and buried it in a mole hill while I was trying to make notes. Specifically I would like to thank Tom Cholmondeley for ignoring the obvious chaos in the background; and Alison Cholmondeley, who not only welcomed me into her house on several occasions, but kept up my strength with coffee and muffins at suitable intervals. Let's hear it for the box room!

Ruth Plowden has been a hilarious and supportive correspondent, and has filled in various gaps, as well as supplying copies of family portraits. Matt Ridley kindly allowed me to photograph the scrapbook collected by his grandmother Lady Ridley at the Carlton House Terrace Hospital during the First World War.

Canterbury Christ Church University allowed me a term's research leave when I was completing this book, and I am grateful for the enthusiastic support of my Victorianist colleagues: Adrienne Gavin, Peter Merchant and Andrew King. Further afield, I have encroached mercilessly on the time and enthusiasm of SueAnn Schatz and Marlene Davis.

I would also like to acknowledge the following for their generous help and good humour: David Sutton of Reading University, without whom I would still be trying to find Cholmondeley's copyright holder; Kathryn Campbell, for research in the Liverpool Records Office; the residents of Ufford, especially the two boys on bikes who showed me round the village, also Mrs Race, who told me where to find Cholmondeley's house, and Twig and Adam Thomas, who promptly invited me into their home when they caught me snooping around outside, and Christopher Hurst for information and photographs of the house; Janice Parker, who gave up her time to show me Hodnet Church and the parish registers; staff at the Shropshire Archives, who answered numerous email enquiries and kept me supplied with documents for a frantic three hours one Friday afternoon; Derek Williams, who sent me an article I had not been aware of, and which threw light on the aftermath of Cholmondeley's fame in Shropshire; Michael Meredith of Eton College Library; Alexis Weedon, who had never set eyes on me and was on leave at the time, kindly translated publishers' archives that had continued to defeat me; Mark Connelly and Hazel Basford for help with First World War queries; David Bedford and Paul Farmer of Canterbury Christ Church University Library, whose sympathy with my appetite for inter-library loans and microfilm was seemingly inexhaustible; Anselm Cramer, the Diocesan Archivist for Shrewsbury, Margaret Lightwood, Personal Assistant to the Bishop of Shrewsbury, and Gerard Boylan at Oscott College, for informa-tion on Canon Charles Cholmondeley; Toby Neal of the *Shropshire Star*; Zoe Stansell at the British Library, who is doubtless praying she never hears from me again; Richard Stileman, erstwhile of Edward Arnold Co.; David Holmes for a transcript of one of Cholmondeley's letters in his collection; Jo Outthwaite, for information on Richard Hugh Cholmondeley's time at Rugby school; and Ann Heilmann, the editor of the Gender and Genre series, for responding in record time to my (increasingly late night) queries while revising the manuscript.

Thanks are also due to staff at: the British Library; Suffolk Record Office; Bournemouth Record Office; the Red Cross Archive and Museum; City of West-minster Archives Centre; Torquay Reference Library; the Railway Museum; the National Archives at Kew; John Rylands Library, Manchester University; Cam-bridge University Library; the Harry Ransom Research Center, University of Texas at Austin; New York Public Library; Cheshire Records Office; the Bod-leian Library, University of Oxford; Canterbury Museum, New Zealand; and the National Library of Scotland.

PROLOGUE

A recent article in the *Guardian* lists the ten bestselling writers in the United States from the year 1900 – a list it describes as 'ghostly' – and asks the pertinent question of what happened to these books, challenging its readers to have heard of them, let alone read them.[1] But in the spring of 1900 the same newspaper, like so many others, was hotly debating the sensational success both in England and America of one of them, Mary Cholmondeley's *Red Pottage*.[2]

Her name itself – pronounced Chumlee – is a trap for the unwary, and it is now largely unknown, but her bestselling novel, currently out of print and read only by academics and English literature students, was one of the best loved scandals of 1899 – 'Have you read Pottage?' ran the joke in literary circles.[3] The story begins with adultery and a terrifying scheme of revenge, as one character is forced into an agreement that he will end his own life within a period of five months. His subsequent love for another woman as the time starts to run out provides much of the suspense of the novel. But the most memorable passages are those in which the writer heroine Hester Gresley insists on her independent right to work, even at the cost of her own steadily dwindling health, and to the fury of her narrow-minded clergyman brother, who insists on interpreting her writing as immoral. More than one reader took this as an attack on the Church, and while Cholmondeley was publicly defended in St Paul's Cathedral, there was a storm of protest from more conservative readers and she was denounced by name from at least one pulpit.[4]

The unmarried daughter of a Shropshire rector, Cholmondeley was often presented in the press as an unworldly spinster in the tradition of the Brontë sisters, and the myth of her secluded existence (largely perpetuated by herself) doubtless added something of its own to the fascination with her novel – by the early years of the twentieth century accounts in the press tended to focus on her having written her first novels while living in rural isolation, occluding the rather less romantic fact of her move to London in 1896.[5] In fact this reclusive spinster, as the familiar myth would have her, had been spending much of her time in London from the 1880s onwards, and was by the late 1890s the friend of such celebrated figures as Henry James, Mary Braddon and Howard Sturgis;

she knew various political luminaries, including both Asquith and Churchill, and received a warm tribute on her bestseller from James Barrie, the creator of Peter Pan. She was rumoured to have won over Queen Victoria with this her most scandalous novel,[6] and her books would be read in more than one war zone before she died.

Her life itself spanned the most extraordinary period. Born into a world thrown into uncertainty by the challenges of scientific debate to biblical literalism, most recently Darwin's *On the Origin of Species* in the year she was born, she was still writing in the years immediately after the First World War. A controversial and mysterious figure, she was reticent both in her dealings with journalists and in her private life. Nonetheless for later readers there was the titillating knowledge that she had written a series of private journals which disappeared from sight shortly after her death in 1925, but the published extracts from which hinted at a tragic love affair and a deep determination, in an age when women had, as she said herself, 'few incentives to perseverance'.[7]

In many ways her story is the familiar myth of the Victorian heroine as modern, feminist-orientated readers have reformulated it. The unmarried eldest daughter denied an education comparable to her brothers' and predestined instead to live at home and care for her ageing parents, Mary battled her own illness, the incessant demands of a large household and eventually her long-dreaded addiction to the painkiller morphia (an opium derivative), in order to fulfill what she saw as a heaven-sent vocation. Admired by many, she was derided by others, and she knew herself that even if she had been able to marry, it would have brought an end to her own ambitions. But if this was the cost of her writing, she knew that it was a price she was willing to pay. The worst disaster she could conceive, as her semi-autobiographical masterpiece devastatingly conveys, was not personal unhappiness but the permanent loss of a writer's best work.

1 'WATER TINTED WITH GOLD'

She spent nearly thirty years living in a series of London flats, but Mary Cholmondeley, as appreciative journalists never tired of pointing out,[1] came from an old and illustrious county family complete with ancestral acres. She was in her own person a powerful symbol of the ongoing shift in class power relations in late Victorian Britain, born into an aristocratic clan at a time of middle-class expansion, an encroachment of which she was always more than half aware. For the Cholmondeleys had been established in their own castle in Cheshire since the Conquest. In the early seventeenth century a younger son of the family was settled by one Mary Cholmondeley, 'the bold lady of Cheshire', at Vale Royal in the same county, and it was a descendant of his who became the first Lord Delamere in 1821.[2] Rather less glamorously, another descendant, Charles Cowper Cholmondeley, went into the Church, establishing himself in Hodnet, Shropshire, in the early nineteenth century. It was a lovely but small village north of the capital town Shrewsbury (to this day many residents of the town profess not to have heard of it, and only manage to give directions if asked for the slightly larger adjoining village of Market Drayton). There were few cottages in Hodnet and only a handful of suitable houses to provide a social life for the local gentry. The church, a surprisingly large one for such a small parish, still retains the family pews of its patrons, the Heber-Percy family.

The rector of Hodnet from 1807 was the famous hymnist Reginald Heber (best remembered for his still popular 'Holy holy holy', composed in 1820), and it was he who was responsible for building a new rectory in 1812. Within a few years it had become the scene of its first frustrated romance, when Maria Hare (aunt of Dean Stanley, who became Dean of Westminster in 1864) was not allowed to marry Martin Stow, the curate, on his departure for Calcutta with the newly appointed Bishop Heber in 1823.[3] But at the same period the love affair of another, better-connected local curate was to have a happier outcome. A letter from one Mary Heber of Hodnet Hall, herself the sister of the famous hymnist, gives a telling if somewhat prim view of Charles Cholmondeley from the cadet branch of the family, in 1820:

Our new Chaplain at Moreton, young Charles, goes on remarkably well and is very much liked by all his parishioners high and low. He is a rather shy odd fellow, but when well known is highly to be valued for his numerous good qualities and excellent disposition.[4]

Two years later they were married and their first son, Thomas, was born in November 1823, followed by Charles in February 1825. Reginald Heber lived for only a few years after being appointed to the Bishopric of Calcutta, and on his death at Trinchinopoly on 3 April 1826, Charles succeeded him as rector of the parish. On 20 April a third boy, Reginald, was born, and some time in this year the family moved into Hodnet Rectory.[5] Moving into a new house with two or possibly even three small children is unlikely to have been a relaxing experience for the parents, but it seems a fitting, if inopportune start to life for Reginald, a man who would later prove to be disorganized to the point of being actually irresponsible. Two years later, on 24 August 1828, a fourth son, Richard Hugh Cholmondeley, was born to the family at the rectory, 'a noble lad indeed' as his proud mother later wrote to her half brother Richard Heber.[6] The death of her husband in 1831 would mean that the family had to leave the rectory, but Mary Heber was in any case a capable, even formidable woman – inheriting the greatly indebted Hodnet Hall for her lifetime when the impecunious Richard died in 1833, she sold the celebrated library and succeeded in virtually freeing the estate from debt by her own death in 1846,[7] when it passed to her niece Mrs Emily Heber-Percy (she had married Algernon Percy, a grandson of the fifth Duke of Northumberland, in 1839, but the Heber family was important enough in its own right for the name to be added to Percy when she married).[8] However these events did not leave the young Richard Cholmondeley homeless, as he might otherwise have been. On 18 May 1841 his mother had married the new rector of Hodnet, Samuel Heyrick Macaulay,[9] who seems to have provided a home for at least one of the Cholmondeley brothers for some years after Mary's death.[10] Surprisingly, given the close connections with Hodnet Rectory, where she herself was born and later spent over two decades during her father's tenure, the more celebrated Mary Cholmondeley completely ignored this second marriage in later accounts of her grandmother.[11] In 1832 meanwhile another Cheshire family would be celebrating the arrival of a daughter. The oldest of five girls in what would become a family of eight children, Emily was born in March of that year to Henry Ralph Beaumont of Newby Park, also a younger son, and Catherine, daughter of the famous aviator George Cayley.[12] Four years younger than Richard Cholmondeley, Emily was six when her father died and thirteen when her mother married her second husband, James Anlaby Legard, and had two more boys, James and Allayne (who subsequently became Uncle Jimmy and Uncle Ally to her own children).[13] It is not known what the young Emily thought of her stepfather, but it was later remembered that she had not had an entirely happy childhood – apart from the death of her father, her beloved younger sister had fallen from her horse and become a permanent invalid when she was still young.[14] In Hodnet Richard Cholmondeley was part of an expansive family network, growing up between the rectory during his father's lifetime, and Hodnet Hall until his mother's death in 1846, the year before he went to Cambridge. The Owens of Condover Hall, on the other side of Shrewsbury, were relatives, as of course were the Heber-Percys who inherited Hodnet Hall, and who enclosed a considerable portion of the common in 1850.[15]

Like his future wife, Richard had lost one of his parents at a young age. But their early lives would have been different in other crucial respects, Richard going to Rugby school with his older brothers[16] while the more intellectual Emily received such education as she may have had at home. In their first year or two at Rugby (where none of them seems to have distinguished themselves, except for Charles's winning of the fifth form prize for Latin verse in 1843)[17] the Cholmondeley boys would have come under the influence of the famous Dr Arnold, celebrated in *Tom Brown's Schooldays* (1857), the novel of another old boy, Thomas Hughes. Richard then went on to Trinity College, Cambridge, was ordained deacon in 1852 and became the curate of Hodnet, before being fully ordained as a priest in Lichfield in 1853.[18] He was on excellent terms with his stepfather, who was also his father's successor as rector, Samuel Heyrick Macaulay; indeed it seems likely that he was living at the rectory from the time of his graduation from Cambridge.[19] It was probably shortly after this that he first spoke properly to the strikingly beautiful Emily Beaumont, at a dance.[20] It seems that he was the most orthodox and unadventurous of his brothers, content to fall into the clerical way of life and superintend the Hodnet parish, as his father had hoped at least one son would do – it was suspected by his children that, while his faith was deeply felt, he had given little or no thought to the debates that were so prominent a feature of Victorian intellectual and religious life from the 1840s onwards.[21] Certainly he remained on excellent terms with the locals of all denominations, an achievement that testifies to his tolerance and good humour, if also perhaps to a certain unreflecting acceptance of theological differences.[22]

In one sense this open mindedness was just as well, as in the meantime Charles was breaking with family tradition, studying at the Roman Catholic Oscott College between 1850 and 1852.[23] At Balliol College, Oxford, in 1844 he had intended to go into the Anglican Church. But at this point he came into contact with leaders of the Tractarian movement, an encounter that permanently unsettled his belief in Protestantism. In 1845 G. W. Ward, a fellow of Balliol, was condemned for his anti-Protestant teaching, and in the same year Newman spectacularly seceded to Rome. By now Charles had transferred to Cambridge, where it was later reported that he took counsel from the future Cardinal Manning, then Archdeacon of Chichester. Manning is supposed to have taken him into the church and told him to settle the matter with God, the result being that Charles converted to the Roman Catholic faith. After Oscott College, he published *Sixteen Articles on the Protestant Doctrine of Justification by Faith* in 1854. Between 1856 and 1860 he was in Rome studying his new faith with the Jesuits and he was finally ordained priest for the Diocese of Shrewsbury in August 1871.[24] It may not have been an entirely comfortable situation, so close to his Anglican brother (by then the vicar of Leaton) and shortly afterwards he moved to Chester, where he was ultimately made a canon, retiring in 1892 due to failing health. It is to the credit of both brothers that Richard's children grew up with little sense of a division between the Anglican and Catholic forms of worship. What they may not have known is that on Charles's conversion, Richard met his brothers to agree that he would be cut out of all their wills,[25] a decision which meant that he did not inherit the impressive Condover estate a few years later.

At around the same time, in 1851, Thomas was enterprising enough to take ship for New Zealand with a view to setting up as a farmer. His first months as an emigrant prompted some pitiful letters home, about prices being higher than in Belgravia, and the abrupt disappearance of an acquaintance to whom he had lent rather substantial amounts of cash. An asthmatic, he was relieved to find the climate suited to his constitution, but confessed to his brother Reginald that he was still suffering from a kind of hypochondria, or what would once have been termed 'the vapors'. In the summer of 1852 he wrote,

> You may have observed for some time before my leaving England that I was subject to a nervous disorder which I cannot well account for or explain. It first made its appearance a little before the death of our dear mother – since when it has been gradually creeping on.

In short, he found it difficult to eat in company. In an age less attuned to the effect of phobias on the sufferer, he feels obliged to go on, 'This is not a fancy – I say it gives me positive misery'.[26] It is hardly surprising that one resident observed of him,

> he is not well and will not come out (visiting). He is quite a gentleman, though, in every sense, and has only come out to settle a young cousin, I believe, but no one knows much about him. I suspect he lived rather delicately at home, for his work here has quite knocked him up ... fond of books, speaks slowly and softly ... and is in most respects very unlike one's idea of a colonist.[27]

The young cousin was George James Cholmondeley, whose daughter Mary would later keep track of her famous namesake, lovingly compiling a scrapbook over the decades to memorialize her English as well as her New Zealand relations.[28] It is also perhaps interesting to note that Thomas resembled other members of his family in his liking for books. Indeed his time in New Zealand inspired him to share his experience in *Ultima Thule; or Thoughts Suggested by a Residence in New Zealand*, published in 1854. An uninspiring read at this distance of time, it was nonetheless a useful guide to emigrants of the period – they were warned not to overload themselves with needless supplies, which could be bought on arrival, nor to assume that they could succeed at sheep farming without previous experience. These and other relevant matters safely dispatched, it returns to a familiar justification of the colonizing habit, and the greatness of the old country,

> I would commence, as a general rule applicable to almost every Englishman, by impressing upon the minds of my fellow citizens the vast superiority of the country, which so many are without due reflection leaving, over any other country, whether in the Old or New World.[29]

Writing aptitude aside, there was no doubting Thomas's enjoyment of literature. It was a bent that Mary Cholmondeley would later imply had been shared by her father but rather less so by her mother, Emily Beaumont.

There is no contemporary evidence against which to measure Mary's further insinuations that her parents' marriage was not a happy one,[30] but certainly it seems that from the start of their marriage in 1855, not all of Richard's relations were prepared to approve of his young wife. In the early years of their marriage, while he was still curate of Hodnet, one cousin ticked her off severely for the way she dressed her hair, telling her that it was not in keeping with her position (before adopting the offending hairstyle herself when it came into fashion a year later).[31] Emily, however, never wore her hair in this style again, adopting one that was, if more respectable, considerably less becoming. No known photograph of her survives, but one taken some time after her marriage apparently showed her as 'very handsome, with parted hair and noble brow, and magnificent dark eyes, but sad in expression'.[32] She took an informed interest in politics and scientific advances, and may well have found it difficult to adapt to the life of a country parson's wife, with its circumscribed society and the often tedious obligations in the parish. In fact very little is known about her at this stage of her life, although Mary Cholmondeley's highly critical sketch twenty-two years after her death has led to her being branded a mirthless puritan, 'this grimly repressed woman' as one scholar expresses it.[33] But whatever her reservations about or suitability for her new position, Emily had a determined sense of duty, and possessed in addition both intelligence and courage – qualities she would pass on in full measure to her children.

It is not certain where Emily first set up house in Hodnet. She and her husband make no appearance in the census of 1861 or in surviving post office directories of the time, but letters from the early 1850s suggest that both Richard and Reginald had been living with the Revd Macaulay at the rectory, a short walk from the church, and it seems most probable that Richard brought his wife to live there after their marriage. Their daughter Mary would tell readers nearly seventy-five years later that she and her older siblings had been born in the rectory, and that her uncle Reginald was a member of her parents' household for a while at least.[34] Again, she claims that in the early years of the marriage, an eccentric aunt, Georgiana Cholmondeley, was living with them as well, having been brought up by Richard from Torquay, and a Georgina Cholmondeley is registered as having died in neighbouring Market Drayton in 1886.[35] What they felt about these arrangements in the early years of their marriage is not known, except through Mary's much later comment that her mother found Reginald trying and bore with his presence patiently.[36] As she was herself a child at the time it is not certain from whom she is getting this information. Otherwise almost nothing is known of the relationship between Emily and her new husband, except that eleven months after their marriage, in May 1856, she gave birth to her first son, Thomas. Reginald was born in October of the following year, followed by Mary on 8 June 1859. By 1861 Richard had left Hodnet to take up another curacy in Farnborough, moving into the vicarage with his growing family.[37]

Caroline Essex (known as Essex), who would herself become the mother of a celebrated writer, Stella Benson, was born to Emily and Richard in January of this year, and just over a year later came Richard (called Dick in the family), in February 1862. The following year the fortunes of the children's uncle Thomas took a dramatic turn, when the male line of the Owens of nearby Condover Hall ran out and he inherited the house on the condition that he take the name of Owen, a condition he sensibly accepted.[38] In the same year another daughter, Diana, was born to the Cholmondeleys in Farnborough. In the spring of 1864 Thomas married a local girl of good family, as he had once urged Reginald to do in a letter from New Zealand.[39] Victoria, the daughter of Lady Louisa Cotes of Woodcote, was a god-daughter of the Queen, from whom she took her name, and her pedigree was unimpeachable. Local newspapers gave a rapturous commentary on their wedding in March. Beginning with fog and drizzle, the day brightened up as the bridal party, with Mary Cholmondeley among the twelve bridesmaids, and the bride dressed in silk and Bruxelles lace, reached Hodnet Church. The tenants turned out in force to wish them well, 130 Condover schoolchildren were given tea in the school room, and after the departure of the bride and groom, a ball in the Corn Market finished off the day for their well wishers. Indeed all the neighbouring villages vied with each other, subscribing for presents and hanging banners from the cottages. After the day itself had passed there was a public dinner at the Red Lion in Westbury to celebrate the marriage.[40]

Then, quite unexpectedly, Thomas died of malaria on his wedding tour in Florence. She had not been one of the family for very long at the time of her husband's death, but 'Aunt Victoria' would remain close certainly to Mary for the rest of her life. Under the terms of Thomas's will Charles had no claim on anything he had to leave, and so it was the middle surviving brother Reginald who now inherited Condover. His fecklessness would ultimately lead to disaster and even during his lifetime the long and involved series of loans and mortgages on the estate must have caused considerable anxiety to the rest of the family.[41] But when he first came into it, the Condover property was worth something like £4,000 a year.[42] From the security of this position he would be able to pursue his interests in exotic wildlife and art (he was the sculptor of an effigy that still lies in Hodnet Church among memorials to various Heber-Percys), and he made many noteworthy friends, including Mark Twain[43] and Edward Lear. It was at about this time, in 1865, that Richard became vicar of Leaton, and it was here that a fourth daughter, Victoria, would be born in January 1868. In October 1867 Reginald had married the Hon. Alice Mary Egerton, but again this marriage was to end in tragedy when Alice died little more than a year afterwards, leaving an infant daughter who also died just over two weeks later. It must have been difficult for him to watch his brother's growing family, especially when an eighth child was born to Richard and Emily in November 1869. They called her Hester and she would give her name to her sister Mary's most celebrated heroine.

Richard and Emily would spend nearly nine years in Leaton Vicarage with their eight children. Again, later events have all but hidden Emily's early relationship with her children from view. She is portrayed as having lived 'a life of almost puritanical severity, denying herself pleasures and relaxation, imposing the same rigorous restraints on her children, constantly in conflict with her mild-mannered, easy-going husband'.[44] Emily may have been the stricter parent of the two, but if she sometimes appeared anxious and ill at ease, this may have been at least partly due to ill health. In keeping with the ideal of the archetypal Victorian family, she had given birth to eight children in less than fourteen years, the last when she was herself approaching thirty-eight. Shortly after Hester's birth came the onset of a creeping paralysis which would eventually leave her a permanent invalid.

There were apparently few toys for the children to play with, but the household was certainly not as austere as this might suggest – even through the double filter of Mary's memory and an editor's recasting, one can hear the pride in Emily's voice as she claims that she had only to arrange a few Noah's ark animals in a picturesque attitude and her children would at once begin to tell stories about them.[45] As a child Mary was given a ruled composition book by her governess, which she filled with stories, including the adventures of the family dog. In the mornings before lessons the children would read religious works with their father and in the evening he would read aloud from the novels of Walter Scott, Jane Austen, William Makepeace Thackeray, Charles Dickens, George Eliot and the then popular Edward Bulwer Lytton. That they were loving and involved parents is not in doubt. Richard's appreciation of old china appeared both in his daughter Mary's collecting habits (in an early article she mentions buying up unwanted china from the less discerning Hodnet cottagers)[46] and in an affectionate portrait of the Revd Allwyn in her novel *Sir Charles Danvers* (1889). There were also of course close ties with Condover, where several of the family, including Mary, seem to have stayed for nearly seven weeks in the autumn of 1871 – a dreamy child, she describes herself as standing on a bridge 'for ever so long, watching the water tinted with gold by an autumn sun, the little fishes darting about, or the big trout finning quietly along.'[47] Clearly she was deeply conscious herself of the idyllic nature of such interludes.

A recently discovered almanac of Mary's for 1872 offers a necessarily brief but near daily record of life in Leaton. There are outings to Shrewsbury (incidentally the birthplace of Charles Darwin), but the family is bothered by constant colds, with Mary and her mother being the most regular victims. Mary had been a healthy and robust child until at the age of seven she fell a prey to asthma, when 'The hereditary taint came out, and my health fell like a pack of cards' as she later put it.[48] It is uncertain whom she held to blame for this hereditary taint – her uncle Thomas was asthmatic,[49] it is likely that Emily was a sufferer, and certainly her maternal grandmother used a respirator. But from that time onwards she would suffer from weak health and painful bouts of asthma, which left her bedridden for up to a fortnight at a time. Her mother sympathized with her least healthy child, and with reason, even as she enjoined her to try and conceal her sufferings rather than upset the rest of the family on her account. It seems not to have occurred to either of her parents that her symptoms could be substantially alleviated. While Mary did in fact use a respirator, she later claimed that in her youth asthma was thought to be incurable,[50] and as late as 1895 she was clearly unacquainted with the ideas in the standard work on her condition, Henry Hyde Salter's *On Asthma: Its Pathology and Treatment*, first published the year after she was born.[51]

Even at this early stage Emily's own health was already a source of constant concern. Her precise condition is not known, but in addition to the wasting disease that would eventually leave her unable to move about freely, she seems to have suffered from what contemporary accounts term 'neurasthenia', an almost endlessly expandable term that covered the spectrum of mental and nervous ailments. In the brief accounts in Mary's 1872 almanac her mother is often away seeing doctors in London – at one point she is absent for ten weeks.[52] She is known to have placed herself at one stage under the care of Dr Charles Radcliffe, the famous specialist in neurasthenic illness and proponent of electric therapy after whom the Oxford hospital is named.[53] Richard seems often to have accompanied her on these journeys, which helps to explain why all the Cholmondeley children felt such a strong lifelong bond with their old nurse, Frances Coupland, or Ninny. A widow, Ninny had been with the family since she came as a servant with Emily Beaumont on her marriage and she seems never to have considered leaving (turning down at least one offer of marriage in 1889, from a man who apparently made enquiries about her on the way back from his last wife's funeral).[54] Mary would recall her strictness and fiery temper, but also her unswerving loyalty to the family and her unselfish love of the eight children in her care. Still, Mary also clearly felt close to her mother at this stage, recording that she has written her long letters and less frequently that she has received one in return. One entry from 24 April includes the information 'Got a letter from Mama, oh such a nice one very kind.'[55] At one point Mary, herself a keen rider, notes that her mother has been given a wide saddle to enable her to ride too.[56] In this year she also remarks that her uncle Regie is furnishing a house in London, and there are brief references to visits from her grandmother and her uncle Charles.[57] During this year she began to learn German with the governess, Miss Parr.[58] But already the keynote of her life is beginning to emerge. The boys attend a dance at Hodnet Hall, and Mary's illness prevents her from going with them.[59] She cannot attend Sunday worship on 3 November because the prohibitive cost of fuel means that the church cannot be heated. Again, she is full of admiration for the scenery in Aberystwyth, where she has gone with her mother, Essex and Diana, but registers no surprise that she is unwell during the visit.[60] Illness would come to dominate Mary's life and it would ultimately all but destroy her relationship with her mother in ways that neither of them could have foreseen.

But if impaired health was a source of intermittent woe to the young Mary even at the age of twelve, the suggestion of monotony in this first almanac seems not to have affected her as yet. She comes across as an affectionate child, secure in her relationship with her parents and full of affection for her brothers and sisters, whose birthdays are carefully noted along with the receipt of any letters from brothers at school. There is the occasional moment of worry, as when Hester is diagnosed with whooping cough, but there are eggs to collect and ponies to learn to ride, as well as the perpetual correspondence that suggests so forcibly to a modern reader just how much time there was to be filled in a day.[61] In a redolent phrase on Victoria's birthday in January, she comments that her sister is now four and 'old enough to start lessons.'[62] One would rather like to know what the lessons comprised.

Given the heritage of Reginald Heber, it is not altogether surprising to see a literary bent in the family, and Emily herself was apparently a notable composer of dramatic verses.[63] Certainly all the Cholmondeley girls enjoyed books, and at least three of them painted as well – Mary would briefly consider a career as an artist, Victoria exhibited watercolours many years later, and Hester's extant picture of Hodnet Rectory testifies to her skill in this direction.[64] There is no evidence to show whether the men of the family shared this aesthetic bent, although Richard evinced a certain skill in arranging flowers and china.[65] If the boys entertained literary or artistic ambitions, there is no surviving record to prove it. It is in the more circumscribed lives of the girls that the family instinct for beauty seems to have provided an outlet for considerable and otherwise almost unemployable energies.

2 'ONE GREAT HOPE'

Whether the almanac had cramped her thoughts, and she had made complaints to that effect, or whether it was simply a kind idea and a suitable present, is not known. But it was over the Christmas of 1872 that Mary, like many girls of the same age before and since, began to keep a personal journal, in a leather-bound book given to her by her governess Miss Parr. It would be the first of three such volumes, spanning a period of over thirty years and breaking off only in the years immediately before the First World War. Their existence was known of afterwards because, at her death, Mary bequeathed them to a younger friend,[1] the distinguished critic and memoirist Percy Lubbock, who used them as the basis of a memoir published in 1928. They were then thought to have disappeared for the better part of a century, before correspondence with members of the Cholmondeley family in the summer of 2005 led to the rediscovery of two of the volumes. Together they make an extraordinary document. It is not just that they give a privileged view of Mary's character, as she carefully delineates her own personal development; her descriptive powers are such that certain scenes almost seem to have been composed in colour, literally inviting the reader to see pictures behind the words. It comes as no surprise that she once wanted to be a painter,[2] and it is less surprising still that she would eventually make her name in literature.

But the first entry shows no prescience of these things, beginning instead with a time-honoured formula and a certain lack of punctuation, 'Miss Parr has written my name in this beautiful diary which she gave me yesterday namely Christmas Day.'[3] She then goes on to her other presents, a book from her aunt Percy and a pencil case from her mother among them. There had been carol singers in the evening and fireworks on the lawn, a surprise thought up by her brothers. Two days later her mother is away in London, but she is able to report a dress rehearsal of their play 'The Queen of Hearts', for which their father has taken great trouble with the costumes. And on New Year's Eve there are bonbons under the children's pillows – their mother still being away, Essex is 'misguided' enough to recognize her sister's handwriting among them, but Mary is insistent that it is the fairies' work. It is worth noting, given her daughter's later damning

portrayal in the 'Mother' section of *Under One Roof*,[4] that Emily was the usual
director of plays and distributor of fairy comfits. There would come a time when
Mary would deeply resent this mother whom she closely resembled, and whose
household role she was forced to take on only a few years later. But this first diary
shows an affectionate mother, involved as a matter of course with her children's
amusements and not yet showing the nervous strain of an illness that had already
partially paralysed her.

It is Mary's own ill health that first threatens to overshadow the buoyant
descriptions of plays and the notes of 'We're all jolly good fellows' drifting up the
stairs to bed.[5] Early in the new year she has been unable to accept an invitation
to tea because, the horse being under physic, she has no means of getting home
again – she is herself too weak to walk both ways.[6] And then, to her chagrin, she
finds she could have gone after all, because a horse had been borrowed to pull
the carriage. But soon she is reporting on another outing, to lunch with a family
called Adams, and how the older son, 'seemed desirous of impressing on me the
number of balls to which he had gone and was going. He must have mistaken my
age or forgotten it.'[7] This readiness to laugh both at herself and the people she
met (the unfortunate Master Adams had 'a nose which would have amply served
two persons') was a trait Mary would take with her through life, and she would
use it in middle age to write a bestselling, mildly scandalous novel. Already in
1872 she was practising satire, through the medium of the family dog, who is
made to say in 'Jet's Story' that 'My mistress has two brothers older than herself
namely Tom and Regie. They are both at Wellington College, and come home
for the holidays which always seem to me much too long.'[8]

That June Miss Parr announced that she had enough money to set up house
on her own and was therefore leaving the vicarage. Bizarrely she seems to have
laid claim to the dog on her departure, but Mary, who seems to have slept with
Jet literally by her bedside, reports with some relief that her father stuck up for
her and said she should keep the dog if she wanted (this beloved animal was
deemed worthy of black-bordered mourning cards when she died a few years
later).[9] Her mother was in Brighton, presumably for her health, and Mary and
her father joined her there shortly after the settling of the dog incident. But again
illness disrupted their plans – after an arrival in the rain Mary was forced to
remain indoors and take her breakfast in bed.[10] A few weeks later she comments
with sardonic humour, 'It is needless to say that I did not get better at Brighton
but worse, and came home with Papa.'[11]

On this occasion at least the return home seems to have been beneficial – this
would not always be the case in future years – and she is soon writing about the
putting on of a puppet show for the maids and some neighbouring children.[12] It
is a commonplace that the Victorian family went to lengths that seem extraordinary in a media age, in their efforts to entertain each other. In the midst of the

preparations for this lavish drama the new governess, Mlle Keller, arrived, and was quickly pressed into service dressing sixteen fairies, to be managed by Mary and her mother in an improvised theatre in the boys' room.[13] It must also have been at about this time that Mary began, in dryer vein, her History of England as far as the time of Elizabeth,[14] and a complete History of Greece, desperately trying to fix the facts in her mind from a five-volume edition of Gibbon's *Decline and Fall*. No vestige of this information, she later admitted, had she ever been enabled to stick in her mind.[15]

Shortly after the puppet show in August she became ill once again, with an attack that lasted this time for three months. By late October, plans had been made for her to go to London with her parents, where she could stay with her grandmother while medical advice was obtained. But, saying goodbye to her family, Mary knew that she would not be returning to the vicarage at Leaton.[16] For after the death of the previous incumbent, Samuel Macaulay, her father had suddenly been appointed to the rectorship of Hodnet, in the gift of his cousins the Heber-Percys. It was a post previously held by his father and grandfather, and in the village where he had himself served as curate. It was moreover a splendid opportunity. As Mary herself acknowledged,[17] even with a reduction of £600 per annum, it was still one of the best livings in Shropshire. Although the value of the living would decline from a net figure of £1,800 in 1879 (the first year for which it is possible to obtain details) to less than half that amount in 1896, it would initially have been a lucrative post, providing a welcome source of income for the family of ten.[18] Richard would be returning to the house where he had first lived with his wife and where several of their children had been born. However, his eldest daughter for one was not anxious to return, in fact her comments in her diary give the distinct impression that she had no recollection of the house and acknowledged no personal connection with it.[19]

As she said goodbye to the rest of the family, Victoria realized with surprise that her sister was actually going, the nurse cried and even Mlle's eyes were wet. In fact the only collected person seems to have been the young Hester, who at less than four was too taken up with Mary's respirator to comprehend the fact of her imminent departure. Mary remembered a mournful parting from the house, in which she lingered over every field and tree.[20] But even in this emergency she was constantly taking in events and passers by, remarking in her diary some time later how they had nearly run over an old man who began crossing the road only to change his mind and begin walking the other way: 'His only excuse was that he was old and perhaps silly', is her somewhat dismissive remark.[21]

They arrived in Hyde Park Gate in the fog, to find Mrs Legard busy packing for a winter in Cannes. Mary reports with interest that the two doctors she saw both ordered her to Hastings, and both gave detailed and exactly contrary directions as to her diet.[22] To Hastings she duly went, where she was soon joined by Mlle Keller, who seems to have operated as a kindly presence, surprisingly so in the light of her later behaviour. Her mother had to return to Hodnet before Christmas, collecting Dick from school on the way, and it was Mlle who was surprised decorating the table on Christmas morning, insisting that Mary shut her eyes until all was ready. Mary herself is remarkably uncomplaining about being stranded in the town with only her governess for company over the festive period; her aside, 'When I was having my breakfast in bed this morning as I always do now' simply introduces a bunch of violets sent by a new acquaintance, one Mrs Wallace.[23]

In the new year her father and Tom came down for a night, and in the following month her diary records both this visit and her distress on receiving a letter from her brother admitting that he had failed his matriculation. He had told her that it would be a disgrace to the sixth form if he failed, and now she was convinced that shyness and nervousness alone had been his undoing. As she wrote she was waiting anxiously for the next day's post, when there might be a more detailed account from her mother.[24] But her mind was also on events of more national importance. She had just heard that the Liberals had won the local election, and she was full of enthusiasm, damped only by fears that the Conservatives would yet gain the majority, which 'for England's sake' she hoped they would not. She herself was staunchly Liberal and damning about her neighbours in Hastings who had no reason to give for their Conservatism. She remarks acidly that 'there is a heap of Conservatives in North and South Shropshire', and interestingly adds 'I know Mamma is Radical, but I wonder what Papa is'.[25] At a time when women could not vote, and were supposed by many to think with their husbands, it is significant that Mary has evidently discussed politics with her mother rather than her kindly but less intellectual father. In the event Disraeli's Conservatives went on to win the election with a majority of 112 in England alone.[26]

It is shortly after this entry, in which Mary is so enthused with the cause she supports, that her diary gives the first sign of another, sadder characteristic. Like her mother, she was to suffer from serious depression in later life, and on 19 February she reports the death of another Mary, one of her many cousins, on the Isle of Man. It had been a sad life, full of suffering, but hearing of the death, this Mary's first emotion was not pity or relief. Herself only fourteen, she admits that her first feeling was one of envy:

> Envy for the quiet grave which is now hers, and for its peace. It is a wrong feeling, but it will come. I feel as if she had finished all her task here, and is now in peace, while I must toil on for years and years perhaps before I can attain to what she already possesses. It seems such a long time to look forward to, how near, or how far away who can tell. And in the grave there will be peace and there will be rest.[27]

A few weeks after this she resumes her diary as if these thoughts had never been expressed, with a commentary on the local fireworks to celebrate the arrival of Duchess Marie of Russia, who had married Prince Alfred on 23 January 1874.

Over the Easter holiday her mother brought Dick and Essex to see her, and they all travelled back via Wellington to see the boys. It was here that Essex developed some mysterious malady and had to be left behind, while the others travelled on to Tenby to rejoin the rest of the family. But when news came through that Essex had been diagnosed with the measles, it was her mother who at once returned to look after her.[28] Within a year of her death Mary would regret the gulf that had grown up between this stern woman and her children.[29] But there is no obvious sign of discord in the record of these earlier years. Mary's account of what happened next is characteristic: 'I think I need hardly say how we had the measles, and in August were installed in Hodnet Rectory, half of which was then roofless and open to the sky'.[30] There is less romance in this comment than she had accorded the departure from Leaton, which felt as if she had been born in it and which she could not leave without almost breaking down. Her first description after a silence of nearly five months is a retrospect of the scenery round Leaton Vicarage, with a lament that it may all be changed even if she does set eyes on it again. But if she was not immediately taken with her new home, as she perceived it to be, she was more impressed by Bishop Hobhouse, who confirmed her in Hodnet Church in October. Just up from an asthma attack, it was uncertain until the last minute whether she would be able to get through the service, but she remembered with awe his sermon on serving God not in our own way, but in His.[31] It was a theme that would have particular resonance for her over the years.

That November she finally offers her impressions of the rectory where she would live for the next twenty-two years. They had had snow and frost, and the building work was still going on, 'slowly, and therefore we will hope surely'. They had earlier invested in a stove to protect them against the excesses of the winter weather, and '[t]he day it arrived it was lighted as soon as possible, and it had not burned long before the house was densely full of thick smoke, much of course to our satisfaction'. Luckily it had now been cured of this trick, but there was more serious work to come, before the family took refuge at the Hall and the dining room door was broken in on to the stairs. Mary alone would remain among the debris, as it was considered, for some unspecified reason, 'best'.[32] Then the stove broke down again, in spite of 'incessant bangs and thumps', and had to be replaced with another, which luckily settled down after the first day, when it 'nearly stifled us'.[33] But, Mary told herself pragmatically, how much stronger she must be to bear the cold of this house, when only the year before she had been obliged to leave Leaton, warmer than this, for the safety of Hastings.

Mary would come to love Hodnet Rectory, although the life of a rector's daughter appealed to her no more than the wifely responsibilities suited her mother. A stone's throw away at the Hall were the Heber-Percys, her relations through her paternal grandmother. Mary never became close to this large family of cousins, with two possible exceptions, Algernon and Alice. But inevitably over the years there would be visits to Hodnet Hall, and Mary would even accompany her uncle and aunt on holiday, which admittedly she seems to have found something of a strain.[34] Nearby also were the rector of Stoke, Rowland Corbet, and his wife, who became close to all the family. Uncle Regie of course was fairly local too, and repaid past assistance with regular hospitality at Condover Hall.[35] It was at about this time that he seems to have started accumulating debts.[36] It has been said in explanation of such indebtedness that 'the basic aristocratic problem of reconciling income and expenditure, which fluctuated independently of one another, persisted through the nineteenth century',[37] the reasons for this being the need for family portions, house building, purchase of land, agricultural improvement and non-agricultural enterprises. But Reginald seems to have engaged in none of these activities. Far from improving the estate, he was away travelling for much of the time, in pursuit of exotic plants,[38] and he had no children on whom settlements would need to be made. The estate itself was a large one, but Reginald himself was not good with money and failed to supervise the management of his affairs as closely as he might have done. By 1874 he was already auctioning furniture and valuables.[39] It was a portent of worse to come. The 1880s ushered in a period of agricultural depression, and indeed landowning families were increasingly turning to middle-class money to bail them out. The sons of gentry were increasingly likely to go into business or to marry the daughters of commercial men.[40] Of Mary's three brothers, Regie made a traditional choice in going into the army, but Tom became a land agent and Dick would become a successful vintner,[41] both professions more associated with the middle class.

For now though Mary was surrounded by family, and the greatest drawback to life in Hodnet was its isolation from the social life of London. It was a small village by any standards – the census for 1871 gives a figure of 1,750 for the township and by 1891 the civil parish (numbers for the township are not given) comes out at only 1,587. Mary would later tell a journalist that she could only socialize within a radius of five miles, the maximum distance that the family pony could manage.[42] In effect this would have meant a severely circumscribed round of visits among the few families of her own class, relieved only by the visits of friends and acquaintances from further afield. As she got older she was expected to play a part in the life of the parish, including the traditionally aristocratic 'cottage visiting'. Again there was not a large number of cottages to visit, but her later accounts of ponderous village talk suggest a patient tolerance on her part, and more than that, a long familiarity. She would later turn her powers of close observation to good use, capturing something of these visits in fictional form.[43] But for a young girl of exceptional intelligence and weak health, this aspect of country life was dreary enough. The – to a visitor – idyllic seclusion of Hodnet over a hundred years after she left confirms that she was not being entirely fanciful when she described herself as being cut off from contact with anyone she might have wanted to talk to.

At this point, however, she was of course still in the schoolroom, and full of the first Christmas in Hodnet. The weather was seasonal (i.e. extremely cold), and regrettably one of the robins who took shelter in the house was summarily eaten by the cat. There was a Christmas dinner and then Mary, Essex and Diana went with their parents to the Heber-Percys at Hodnet Hall, where their cousins chased them with mistletoe. But Mary herself could not join in the more boisterous entertainments, drawing the line at such games as 'Walk, lady, walk', in which whoever was caught was made to run a gauntlet of knotted handkerchiefs. She and her sisters were to stay the night, but Essex and Diana had forgotten their petticoats and consequently could not get up the next morning. How they got home is not known. Mary professed herself quite well and was anxious only to be allowed to return on the 30th, when there would be a conjuror.[44]

Whether or not she went is not recorded, but ominously on New Year's Day she was alone in the study at home, the drawing room being too cold to sit in. She then admits that Hester, Diana and Victoria are likewise left behind, but the others have gone to Condover and, despite the specific invitation of her uncle Regie, her mother has not seen fit to let her go in such cold weather. Instead she confides to herself somewhat sorrowfully that she is now considered too old to be left bonbons by the fairies, although she has left little packets for Hester and Victoria under their pillows. Having given vent to this small sorrow, she then goes on to question the future:

> why am I always looking forward to when I am older[?] I do not hope rationally to be happier then, than now. I am very happy now, yet I never really enjoy the present, from looking forward to something I shall enjoy more in the dim future. I have not the least idea what it is that I look forward to, at least, directly I think of anything, it does not seem to be quite it, and the nearest approach to it is the delight of getting older, which after all is quite without a reason, for I am sure I shall want to stop once I am eighteen or at any rate twenty.[45]

These bewildering shifts in tone and mood are, as Mary herself was well aware, indicative of her age in writing – she was fifteen at the time. Nor is her setting of a personal horizon at twenty entirely arbitrary for a Victorian girl, aware that youth and virtue should be her most prized attributes. But the concern with what her future was to be would persist, and eventually stimulate her to escape the constraints of being simply 'the rector's daughter'. Next she turns her attention to the news of a recent disaster at sea, when an emigrant ship lost all but three of its four hundred passengers and crew; she cannot help picturing their last moments and thinking in turn of the homeless in the freezing snow now covering Shropshire. 'And what have I done that all the good things of this earth should be lavished on me while they perish from cold and hunger[?]'[46] While the last sentiments are recognizable as the conventional guilt felt by a privileged class confronted with the suffering of the poor, the sympathetic impulse is nonetheless genuine. Indeed the rapid change of mental direction, beginning with a grievance about confectionary and ending with the imagined horror of being out in the dark on a freezing night, is relayed almost as if in 'real time'.

Mary began 1875 by looking forward uncertainly to the future; by the end of it she would have formed plans for a career of her own and her formal education would have come to an end. It was early in the year that she first met her uncle Regie's friend the artist John Nettleship, celebrated for his pictures of animals. He had come to make a sketch of Victoria's face, to be inserted into an unfinished picture abandoned by Regie, himself a talented amateur artist, some years before. Ironically Victoria, who would later become an artist in her own right, was the one to entertain Nettleship with impromptu stories (she also whiled away the five-hour sittings by sketching the artist himself), while Mary picked up tips on how to draw a horse's leg or a man's arm.[47] At this stage it was art and not writing that attracted Mary and, not having drawing lessons as her Heber-Percy cousins did, she was keen to learn all she could from this unexpected opportunity. The criticism of Mary's drawing incidentally seems to have been more honest than the painter's own work – Emily thought the picture of Victoria too flattering to be 'quite like'.[48]

But what is immediately apparent from this entry is the humour of Mary's narrative style and her delight in mimicry. She records in detail the insights into horses' muscular movement, for her own reference; once this subject is disposed of, she gives a no less minute but exuberantly funny account of a dinner given by her father for the workmen. She herself was not present but listening from Diana's room:

> 'Oh come Jim you know you must sing.'
> > 'Oi've got a cold.'
> > 'Oh nonsense.'
> > Great clatter of fists and heels.
> > 'Oi don't know a song.'
> > Great noise. Someone tells him of a certain song 'as he knows'. At last he is persuaded to sing the song which he has intended to all the while[49]

The following day there was another dinner for the choir, at which Paul the coachman, who had been with them at Leaton, sang and 'Every instant we thought he would break down, and it really was a great relief when he got safe to the end, when we all clapped vigorously to make him think we had liked it'.[50]

Then in the spring Mary was ill again with what she describes as 'an attack of asthma and biliousness', but she rallied in time for a visit from her cousins, when she put on a puppet play of her mother's devising, with Regie and Essex. As Mary expressed it with some satisfaction, 'None of the dolls fell on their faces and Regie's hands were only seen once'.[51] Again it is significant that Emily had never before seen one of her own plays performed, as she had always been behind the scenes assisting with the dolls. She was also supportive of Tom, who was now off to Cambridge to retake his matriculation (successfully this time). In the last years of her life she seems to have been morbid and distanced from her children, but such evidence as there is suggests that what Mary remembered as a stern temperament was in fact the result of her long illness, resulting in a depressive complaint.[52] At this point Mary seems still to have enjoyed a sympathetic relationship with her mother, but the year would end in catastrophe, marking the beginning of the rift between them.

For now life at Hodnet went on much as ever. In April Regie joined the Faithful Military Academy in Storrington, near London,[53] and some time in that spring Mary herself went on a visit to the metropolis. Over the summer Paul fell off a hay bale and broke a rib – Mary's concern for this old servant as a member of the household is something to set against the exclusiveness she routinely assumed in matters of class.[54] Then there was a week at Condover, where Mary met Nettleship again, and was 'foolish enough' to confide to him that she wanted to be a painter, while he in turn was foolish enough to flatter her about it, before their rapport unfortunately foundered on the social status of actors and the appropriateness of training as an animal painter by working on bowls of fruit.[55] Then there was hospitality to be shown to visiting cousins, before she could return to her painting, which she now looked to as both vocation and release, her 'one great hope':

> I feel so eager to work hard with this in particular, to work and get on, get up one step of the ladder ... I think it must be a bad thing to dream and build castles as I have been doing lately, dreaming that I am a great painter, that beautiful forms rise on the parchment at my will, and fame smiles on me and beckons me on. Then I wake up and torture myself with doubts, whether I have enough talent. I cannot bear to answer myself that I have not ... I still cling to my bright castle in the air, which always fades when I look straight at it.[56]

It was in December that the first sign of trouble came. Mary was excited about the Drayton Ball, they were to have a house party for a dance at the Hall, her brothers were coming home for Christmas. Then her mother became ill and was consigned to bed for a month. Mary found herself acting as housekeeper, a role she never enjoyed but which she commented ominously, would probably continue 'for some time to come'. They decided to go ahead with the plans for Christmas, but then the dance had to be postponed when a great aunt of the Heber-Percy cousins died. And just as Mary was attempting to cheer herself up with holly to decorate the house, Mlle came into the drawing room and asked for 'a little conversation'. Apparently without warning she began by saying she could not continue with the present state of things, that Mary was 'vulgaire', and 'grossière', so unladylike, and that it made her ill to feel she was always being criticized, winding up with an attack on her impertinence in the schoolroom and demanding a promise that Mary would not report this conversation to her parents. Mary would make no such promise, and went straight to her father to tell him what had happened. He in turn did not seem surprised and was particularly kind to her all morning, helping her to mount a picture of Victoria's face that she had drawn for her mother's Christmas present.[57]

Then just at this crisis it transpired that Dick, in bed with a sore throat, had scarlatina, and the other boys were written to at Condover with orders to remain where they were for fear of infection. It was a dull enough Christmas, although Richard did his best, reading *Nicholas Nickleby* to the girls and handing out presents. On going to bed, Mary stopped in her mother's bedroom to wish her good night and noticed that she looked unusually ill and tired. She was informed that Mlle had been in to complain for the second time in two days, and Emily had been exhausted by the strain – it would kill her, she said, if this went on, she thought both sides wished to do right and they must simply try and get on for her sake. Terrified for her mother by this latest scene, Mary made a mental vow on the spot to give way to Mlle in everything if she would only leave her mother alone. But when she went to find her governess to offer this resolution, she was met with a volley of abuse, to the effect that Mary had been unable to please any of her former governesses (which was patently untrue, in fact she still corresponded with Miss Parr's predecessor) and must therefore be the one at fault. With admirable self-control, Mary repeated her willingness to obey her governess in everything, and an hour after she had been in to see her mother, was finally free to go to bed. But she could not rest after what had happened, and instead went back to the drawing room to seek consolation from her father, who was annoyed on her behalf and offered what comfort he could. So ended Christmas Day 1875.[58]

By the spring of 1876 Emily was no better, and had gone to London to be in close touch with Dr Radcliffe, while her husband divided his time between her and the family in Hodnet. At least Mlle Keller had now left, which must have been a relief all round. But Mary's excitement about her own visit to London to see her mother is coloured by a weary acceptance of new responsibilities at home, 'I suppose I am now out of the school room though I am not yet seventeen, but

I know that I have hard work still to do for a year or two, and probably I shall be much busier than I have been yet'.[59] From this time onwards she found herself responsible for the running of the household, with eighteen people including the servants to be considered. She would later recall that her mother gave her no advice in this emergency, having apparently none to give.[60] What she fails to point out in this bitter retrospect is that her mother was not simply incompetent or uninterested, as such a comment implies; she was seriously ill, indeed bedridden for much of the time. Elsewhere Mary would pay tribute to the stern sense of duty that upheld her mother in these years – often in great pain herself, she once told her daughter that the two of them should attempt to conceal their suffering from the others, for duty was all there was. But she could not reconcile this 'austere appeal'[61] with her own sense of abandonment, forced into a domestic role for which she was no more suited than Emily herself.

Even the few days in London to which she had looked forward were nearly taken from her, when Tom came back from a conference with their father suggesting that she might go 'another time'.[62] This rather peremptory announcement seems to have been based on concern for Mary's health, so often the cause of missed pleasures over the last few years. But, in the event, she was well enough to accompany her father and brother. She was delighted at the thought of seeing her mother and the Beaumont cousins, but already the mere thought of leaving Hodnet, if only for a few days, appeared to her 'perfect happiness'.[63]

She found her grandmother ill with a cold and her mother less fully recovered than she had hoped, a disappointment which she attributed to the failure of a course of galvanism (a popular treatment for asthma at the time was the passing of electric currents through the chest). But she saw her cousins, ordered a new bonnet and dress, visited art galleries, the Kensington Museum (now the Victoria & Albert), travelled on the new Underground and went to her first play, featuring an elderly Charles Matthews, before being driven home by a tipsy cabman. The following day her father returned to Hodnet, Tom left for Cambridge and Regie, who had also been staying, returned to Storrington. Mary remained to keep her mother company and promptly caught cold – luckily it did not turn to asthma 'thought it tried its best'; after a few days her grandmother re-emerged from her bedroom and her mother claimed that she felt 'another woman'. Now, after her desperation to escape, Mary found herself missing Hodnet. She felt she had had sufficient rest and holiday to last her all year, and felt restless to be 'back in the saddle' as she put it.[64] In the event she stayed in London for a month, including a fortnight with Essex and Diana. She went to the Academy – her old acquaintance Mr Nettleship had no picture in, although her aunt Victoria, widow of her uncle Thomas, said he had taken great pains; then to hear Rubinstein, and various other entertainments. On her return to Hodnet at the end of May, she might well say that she had had 'quite a season in London'. It was

London to which she was so anxious to escape during the next fifteen years, and yet she already realized herself that the country was necessary to her too. 'It is delightful to go to London if only to come back home' she wrote now.[65]

She was also able to report that a new governess, one Miss Gates, had been employed and seemed 'a quiet, gentle little woman'. But Mary herself was no longer in the schoolroom, although she was still just short of her seventeenth birthday; instead she was in a new routine of taking breakfast with her father and doing lessons by herself. It was, she commented ruefully, 'rather uncomfortable this half and half, neither in the schoolroom nor considered grown up'.[66] A distraction soon offered itself in a welcome visit from her grandmother, and, yet more welcome news, she learned that she had won the class prize from her drawing club.[67] This club comprised anywhere between about six and twenty active members, each set the task of producing a painting or drawing a month on a prescribed topic. The subjects included abstract titles such as 'Alone', a passage of choice from the poetry of Macaulay and the ever welcome 'Old china'.[68]

She would keep some of these drawings for the rest of her life, and decades later she still remembered with rage how jealousy and spite had led one of the other, less talented pupils to deface several more of them. 'I am so proud of this' she wrote delightedly when she heard the news of her win:

> I have won the prize in spite of having my drawings so often spoilt, in spite of effaced notes, in spite of never having had a lesson, as Maude and May [two of the Heber-Percy girls] have. Of course I think too much of this little success, but it is very pleasant. I cannot help looking on it as a first step, however small a one.[69]

And then once again self-doubt sets in. 'I trust but I fear, vainly, I shall one day do greater things than win a prize in a drawing club.'[70] She would do greater things, but not, as she anticipated, in art.

There was little time for introspection before she was swept off to Tenby for a holiday with the Heber-Percys. Tom saw her off at the station, between them they somehow left her luggage behind and 'I found that my wardrobe consisted of a sponge, a tooth brush and a scent bottle'. Everyone was kind to her, although she wished her aunt and uncle would not appeal to her as a matter of course in their marital differences. But if her relations could be trying, the scenery was beautiful, and she was most amused when they sometimes had to turn back from a walk through the apparently deserted landscape, because of gentlemen 'in the costume of Adam' emerging from what they had thought was a solitary bathe.[71] If Mary was in many ways a product of the late Victorian period, she was certainly no prude.

There were days of intense heat spent mainly reading under a tree, services in the local church, with the vicar 'a sort of big bouncing, honest looking sort of old school boy, who fired off the commandments ... swung himself into the pulpit,

stood with his arms akimbo and preached us a most original sermon extempore'
– and in the middle of the service, a crisis involving a spider that made Mary and
her cousin Gertrude nearly choke with laughter at an inappropriate moment.[72]

The next big event after this holiday was Regie's success in getting to Sand-
hurst, to everyone's great relief. As they waited in their mother's room for the
arrival of the paper, Regie plunged in with Dick, nearly knocking them all over.
As Mary recalled, he had not seen his name at first because he was looking at the
bottom of the list, and it was left to Dick to point it out almost at the top (that
it was in fact 27th out of the hundred names, in no way detracts from his sister's
pride in the 'dear old boy's' achievement).[73]

It was after Regie's departure that Mary went on a visit to Farnborough, a
great event to her although she thought it might not appear so to anyone else. As
luck would have it the Vicarage was uninhabited and she was able to go all over
it, recognizing much but finding the nurseries smaller than she remembered. As
she stood looking out of the window she thought of how she had stood in the
same spot thirteen years earlier. 'The contrast felt so odd. The big, tall thin, growing up girl, with the little stout thing of five, something like Hessy is now, only a
year or two younger.'[74] Her old garden was intact but sadly overgrown – it may
even be this sense of desolation that reappears in *Notwithstanding* (1913), when
a young Edwardian girl looks on sorrowfully at the abandoned garden of a dead
child. She wrote now:

> I do not know what it was that made me so sad as I looked at the poor little plot of
> ground, but I somehow felt those were light hearted days without the responsibility
> and the little worrying troubles and anxieties and <u>sins,</u> that must come as one grows
> up into life ... I have youth, better health than I ever thought possible, the love of
> those I love, and bright rainbow hopes, very pleasant though of course I know they
> must fade. A great many treasures I have, and I would not be five years old again if I
> could. Yet I suppose one cannot help feeling a little sad when one looks back at the
> first dawn as it were of the early morning, when one feels the sun a little later on,
> beginning to beat a little hotly[75]

The church itself she did not remember, although she did recall stroking a lamb
on one of the graves. Then suddenly she recognized a walnut tree in the garden
and as she walked back to the Hall, where she was staying with the Holbech
family, she found the scenes of her early childhood, before she had become ill,
coming back to meet her.

The afternoon she found dull enough, walking up and down by herself in
the cold, as the others played lawn tennis. But in the evening she derived some
satisfaction from a new dress – although she complained that the fashionable
skirt was so tight she could hardly get into it – and a new silver bracelet, a present
from her father. She was called on to play piano, at which point the son of the
house carefully arranged her foot on the pedal and held it there, apparently

in the belief that it needed to be perpetually down. Mary complained that he
treated her more like a five year old than a great girl of seventeen, but nonetheless she enjoyed the evening so much she found herself shivering with chattering
teeth, and was more desolate than she had expected when she had to leave the
next day for another visit, to the Hickmans at Birdingbury. The wrangling of the
brother and sister at this next house got on her nerves, and she spent the afternoon knitting in the drawing room in 'a state of savage dullness', participating
with difficulty in a conversation about Violet Hickman's pug and chickens. It
was a long three days' visit, and on the way home she was less than impressed by
a visit to her father's old school, when her head ached so that she could not have
enjoyed it 'had there been anything to enjoy'.[76]

That Christmas Mary was looking forward to a dance at the rectory, as she
had looked forward to the ill-fated Hodnet dance a year earlier. Much had happened since then, but this time nothing in the diary comes between Mary and
her enjoyment. She lists games of *rouge et noir* and *vingt et un* among the entertainments for the houseful of guests, and remembers taking them with Tom on
an outing to Hawkestone, coming back to find the carpets up and the house
decorated with holly. She danced every dance but one, when she could not get
past the doors so great was the crush of people. She enjoyed talking to Tom's
friend Mr Hughes and, despite her recurring anxiety about her lack of pretti-
ness, it is telling that 'one was obliged however to be a little distant with him for
he seemed to get so familiar, and it was very difficult to help it'.[77] Mary was in
no sense a pretty girl, but clearly there was something attractive about her. She
barely registers herself the pattern in which she is obliged to keep young men at a
distance, but it is a theme that appears more than once in her journal.

Even more enjoyable than their own was the dance at Hodnet Hall, where
Mary was resplendent in white and gold. But once over this round of dissipation, there was one subject that dominated her thoughts. There were the usual
duties to be got through at home; there was an interlude of a month in London,
involving plays, parties and a viewing of Doré's new painting of *Christ Entering
Jerusalem*; then home with new dresses, causing her mother to go into 'ecstasies'
of admiration. But none of these is the subject uppermost in her mind. For just
at the time of her aunt Percy's dance she had begun the first chapter of a novel.
The enjoyment of that event, and her uncertainty about whether she did or did
not like one Mr Russell, with whom she had danced on the occasion, had temporarily put it out of her head. But she had returned to work on the book and
by May it was finished. *Her Evil Genius* was a source of half satisfaction, half
shame, but Mary would not really know what to think of it until she had secured
her mother's opinion. The book had, she said, engrossed her night and day, she
had lived for it, and now she put herself through a series of imagined scenarios
in which the manuscript was buried at the bottom of a cupboard, returned with

thanks by publishers, published and unread, published and reviled in the press – or became popular. What she did know, or thought she knew, was that if the book was an entire failure it would be some time before she dared begin another. And yet, she goes on:

> what a great pleasure and interest it would be to me in life to write books. I must strike out a line of some kind, and if I do not marry, (for at least that is hardly likely, as I possess neither beauty, nor cleverness) I should want some definite occupation, besides the home duties, though they certainly do engross far more of my time than I could have anticipated. Writing or drawing suggest themselves. Alas! poor drawing! As I grow less enthusiastic, less confident in my own powers, I have begun to see that I could never attain to anything like greatness, perhaps not even proficiency. I had set my heart upon it very much, and I still think I have a certain amount of talent, but oh! not nearly enough, to do more than just fairly well. I must do my best with it too, for, for the first time in my life I am having lessons[78]

Then, in one of her apparently rapid transitions, she recalls herself to a sense of the absurd, detailing the inane conversation of her cousin in London and her own partner at a country ball on her return home:

> he hardly reached up to my shoulder. He was so fiery, and peppery, and amused me by the way he shook his fist at anyone who jostled him, and by the extraordinary contortions into which he screwed a mouth, which would have been amply large enough for a man of six foot three.[79]

The abrupt shift from introspection to mild humour is a new feature here, but in her last diary it is characteristic, as Mary can almost be felt giving herself a shake and pointedly changing the subject.

Within a few weeks of this entry her brother Tom would come of age and she herself would turn eighteen. Tom had been in Cambridge over his actual birthday but came home specially to mark the occasion in June and, despite his best efforts to avoid publicity, the village had subscribed to buy him some plate; Mary was mortified at having missed the presentation and his speech, which was duly reported in the local papers.[80]

For her own birthday on 8 June there was a visit to Leaton. The past had been much in her thoughts over the last year, but as she reached her eighteenth year, the point at which she had once wished to stop growing older, she looked back on the four years that had passed since she came to Hodnet and saw a gulf between her childhood and her now acknowledged womanhood. As she looked back she began to feel anxious about her future:

> I do not like to think I am growing into a woman yet, but I feel it is so, and now I wonder what will have happened before my birthday comes round again … I can see nothing. I can hope much, but I can see nothing, and it is better it should be so,

> though I grow anxious now and then to know what my life is to be, forgetting how
> disappointed I should be, were I to know.

Her cousin Jimmy was engaged to be married that summer and:

> I sometimes wonder whether I shall ever be married. I don't think it likely, because
> I am so plain, and yet if people could once get over that, I think –, but I am writing
> nonsense, I must leave off, and get ready for luncheon.[81]

For a Victorian woman marriage was an inevitable preoccupation, and Mary
must have dreaded the usual alternative, of spending the rest of her life as the
'daughter at home' looking after her ageing parents. Apart from such pragmatic
considerations, she thought 'It would raise myself not a little in my own estimation to have someone who could love me enough to ask me to marry him'.[82]
And several men took notice of her. There was Mr Russell, whom she had met
through the Heber-Percys and on further acquaintance found conceited to the
point of arrogance. She did not, she admitted, like him much, but she enjoyed a
little attention, and was somewhat bitter to find that he had engaged himself to
someone else while paying her that compliment. There was Regie's friend, who
came on a visit and somehow managed to shoot himself while being shown how
to fire a gun (he became a fixture at the rectory for some time afterwards before
he could be safely moved).[83] During this time he merited so high a eulogy and, in
consequence, such an embarrassing lamentation over her own personal appearance that she felt obliged to cut out several pages of her journal when she looked
back on it a few years later.[84] And of course there was the 'cad' Mathias Thomas,
who stared at her at a public ball before trying to put his name on her dancing
card – when she collectedly pointed out that they had not been introduced he
attempted to gain an introduction through her brother, who he saw was with
her; when this failed, he pestered the hapless Regie into buying him a glass of
claret instead.[85] But while she records with considerable amusement these efforts
of young men to engage her at dances, still she cannot believe that they might
genuinely find her attractive. Certainly she felt unable to attract the more eligible, such as the unfortunate Mr Nusse of the gun incident. She was clear enough
where the blame for this lay:

> I could not fall in love with myself if I was a man. I have nothing outside to fall in love
> with. I know I could love steadfastly in return, but who on earth is to find that out.
> No one! Miss Mary I shall remain to the end of my days[86]

Even as she worked on her first stories, still she was wary of admitting to personal
ambition – just as office work would soon become a recognized field for women
who were unable to marry, so she justifies her interest in a literary career by the
assumption that she will remain unsought. She would not yet feel confident

enough to talk about 'the work in which I delight'. For now it was to be simply 'an interest in life' if she failed to marry.[87]

Her state of mind was not improved by her role as bridesmaid at Jimmy's wedding that September. She was shocked that certain parts of the service, presumably the references to conception, should be so publicly gone through in front of the innocent groom and his bride – Mary was not easily shocked, but she was herself naturally reticent and knew how it felt to be embarrassed in front of others. There was a picture of the wedding party, her with her mouth wide open, and then the couple was gone 'in a shower of wine and cheese'. Jimmy declared himself 'perfectly happy' and she wondered whether she would ever be able to say the same.[88]

For the rest of that year she would continue to manage the household as best she could,[89] doubtless assisted by her younger sisters (Diana and Victoria would later take on such tedious work in order that Mary might be spared). Whether or not she was happy it is hard to say, and quite possibly she could not have answered the question herself. In the New Year of 1878 she still veered between a delight in new scenes and acquaintance, and a depressing sense of the relapse sure to follow them. For her first Hunt Ball, the cause of both excitement and terror, she appeared in white silk with a long train covered in a froth of tulle, with a wreath of flowers in her hair. Literally sick with excitement, she was aghast to find one side of her face a deep shade of red, a psychosomatic complaint to which she had been subject for some time. There was consolation to be found in the dances, particularly one with a certain Mr Newfrost, who is never mentioned again.[90] And then the Drayton Ball, followed by a visit to the Hall – it was now that her mother was able to venture out in black velvet and diamonds, for the first time since her illness.[91] There followed a week at Donnington Rectory, home of the Revd John Lander; looking back Mary felt 'as if I had been on enchanted ground, for a few hours, and then set down to think it over in Hodnet on a very rainy day of every day life'.[92]

Perhaps it was the temporary improvement in her mother's health that rescued Mary from this rainy every day existence for a while, leaving her free to go to London, where she spent a welcome couple of months with her grandmother in the spring, and was casually introduced to a young and eligible painter, Bob Bateman. There seems to have been an attraction on his side at least, but while 'No one ever said so many pretty things to me before', Mary could not persuade herself that he meant anything by his blandishments, nor could she talk herself into returning his evident interest.[93] It must have been at about this time that she began making regular trips to Palace Gate, and it was during these visits that she began, under her grandmother's careful tutelage, to lose something of the shyness that had so hindered her first sorties into society. She remembered gratefully how her grandmother had taken her into London society, 'introduced her to new lines of thought' and, more importantly yet, to the works of Ralph Waldo Emerson.[94] Mary would later claim that no one, not even her revered George Eliot, had influenced her as much as Emerson.[95]

Cleary her sallies under the protective wing of her wise and witty grand-mother did more for her confidence than anything in her life had yet been able to effect. By the end of the year she felt polished enough to spend a week at Cambridge with Tom, without absolutely disgracing him in front of his friends. The visit was a great success, apparently one of the last really carefree interludes she was to enjoy. 'How can I describe a whole week of perfect enjoyment, a week that never had its equal before, and will probably remain as one of the bright-est places, in a not very eventful life.'[96] There was a Trinity Boat Club Ball and a Masonic Ball (she was pleased by Tom's rather moderate compliment that she had looked 'creditable' on this occasion).[97] There is also a reference to someone whose name she then felt obliged to efface, but who was in earnest enough to cause some anxiety on her part. She decides with reference to this particular man that she will act for the best at the time, which will be the January Hunt.[98] But with all these indications that she was more appealing to her brothers' friends than she imagined, still she felt depressed as she looked to the future. As she returned to the routine of Hodnet she reflected sadly:

> Surely I must have dreamt it all. It seemed so strange, as I stood there to look back at the brilliant ball room with its excitement and whirl, and to think how short a time ago, I was in the thickest of it, and then to find myself standing in the fresh country morning listening to the bells, in the village. If such is life, life is indeed a riddle![99]

Mary seems almost wilfully to have decided, at the age of nineteen, that the happy marriage she so wanted would never be open to her. Instead, she would write.

3 'IF I FOUND I HAD NO POWER AT ALL':
THE EARLY FICTION

Mary's first attempt at a novel, *Her Evil Genius*, would not make a name for its author and in fact it was never published. Her youngest sister Hester considered it 'horribly vulgar' and it is likely that it formed part of the final bonfire Mary remembered fuelling with at least two early novels when she left Hodnet many years later.[1] In her masterpiece of 1899, *Red Pottage*, she would allow her writer heroine a dazzling revelation, in the sudden realization of her talent, followed by a sensational success only a year later, before she is brought to near breakdown by the stifling regime of her brother's household. But if Mary's own first novel was not to project her into overnight fame, it did at least confirm that writing and not painting would be her career.

It was a direction that she could follow, like other women of the time and in common with her famous heroine Hester Gresley, only with difficulty. The prejudice against female writers was compounded in her own case by class prejudice, as acquaintances greeted her desire to become known as a writer with disbelief. For the boys of the family a career was not only acceptable but necessary, given the lack of a private fortune. As they grew older they would have left home as a matter of course, Tom becoming a land agent, Regie joining the 27th Inniskillings and Dick emigrating to Australia, where he became a successful vintner. But for the girls it was different. While they were all well read and four of the five seem at least to have considered a career at different times, their first priority had to be running the family home and helping their father in the parish.[2]

There were of course the more lively entertainments of village and hunt balls, and visits to Condover and Hodnet Hall. As Mary became old enough to take advantage of these diversions away from home, she was expected on her return to relay tales of her adventures to her 'inexorable' young sisters Victoria and Hester, and while Victoria would listen calmly on these occasions, Hester would punish any unwarranted license with tears of rage. Mary was permitted 'a certain latitude', frequently being kidnapped by brigands on the way to visit their Yorkshire relations, and lions were accepted provided they had escaped from captivity.[3] But she always remembered the outcry when on one occasion she thoughtlessly imprisoned herself in a coffin while taking a nap in a vault, and without a clear idea of how she was to get out again, claimed that she had prised open the lid with a sheet of drawing paper. Victoria shed silent tears as Hester furiously attacked with her fists, and Mary found herself begging for their forgiveness. 'I, with my hair done up, ate "humble pie" to those two pigtails.'[4] Their brothers with their less adventurous lives away from home would return for visits, there were holidays in Europe, and as the girls got older there was the lure of their grandmother's house in London, a sanctuary Mary would later bequeath to one of her most appealing heroines, Diana Tempest. Catherine Legard (Beaumont, née Cayley) would appear in this novel as a kindly and dignified, if occasionally acerbic character. The 1900 edition of the novel pays tribute to her, noting her influence over the young Mary, and the way in which she 'obliged her to overcome her extreme shyness, encouraged her to express her ideas, however crude, never ridiculed her, firmly believed in her ability, of which there was no outward sign whatever,'[5] behaviour that must indeed have endeared her to her granddaughter.

Mary's diary for these years has since disappeared, but her friend Percy Lubbock includes such extracts as he deems fit in his memoir, or 'Sketch from Memory' as he terms it. Her last entry from 1878 is followed, he says, by 'more difficult meditations' but her support lay in her work.[6] The dynamic within the family itself is inevitably now hard to determine. In *Under One Roof* Mary quotes a journal extract of Hester's, in which she claims a tendency to 'melancholy, apathy and dullness' as a family failing.[7] But there is also a sense of jollity and general affection, with letters addressed to one member of the family clearly intended to be read by all. Lubbock, working from Mary's own diary entries of the 1880s, notes that 'the many brothers and sisters were a cheerful band, and their father in his active times was a maker of happiness for all about him'.[8] Clearly they were a close family, but it is certainly possible that for the sensitive and sometimes irritable Mary the banter may have seemed at times a little too unremitting, particularly if she herself was the object of well-meaning jokes about her tendency to nerves and her proneness to accidents. In an autobiographical story she would recall how:

> I had once in a dreamy moment got my gown shut into the door in an empty railway compartment on the far side. And as the glass was up on the station side I had been unable to attract anyone's attention when I wanted to alight, and had had to go on to Portsmouth where the train stopped for good before I could make my predicament known. This trivial incident had never been forgotten by my family. So much so that I had often regretted the hilarious spirit of pure comedy at my own expense which had prompted me to relate it to them.[9]

By the early 1880s she was writing in earnest and had published her first story in the *Graphic*.[10] According to Lubbock she was now meeting 'people of mark', and finding them glad to know her.[11] By the end of 1882 Regie was in Shanghai, where he was posted as aide de camp to the governor and hoping to be promoted to captain. On Christmas Day he imagined the cheerful scene at home, his family eating their plum pudding at half past one.[12] On the night of the same day Mary was writing in her diary, 'But I am learning to expect very little ...'.[13] Discreetly ignoring this comment, Lubbock cheers himself up with accounts of her social success, dining with the painter John Millais (a friend of her uncle Regie's) among others, and her satisfaction in her work.[14] By 1883 she was sending out further work to journals – many years later she would write to thank James Payn for his encouragement when turning down a story she had sent in to the *Cornhill*. She remained grateful for his 'goodnatured encouragement which came at a time when I had few incentives to perseverance'.[15]

In 1884 another story, 'Lisle's Courtship', appeared anonymously in *Household Words*, now edited by Dickens's son Charlie.[16] It would be hard to tell from the buoyancy and evident enjoyment she takes in this story that she was in need of any such incentive. It charts the comic progress of a young man who is not sure whether his proposal of marriage has been accepted or not, because at the moment of response a caged canary chirps loudly and the girl's mother makes an inopportune entrance before he can reiterate the question. Determined not to admit his uncertainty, he sends his younger brother to propose to the girl ostensibly on his own account, in the hope that he will be told of the prior engagement. What actually happens is that the brother's proposal is accepted with evident enthusiasm, intensifying the comic dilemma, and matters are only resolved when the young man's friend intervenes on his behalf. Like the novel that she would begin a year or so later, 'Lisle's Courtship' is humorously engaging, and already suggests Cholmondeley's command of the short story form.

But still she could write only in the intervals allowed by her household responsibilities and the uncongenial work of her father's parish (an appreciative article in the *Bookman* in 1900, long after she had become recognized as a writer of distinction and shortly after the publication of her most successful work, makes no secret of the connection between Cholmondeley and Hester Gresley).[17] For Mary in the 1880s there were sales of work to organize and attend – 'If the reader wants to know what "bed-spreads" and "sheet-shams" are', the narrator of *Red Pottage* comments grimly, 'let him ask his intended, and let him see to it that he marries a woman who cannot tell him'.[18] In addition to the charitable work and the recurring burdens of the church calendar, there were choir practice and meetings with farmers' wives, as well as Sunday school events, to be got through before the work of writing could begin. And of course there was the endless round of parish visiting.[19]

A watercolour cartoon by Victoria from 1885 gives some indication of the sort of commitment that was expected.[20] Accompanied by a poem beginning

'Too many irons in the fire, Mary', it shows Mary sitting by a fire, determinedly toasting 'shawls for the poor', an 'asylum for orphans of the clergy', the Girls' Friendly Society and a secretaryship of the EFS,[21] next to 'essays for the *Cornhill*' and the 'lending library'. In middle age Mary would remember the routine sacrifice of the clergy's womenfolk on 'the altar of parochial work' and, most of all, the sheer tedium of her life in the country.[22] Indeed in *Red Pottage* the most uninviting of events becomes a form of entertainment: 'Why the parishioners had come in such numbers it would be hard to say. Perhaps even a temperance meeting was a change in the dreary monotony of rural life.'[23]

It is likely that by now Emily Cholmondeley had begun to lapse into the depression, almost certainly manifested in an increasingly stringent religion, that would ultimately estrange her from her children. None of her correspondence is known to survive, but a letter from Regie over Christmas 1882 is telling. He is close enough to his mother to tease her that he plans to leave the army and grow a beard, in hopes of attracting a wealthy heiress. But there is an anxious note in his admission that 'I <u>did</u> shoot on Xmas Day by myself ... please dont think it wicked I dont consider it so myself'.[24]

None of the Cholmondeley children seem to have shared their mother's strict religious views, but Mary at least found that her own independence of mind was not necessarily in accordance with her father's unreflecting faith either. The only nonconformist minister in Hodnet, who was on friendly terms with the rector, later recalled talking to him at length just before he left, about 'the deep and abiding things of our faith' and being presented by Cholmondeley with a copy of Geikie's *Life of Christ*.[25] Nonetheless Richard Cholmondeley seems to have lacked his daughter's searching intelligence. Mary recalled many years later that, while his was 'a vital faith', he had never to her knowledge given a thought to the authenticity of the gospels or the apostolic succession,[26] those most divisive questions of the 1860s and 1870s. Mary herself would read avidly the writings of all sects and denominations, from the High Church Pusey to the transcendentalist Ralph Waldo Emerson (founder of his own religion), the better to understand her own position.[27] In her thirties she would be exasperated that there were those who would deny her Christianity if she disputed the authenticity of the miracles, believing that in any case Christ's words were a far higher proof of divinity than his rising from the dead.[28] While she would remain a Christian all her life, her beliefs veered towards the unorthodox, as her continuing admiration for Emerson would suggest. Revd Rowland Corbet, known for his mysticism, was a close family friend and may also have influenced her. She was deeply amused by one conversation between him and her father, when the Revd Cholmondeley had demanded to know whether he was denying a belief in the devil, and Corbet had answered, 'Believe in him! I would not trust him for a moment'.[29] It was a response she liked so much she would later include it in one of her books, and again in a dramatization of another.[30] But tending to the unorthodox as they did, her religious beliefs might well have failed to satisfy a watchful mother. She would later write, with a certain level of frustration, that while the young should listen to the intricacies of religious debate with some consciousness of their own half-educated state, still those among them who had no desire to learn would perhaps suffer less:

> The attitude of the young and thoughtless towards religion has at least the beauty of simplicity. No difficulties are felt. There is no struggle. The religion of the parent descends upon the child, often to the third or fourth generation.[31]

Mary's references to her mother over the next ten years testify to Emily's concern for her eldest daughter's health, and her pride in her literary achievements.[32] But there are no jokes, and discussions on religion are unlikely to have ended happily. Mary herself was prone to anxiety, and suffered a level of religious insecurity for most of her life. She was like her mother in many ways, but for this very reason she may not always have felt comfortable in her presence. Little wonder that she escaped to London whenever she got the chance. And from 1883 she would have the support of Anne Thackeray Ritchie, daughter of the more famous writer William Thackeray, himself the first editor of the *Cornhill*. Like James Payn, Anne Ritchie was quick to appreciate the potential of this young aspirant, and their friendship, crucial to Mary's first success, would last until Annie's death in 1919. Lubbock, who had been reading the sad accounts of many 'hard things', comments that at this stage Mary was still working 'like a man', and turns with some relief to the moment when she 'began to receive her reward'.[33] But what he does not see fit to tell curious readers is that some time during these years Mary had fallen in love.

Very little is known about this interlude, so inconclusive and yet so catastrophic in its effects that twenty years after the final parting, Mary had still not recovered from her distress. All that is known for certain is that at some point she formed an attachment that lasted for seven years, and which she hoped would end in marriage. The available evidence suggests that this relationship began shortly after her last diary entry of 1878 and probably ended some time in 1885. While it is highly unlikely that her 'love affair' was anything other than entirely proper, Mary's longing for affection is obvious from her diary entries of 1878, in which she speculates on the chances of finding someone to love her. In a satirical allusion to the notorious claim of Dr William Acton that a virtuous woman was little troubled by passion, she would later write of 'that dreary level of emaciated semi-maternal tenderness which is the only feeling some husbands allow their wives to entertain permanently for them; the only kind of love which some men believe a virtuous woman is capable of'.[34] The man Mary loved – he is not named in her extant diary entries – was ambitious but not yet in a position to marry. So she waited.

In these years she was only beginning to overcome that shyness that had caused her to flush up so humiliatingly in public as a girl. She was still not confident socially, and she would later remember how she dreaded dinner parties because she was 'sure to be left out'.[35] Yet, as she said herself, she had a certain determined pride, and perhaps a caustic temper. She doubted her ability as a writer, but still, 'I sometimes wonder what I should do if that interest were taken from me, if I found I had no power at all'.[36] This is not the language of someone who has faith in her future or in the support of a happy marriage only temporarily put off. But when she was well enough – which she often was not – she continued to write. And if her love was full of insecurities – unwise as she later said – it was nonetheless 'devoted'.[37]

Then something went terribly wrong. She never forgot the anger of the man she loved, who left her 'bitterly', with a sting in his last speech and in his last letter.[38] The anger, and the writing of a letter when he had already confronted her face to face, might perhaps have persuaded her that he was not indifferent. But, convinced that he was at fault, and both too proud and too insecure to question him further, Mary decided that he was simply too ambitious to marry on an inadequate income, in other words that he had never really loved her. The faithless lover who is put off marrying the woman he loves by lack of ready money appears in two of her most personal novels, *Red Pottage* and *Prisoners* (1906). Both Mr Tristram and Lord Lossiemouth are good looking but already lapsing into fleshiness with thickening waistlines when they are first introduced to the reader, some time after their abandonment of the women they love. Both are artistic and boast a high level of sensibility, but neither is capable of sustained resolution, which may or may not give a clue as to the kind of man Mary herself had loved. When he began visiting at the rectory again after several years of silence, he could not resist complaining to her that all his friends had deserted him,[39] a lament that would resurface in the posturing of Mr Tristram, confronted with Rachel's lost regard. Mary had not stopped loving the man she had lost so abruptly, but again she missed the chance of an explanation because, seeing herself as the injured party, she would not respond to his insinuation against herself.

If she was reserved in her personal life, she could be outspoken enough in her writing. In the summer of 1885, when she was twenty-six, her story 'Geoffrey's Wife' appeared in the *Graphic*. In its uncompromising critique of social values, this story remains one of the most compelling, and disturbing, of all Cholmondeley's published works. It tells the story of a young couple caught in a crowd on their honeymoon in Paris. As the wife is on the verge of fainting, her husband signals to her to climb onto his back and, after falling once, rises and struggles to safety, only to realize hours too late that he has saved an ageing prostitute instead of his young bride. In its exploration of sexual codes, this story foreshadows *Diana Tempest*, in which Cholmondeley uses female sexuality to probe the moral status of male figures. Geoffrey is characterized as earnest and devoted, deeply conscious of 'The awful responsibility of guarding such a treasure [as his new wife], and an overpowering sense of its fragility'.[40] The bride herself is given the name of Eva, recalling the moral rather than physical frailty of the biblical Eve, and the mirroring of the pure woman and the prostitute is further foreshadowed by Geoffrey's own fear of the mob, 'the rough men and the rougher women, whom, do what he would, he could not prevent pressing upon her'.[41] In its images of rising and falling, the crowd scene dramatizes the surge of the mob even as it obscures the exact moment at which a prostitute is substituted for Eva, for whom Geoffrey ironically feels able to endure his own increasing pain and exhaustion.

In the final lines of the story, clothing alone enables Eva's servant to identify her body, a suggestive comment that further elides distinctions between pure and impure women. Geoffrey's sole resource at the end of the story is to keep a symbol of his wife's genteel status, one of the gloves she was wearing on the night of her death. Over the next ten years New Woman novels would repeatedly explore the dynamic between dissolute men, their wives, and prostitutes or discarded mistresses. In Ella Hepworth Dixon's *A Modern Woman* (1894), for instance, it is left to the New Woman Alison Ives to visit the dying prostitute who was initially seduced by her own current suitor, Dr Strange. In Cholmondeley's formulation, Geoffrey's abandonment of his wife is unintentional but it nonetheless prefigures a key theme in New Woman writing; shared contact between the male, his wife and a prostitute endangers the legitimate wife as well as the other two (the specific threat of sexually transmitted disease is most famously realized in Sarah Grand's 1893 New Woman novel *The Heavenly Twins*). Geoffrey stands as an essentially honourable figure who seeks as a matter of course to isolate pure women from their 'fallen' counterparts. His failure to do so is dramatized through his own symbolic fall in the crowd that brings down his 'frail' wife. Written at the height of the purity campaigns, a year before the repeal of the notorious Contagious Diseases Acts that had allowed the compulsory detention and inspection of prostitutes,[42] 'Geoffrey's Wife' powerfully suggests that where male figures stand between the mirror images of pure and impure women, they themselves may become vulnerable to judgement. At the moment of crisis, Geoffrey is unable to distinguish between the two types, and unthinkingly carries the burden of both. Cholmondeley's story, while it figures the death of Eva as tragic, is ambivalent in its treatment of the prostitute who usurps her position on Geoffrey's back. Both women are parasitic, and both cling to him with feeble arms, but the narrator avoids any definite comment on whether the prostitute has pulled Eva away from her husband or simply taken advantage of her fall in the press of the crowd. What is clear in this scenario is that only one woman can survive.

Marriage and its demands may well have been on Mary's mind as she wrote the story. Towards the end of 1885, quite possibly at the very time that her own affair came to an abrupt end, Essex announced her engagement to the brilliant but erratic Ralph Benson, heir to a large property in Shropshire, and whom even a young Hester had admired entirely until he had the effrontery to want to marry her adored older sister. It was, according to their daughter's biographer, an ill-assorted match in more ways than one, but if the twenty-four-year-old Ralph, with his good looks and better expectations, was a catch even without much of a lineage, Essex at twenty-five was simply 'a pleasing-looking, amiable girl enough ... with a lively turn of wit' but 'no distinction but her name'.[43] The marriage would end in an acrimonious separation, but for now Essex was in love, the family (other than Hester) was pleased, and her uncle Charles wrote Mary a delighted letter, assuring her blandly, 'Your turn may come'.[44] She knew better, and even as a writing career seemed finally to be within reach, she succumbed to a serious bout of depression. By the winter of 1885–6 she was 'in the depths'.[45] And yet astonishingly it was now that she wrote one of her most humorous novels. She got the idea while taking part in an amateur production of Tom Taylor's 1854 comedy *To Oblige Benson* at Condover in January,[46] and both house and theatricals reappear in this first book. By now Condover itself had been mortgaged for £100,000 to allow the payment of debts, and within the next few years Richard Cholmondeley would lend his brother £2,500, a sum that remained unpaid at Reginald's death.[47]

It is hard to say how aware Mary was of the cloud looming over Condover. Her principal energy was in any case being directed into her writing. But her work had always to be done within the time allowed by other responsibilities. It is likely to have been in the February of this year that both Mrs Legard and Mary's mother were ill, and Mary's customary visit to London was taken up with looking after them both.[48] While there she gleefully confided to Hester that a certain Mrs Gregory, astounded at the rejection of her own novel and having heard that Mary wrote, was now keen to offer her advice. Mrs Legard Mary personally deemed better, but unwilling to admit it. And she was reasonably confident that her mother was starting to recover, while her grandmother had given her strict orders not to lace her boots or help her into her walking things, as she had done at first. But 'Granny is such very depressing company that I think it is just as well she should come home lest she should become depressed too'.[49] Despite the note of impatience in her last comment, Mary was close to her grandmother, and in later life she would continue to pay tribute to her kindness.[50] Nor would she forget that it was her grandmother who first introduced her to the writing of Ralph Waldo Emerson, whom she claimed later had influenced her as much or more even than George Eliot.[51]

Still Mary relied on the opinion of the women in her family, whose criticism and approval she would continue to need throughout her career.[52] She even claimed subsequently that, as she only included scenes in her fiction that had actually been taken from the life, she was dependent on Diana and Victoria for anecdotes when she herself was too ill to venture into society.[53] Victoria herself must have been reminded of her own childhood, listening avidly to the stories her older sister brought back from the outside world. And in these early years of her career, she also co-opted Hester into copying out interesting extracts that she could use for chapter headings. It seems likely, although if so Mary herself seems to have forgotten it, that this request prompted the portentous 'Quotations from Everywhere' that Hester began at about this time.[54]

In fact Hester too had literary aspirations, and their relationship as they grew older seemed set to develop into one of mutual support and advice. In the summer of 1883, when she was thirteen, Hester had been included in a roll of honour in the children's magazine *Little Folks*, for her entry on 'The Tale of a Shilling'.[55] A few years later she was seeking Mary's advice on her writing, and Mary would confide in return her regrets about her lack of a directed education when she was her sister's age.

> I really do envy you laying such a solid foundation ... If there was one thing beyond all others that I would go back on if I could, it is the two years from 16 to 18 when I was out of the schoolroom, and tried to work, and had no guiding principle as to method.[56]

Hester at this point was immersing herself in a programme of long-distance education, taking advantage of the new correspondence classes for women organized by Queen Margaret College in Glasgow from 1883. Through this scheme Hester could have undertaken courses in a variety of subjects normally reserved for boys, such as geology, chemistry and natural philosophy, as well as Latin and Greek. As she grew older, she could have studied the classics or English language and literature to degree level, although the college was not authorized to confer degrees on women. No records of Hester's enrolment survive, but in addition to the subjects prescribed by the University scheme there was a correspondence class in English writers of the nineteenth century, which may well have appealed to her. It is likely that she studied at a higher level year by year during this period, as Mary recalls her obtaining a number of certificates.[57] It is not surprising that she should have envied this solid foundation.

But it was not just Hester with whom Mary discussed her early ambitions. In the freezing Hodnet winters all four of the sisters still at home would race up and down the schoolroom to keep warm. Each had their allotted 'beat' and as they walked briskly up and down, hands in muffs, they discussed 'books and people and Life, with a big L'.[58] Reading Gaskell's *Life of Charlotte Brontë* later in life,

Mary was surprised, and doubtless touched, to learn of another band of sisters walking up and down talking in much the same way, years before the Cholmondeley girls had been born.[59] But she did not take advice from her sisters alone. Her cousin Edward Cholmondeley was sent *The Danvers Jewels* in manuscript, and Mary made no fewer than sixty minor alterations on his advice.[60] She was pleased that he liked the character of the scapegrace Charles in particular, and valued his opinion enough to entrust him with the manuscript of her follow-up story, in which that character would take centre stage.[61]

Her first surviving novel is admittedly derivative – it owes an immense and unacknowledged debt to Wilkie Collins's *The Moonstone* (1868) – and she confided to her diary that she had hated the task of writing it, forcing herself to go upstairs and write the required number of pages and stopping anywhere once the allotted time was up.[62] But if the narrator is a stock 'old buffer', a modern reader can still enjoy his purblind retelling of events, in which he alone fails to see the suspicious interest of his chosen confidant in the priceless jewels of the story's title, and which he has been charged with delivering. It is left to Charles, the son of the house whose debts as much as his nocturnal wanderings help to throw suspicion on him when the jewels are stolen, to uncover the villain and his accomplice, the apparently vacuous girl his brother is about to marry (bigamously as it turns out). Again there is a sprinkling of Mary Braddon here, as the pretty blonde girl is shown to be wearing a wig – Cholmondeley's readers would have known of *Lady Audley's Secret* (1862), which satirizes the reader's expectation that a blonde, fragile-looking woman with a taste for fine clothes must by definition be innocent. Charles himself finally emerges as the one truly tragic figure, whose love for his cousin Edith is unreciprocated and even unsuspected, and whose father treats him with a contempt he deals with flippantly, rather than reveal his own self-loathing. But like the mid-century sensation novels from which it takes its inspiration, *The Danvers Jewels* derives much of its suspense from the cultural anxieties it exploits. Braddon's Lucy Audley is not simulating her love of clothes and jewels, indeed this frivolity is her central motive for attempted murder. Aurelia by contrast participates in the ideal of the doll-like woman purely to further her own ends, and, at the end of the story, Ralph is significantly screened from the revelation that she has symbolically dark and not blonde hair. As in the work of Wilkie Collins, family members must aid the police in repelling the threat of criminal infiltration into the country house. For Cholmondeley, this threat is not only criminal but specifically middle class, an anxiety she would continue to explore in her later fiction. Marriages between the upper and middle classes are repeatedly shown in her fiction to be little short of disastrous. However she is equally concerned with the reckless squandering of family wealth threatened by such figures as Charles Danvers, the eldest son who stands to inherit the estate.

While her sisters and her cousin Edward were hugely supportive of her writing at this stage, it is not clear how involved the other members of her family were. Mary continued to refer to her mother's pleasure in her writing until the end of her life,[63] but as the sisters became older and their criticism more valuable, it is possible that Emily was no longer asked to comment on her daughter's manuscripts. Similarly Regie would later offer a refuge when Mary needed somewhere undisturbed to concentrate on her writing, but there is no indication that she consulted him about the actual drafts (a later letter offering criticism on *Red Pottage* may or may not have been solicited).[64] But an astute comment by Lubbock suggests that just as Mary would later be surprised to learn that Hester, the youngest in the family, was keeping a journal in which only their parents escaped censure,[65] so the boys may not have taken Mary's writing particularly seriously at the beginning. Certainly the young men around Hodnet were not particularly impressed. As Lubbock inferred, 'There was no want of irony in her attention, but that didn't trouble them: why should it? – for the world was theirs, they had made it, and a good-natured man may be indulgent when a young woman amuses herself and does so little harm'. And if the young woman 'chanced to have ideas and ambitions of her own' then those around her would be pleased and proud, always on the understanding that 'the young woman was welcome to her fancies, but she couldn't expect to upset the world in order to make room for them'.[66] There are irreconcilable contradictions in this attitude, as Lubbock presents it, which would not have been lost on the young author herself. What to her was a laudable ambition, even something like a sacred vocation, would remain a 'fancy' to her Shropshire acquaintance, a stance she would confront with both humour and frustration. Mary remained close to her brothers, writing them and their houses into her novels, and eventually dedicating her memoir to the eldest of them.[67] But it is her sisters whose support she invokes when discussing her writing.

When this sensational story was finished, she submitted it anxiously to Mr and Mrs Ritchie for their opinion. Their response, sent to her grandmother's house in Hyde Park, where Mary was staying, made her 'feel vainer than I should have thought possible'.[68] They advised her to send it to George Bentley, the son of Dickens's first publisher and proprietor of the journal *Temple Bar*; meanwhile she had been offered a recommendation to the critic Andrew Lang, who read for Longman and who had expressed an interest in seeing the manuscript. Publication in *Temple Bar* itself she thought too good to be true, but the firm of Bentley was in some sense familiar, as the publisher of her family's friend the formidable Rhoda Broughton. By the turn of the century they were close friends and Lubbock, who had many chances to watch them together, remembered Broughton's affection for the whole family: 'She adored them, she couldn't do without them at all; she was deeply hurt, and not silently, if they weren't punctual in attention to her; and she watched over their name and fame with a jealous fondness'.[69]

They also had much in common. Broughton's novels had initially caused outrage in the conservative atmosphere of Oxford, where she lived for most of the 1880s, and she worked hard to face down the hostility and disapproval. But at this stage she was known to Mary mainly as a connection of her parents, and as the successful author of romances pedalled by the circulating libraries – the members of an Arctic expedition had actually named Mount Rhoda after her, in gratitude for the relief her books had given them in the long hours of the Arctic twilight. But Mary's own first impression of the famous writer in person had not been entirely promising. Some time in the early 1880s they had met at a large country house party, where the ladies occupied themselves with preparations for a local bazaar. As Mary sat dutifully making pincushions in the shape of a heart and set round with beads, the unoccupied Rhoda, whose own hands were elegant in appearance but clumsy in action, suddenly picked one up, held it between finger and thumb and commented, 'This is Miss Cholmondeley's heart, set round with dull but worthy thoughts'.[70] Somehow they became friends. The writer Ethel Arnold remembered meeting Broughton, with whom she too formed a close friendship, at around the same time, and confirms the sense of her as daunting as well as entertaining. As a girl of eighteen she had been invited to a house where the famous novelist was expected to dinner:

> And what I saw was this: – A woman, obviously in the early forties, with greying hair, largely concealed, as was the monstrous fashion of that day, by a cap of old lace; a thin, somewhat sharp featured face, with a keen aquiline nose, and decidedly truculent chin, held well up and slightly thrust forward, as though in instant readiness for the fray; large, prominent, 'noticeable' grey eyes, with humorous lines about the corners; a somewhat large mouth which looked as though it could readily develop a sarcastic, almost sardonic twist, yet wore a kindly expression at the moment; the head small and carried erect and slightly thrown back upon what I think were the most beautiful neck and shoulders I ever saw upon a woman – certainly upon a woman of her age. Add to all this the air of an accomplished woman of the world, at home in any company, and filled with the blessed consciousness of being remarkably well-dressed[71]

It was a year or two after this, confronted with the dilemma of where to send her novel, that Mary put herself in the hands of the Ritchies. She herself inclined towards Lang, but she was aware of her own inexperience and, as she said ruefully, 'I can do nothing for myself. I am nobody, and what it worse, a nobody buried in the country (the funeral takes place on Saturday).'[72] Their help at the beginning of her career was, as Mary recognized, of enormous value. Less helpful in the event was Mrs Ritchie's opinion of the Society of Authors, which for some reason she dissuaded Mary from joining. As to a publisher the Ritchies urged her to approach Bentley, although as Mary remembered anxiously, he had turned down an essay of hers two years previously when Mr MacColl of the *Athenaeum* had offered her an introduction.[73] In the event she secured a second champion in the person of the formidable Broughton – whose readiness to support her Mary in no sense took for granted – and in August Bentley himself wrote to tell her how taken he was with this 'bright and humorous story', a description that Mary received with bitter amusement; offering her the 'handsome' figure of £50 for her first story, he lost no time in asking her for more of the same.[74] It was the beginning of an important association that would benefit both parties for the next ten years. But she would not write another *Danvers Jewels*. There was, she felt sure, 'better stuff' in her than this.[75]

This was the summer in which Mary's cousin Henry Heber-Percy officiated in Hodnet Church at the wedding of her sister Essex to Ralph Benson, a union that would one day produce the feminist writer and suffragist Stella Benson. And it was also some time in this year that Mary herself received a proposal of marriage from 'a clever man'[76] – it was this rather than her literary success which she thought raised her somewhat in the estimation of her family, as well as in her own. She was perceptive enough to realize that she pleased others better now as she became less displeased with herself. But she did not intend to marry the clever man and wrote to tell him so.[77]

It was in this context that she seems to have finally decided the direction of her life, a life that she knew would not now contain marriage:

> I am constantly driven back upon myself. I seem to be checked at every point. I cannot go where I would, or among the people with whom I would associate. I am turned back, quietly, time after time, to a quiet life, monotonous, without any outlet to thought in the way of conversation, turned back to the silence of a country life, without interest in country life. And these I know in my own heart are the conditions in which I can (at times) work. I would go abroad, I would go to London; I would try and escape from the yoke and the harness. As if without the yoke and the harness I could draw a pound's weight – and as if, when I am sane, there was anything in heaven above or earth beneath I really prefer to following the Hand that points so plainly, that points in the direction my own soul prompts me to walk in. Happiness for me is *work*[78]

It is at once a lonely and an inspiring declaration. Lubbock refuses to reveal what she wrote between this time and his own meeting with her at the turn of the century, beyond a general comment that the intervening years were long and arduous, broken up by the social life at the rectory and sustained by Mary's continuing passion for her work.[79] But something of her life between this point and 1895, when she began a third volume of her journal, can be recovered through her extraordinary correspondence with the man who now became her publisher and perhaps her most valued critic.

George Bentley, son of the 'Brigand of Burlington Street'[80] as Dickens called him after his own dispute with the founder of the firm in the 1840s, would become as much Mary's mentor as her publisher. It was a relationship she valued enormously, as she explained to his son after his death.[81] Nonetheless these first letters are formal enough and relate entirely to the anonymous serialization of *The Danvers Jewels* in *Temple Bar* between January and March 1887. Mary had been anxious about this arrangement from the start, simply because she doubted that her rather slight first effort could withstand a reading by episode. But encouraged by the thought of a debut in an established periodical, and doubtless reluctant to lose the support of the Ritchies, she had quickly allowed herself to be talked round.

But if the Ritchies were eager to advise her, not all her male relations were as supportive on hearing her news as her cousin Edward had been when she sent him the initial manuscript. Her grandmother's son by her second marriage, James Legard, was by turns astonished, dismissive of *Temple Bar* and delighted at her success, recalling how she had once kept him awake after dinner with her stories.[82] Uncle Charles cautiously wished her success before lamenting that she had:

> joined the large army of female novelists. The fact is they are a <u>nasty</u>, <u>fusty</u>, <u>frowsy</u> lot, – Braddons and Broughtons & all of them! ... I hope you haven't 'took off' your father <u>or</u> your mother. I know that Rhoda Broughton (what a vile thing it is when the public calls a lady by her <u>Chtn name</u> as if they 'was brother or sister') has taken off some of her relations – notably old Sir John Broughton of Staffordshire, – the nasty thing! After all thank God it is not poetry![83]

The allusions to Rhoda Broughton were particularly unfortunate, a fact of which the writer in his own indignation seems entirely unaware.

Mrs Legard died just as the final instalment of her niece's first book was running in *Temple Bar*. No sooner did it appear, than the story was complimented on all sides, and in answer to constant questions about its forthcoming appearance in book form, Mary was forced to write again to Bentley to ask him what his plans actually were. The story had been written with volume publication in mind, but, she was quick to point out, she did not underestimate the value of an appearance in *Temple Bar*, she simply wanted to amend the proofs if he intended to reproduce it.[84] Even her uncle Charles was forced to admit that it was 'a very clever and creditable performance' in '<u>very well written</u> English' and that every page of it might have been written by a man. He hoped she would use a pseudonym of course if she continued to appear in print – 'If you had taken to the stage or appeared before the public in your own name it would have been the death of me!'[85]

The Danvers Jewels was duly published, still anonymously, in one volume, but, with the 'witty but unfavourable'[86] exception of *Punch*, the reviewers were slow to take the bait. When it began to be discussed, much later, as an early work by 'Miss Mary Cholmondeley, the author of *Red Pottage*', it was not discovered to be a neglected masterpiece after all. Nonetheless her first book had a reasonable success among readers (it was subsequently serialized in an American paper and translated into German, and was still in print with Macmillan until 1902).

It appeared in two further editions from Bentley, one as a sort of prelude to her next novel, *Sir Charles Danvers*.

To Mary's continuing irritation, her success caused little stir in her own part of the world.[87] But even where her book was known and admired, the absence of her name on the title page gave rise, perhaps inevitably, to misunderstandings and even attempts at usurpation. Many years later Mary recalled hearing her first books discussed in front of her and the authorship assigned 'on good authority' to other people, usually men. Indeed in the first enjoyment of fame she could not resist divulging her authorship to at least one kindly old man at a dinner party, only to be met with the grave reply, 'I know that to be untrue', before he tactfully changed the subject.[88]

The experience of writing *The Danvers Jewels* had not been a happy one. But shortly after hearing that it had been accepted for *Temple Bar*, Mary was set to begin again. 'Happiness for me is *work*'[89] she told herself at the time, and besides, Bentley did not encourage idleness. Throughout their relationship his presence can be felt on the sidelines, urging her on to greater work, reminding her to capitalize on recent success lest she be forgotten among the crowds of women writers crowding the *fin de siècle* press.[90]

And so, probably in the autumn of 1887, she began again, with a novel she intended to be entirely different from her first. *Sir Charles Danvers* regenerates Charles, the charming scapegrace of the first novel, who with his mountain of debts and suspicious behaviour was first suspected of having stolen the Danvers jewels. At the beginning of this sequel the woman he initially loved is married to his younger brother Ralph, and his father has spitefully left everything that was not entailed and so was in his power to leave, to Ralph. In *Sir Charles Danvers* Charles is transformed into a hero, who falls in love with a local girl. By the time he makes his declaration, she has rashly become engaged to the new owner of an encumbered estate, Dare, in a gesture of pity mixed with social conscience. In its focus on the life of a county family and the idealistic young girl who nearly marries the wrong man in order to persuade him to build model cottages for his tenants, the novel confirms Cholmondeley's own comment that George Eliot was a major influence.[91] The anxiety about the fate of aristocratic estates that informs *The Danvers Jewels* is further developed in Dare's failure to retrieve the position of his tenants during this decade of agricultural depression. The pre-story sees Charles miraculously rescued from debt by the bequest of a family friend, which potentially saves him from a mercenary marriage. In this second published novel the threat to upper-class control of the landscape lies not in middle-class encroachment, but in the very past Cholmondeley was always anxious to preserve. A Dare ancestor has plunged his estate into such ruin that it has become virtually impossible to rescue, a state of affairs that mirrors what might have happened to the Danvers estate had Charles not been redeemed.

Again taking up a theme from the first story, the portrayal of Ruth offers an extended critique of gender roles in this world. Where Dare promises far more than he will fulfil, Ruth resignedly meets her responsibilities in the parish, sitting out tedious cottage visits and helping at dolls' bazaars. She comically defines her own role and that of Charles in terms of gender, telling him, 'No man who respects himself makes himself common by attending village school feasts, and attempting to pour out tea, which he is never allowed to do in private life'. When he protests that he could hand out buns, she responds with, 'I only wished to keep you in your proper sphere'.[92] This raillery certainly suggests Cholmondeley's own awareness of gender status, and the ways in which masculine and feminine 'spheres' might become subject to fracture. Nonetheless, Ruth goes on to deride women who would attempt to engage in political debate. Despite the author's own interest in politics,[93] she will only allow Ruth to question gender roles by subverting feminine discourse, not by appropriating that of men.

In terms of her writing itself, she was still prepared to take criticism. Hester found Mrs Alwyn capital, but pronounced the tenants' supper poor and decided it should come out. 'I think it will, for we have made her see it is weak and uninteresting'. Quoting this extract from her sister's journal, Mary notes resignedly 'The tenants' supper had taken a long time to write, but it came out'.[94] While there is an emphasis on the exigencies and routines of country life that was virtually absent from the earlier story, still Mary includes an exciting plot that was to become something of a trademark in even her most serious work. The climax of the story is reached when, a despairing Charles having failed in a moment of weakness to persuade Ruth to elope with him, a strange woman appears from America claiming to be Dare's wife, despite their having gone through a divorce. The suspense builds as Dare investigates the claim, and in the midst of the drama Ruth's criminal brother reappears and declares that he has proof that the woman's claim is legal, despite her having already had a husband whom she believed to be living at the time she married Dare. Ruth's brother urges Charles to conceal this revelation in order to marry Ruth himself. In yet another twist, Ruth learns the truth and decides that while she would not in any case marry a man who has divorced his first wife, nor will she marry Charles if he fails in integrity by keeping his new knowledge secret from her. This dilemma begins a pattern discernible in almost all Cholmondeley's later fiction, whereby the moral status and ultimate happiness of a central figure depends on the revelation of a secret, at whatever personal cost.

It was some time in this year that Dick Cholmondeley paid a visit to Hodnet from Australia. Hester recorded in her journal how much noise they made at dinner and how handsome everyone looked, 'which shows that even her critical eye could occasionally take a roseate view'.[95] Mary herself remembered this occasion, and 'I am afraid there is no doubt we *were* noisy. Father and Mother smiled tolerantly at us from either end of the table. It was the last time we were all together.'[96] The following year Essex's first child George was born. But on the last day of the year, Hester wrote in her diary, 'is it coming on slowly and surely that thing I sometimes think of? ... all seems very good as it is, and changes are cruel things.'[97] Slow, as Mary sadly remembered, to take the alarm, the family became worried about Hester when the accustomed asthma simply failed to go that winter. In the end she was taken to a London specialist, who confirmed that one lung was slightly damaged.

4 'THE ONLY LIFE I KNOW': *SIR CHARLES DANVERS, DIANA TEMPEST* AND *A DEVOTEE*

Mary had come a long way since the days when she gave up her artistic aspirations and began to turn her storytelling powers to account in the writing of *Her Evil Genius* in 1877. Still some months short of her twenty-ninth birthday, and with her second novel now safely completed despite her perpetual lapses in health,[1] she had every reason to feel pleased with herself. But still she doubted her ability. She had achieved a great deal, but she remained uncertain about the future, and in March 1888 she sent the manuscript to her cousin Edward Cholmondeley, who had given valuable advice on her previous novel. His self-mockery in the *Cornhill*, where he would claim to be a 'briefless barrister' making desultory efforts at verse because he had nothing else to do, is at odds with the painstaking commentary to which he now subjected Sir Charles. In his own account of a day spent in his Birmingham chambers, the monotony is broken only by importunate sellers of furniture polish and annotated volumes of Shakespeare; his sole correspondence turning out to be from his aunt, whose servant wants to take a lease of a cottage at Peckham, 'Would you, like a good boy, run through the copy.'[2] To Mary he wrote that he was 'in a great hurry', and had been forced to skim the last part of the manuscript because he had to go on circuit the following week. But his proofing was punctilious – he pointed out that a Frenchman should be treated to a capital F, and went through with a pencil lightly making alterations which he tactfully assured her a piece of India rubber would soon remove. He reassured her about the point of law governing Dare's marital status, and pointed out that gentlemen did not generally go riding in knickerbockers. He admired the novel more than *The Danvers Jewels*, finding it showed 'more thought, more power, & in some respects more of the novelist's art'.[3]

Soon afterwards she wrote to the Ritchies for further advice, admitting apologetically that 'I cannot remember <u>exactly</u> what I was to do beyond being very careful. I don't know how I can be very careful except by applying to you.'[4] She must have envied the Ritchies their accepted position in the literary circles of London, where she herself could only go for visits before returning to the demands of life in Hodnet. Later in life she would come to realize that both the

city and the country were necessary to her at different times, but at the beginning of her writing career she thought mainly of escaping the provincial attitudes
and lifeless routine of her rural existence. Still she was always alive to the literary
opportunities even of her own despondency and, mindful of her correspondent's
former advice, she had carefully avoided too many sensational elements in her
new book and had stuck to describing 'real life, the only life I know, the life of
country people'.[5] Now she was in need of reassurance. The book had taken nearly
a year and a half of severe manual labour – throughout her career Mary would
be grimly conscious of the *physical* cost of her writing, as it drained her of her
already feeble health – and she was apprehensive about her publisher's reaction
to this very different story. With the self-doubt common to most writers and
that would return with increasing persistence as her fame grew, she wrote now:

> It seems to me that to write a book at all is an act of faith. One cant tell whether all
> one's time spent in laboriously digging it out may not be thrown away, I mean I cant.
> I have dug out something, but whether a nugget of silver or garden clay I don't know,
> and the more I turn it over the more I don't know.[6]

Despite having once said it was 'too good to be likely to be true', she was not
keen for this new story to appear in *Temple Bar*, thinking that it was not substantial enough and would not 'bear the strain'.[7] But she was otherwise unsure
how to deal with Bentley. Evidently she felt out of her depth negotiating with
businessmen for the rights to her work, which meant far more to her than it
could possibly do to them, but the success of which she was already inclined
to measure in terms of payment and subsequent sales. As the years passed she
would develop an extraordinary relationship with George Bentley, based as
much on their shared subjection to asthma as on her respect for his critical acu-
men. Although they only met once, she never forgot his words on that occasion,
when he predicted future triumphs if she would only persevere.[8] He was a thor-
ough and conscientious critic, never scrupling to tell her where he felt she had
not lived up to the potential he had foreseen that day in New Burlington Street.[9]
Mary later confessed that he had the power to influence her writing where no
one else could,[10] and their correspondence remained cordial throughout the
misunderstandings, illnesses and deadlines of the next decade. But while she
formed and would retain the highest opinion of Bentley as a critic, Mary was
always aware that he was first and foremost a man of business, and it was in this
context that she now wrote once more to the Ritchies asking for advice and a
degree of moral support.

In the event it was not Bentley Senior but his son who wrote in May, with the
unwelcome offer of a mere £40 for the copyright, on the grounds that the story
would only fill two volumes;[11] the three-volume format popular at the time was
a particular draw to the large circulating libraries such as Mudie's, who could

charge extra subscription rates to a reader wanting to borrow all three volumes simultaneously. Further royalties would depend on the number of sales. But, as Mary was quick to point out, this would be £10 less than she had been given for the considerably shorter *Danvers Jewels*. Upset by what she took to be a comment on her writing, she nearly refused to publish the book at all if it was considered worthy of no more than this. But she was about to leave Hodnet for a holiday in Brighton and after a few days staring at the sea she was, she decided, 'prepared to be rational'.[12] Accordingly on her return home she wrote a pragmatic offer of acceptance, stipulating simply for another £10 to avoid the humiliating possibility that she might earn less for her second book than for her first in the event of poor sales. What rankled most was that 'Mr Bentley's opinion is of immense insight, and consequently it is very disheartening to me to infer that this more serious effort ... does not meet with much approval from him'.[13] Until his death in July 1895, Mary would continue to seek the approval of her publisher, using his opinion as the most reliable benchmark of her progress. Later in her career she would become increasingly conscious both of the agenda of the publishing world, and of her own market value in that world.[14] But in bringing her second novel to confront a critical public, with the expectations she herself had raised with the success of *The Danvers Jewels*, she was concerned only with the doubt implied in Bentley's unflattering offer for the copyright.

What is likely to have pleased her more was the marriage of her brother Regie, on 5 September, to Florence Mills, the daughter of the extremely wealthy John Remmington Mills of Tolmers, Hertfordshire.[15] Florie would be a source of emotional support to Mary for the rest of her life, eventually figuring in her diaries as a closer friend even than her beloved brother himself. But for herself, Mary was anxious. She was understandably worried about her novel, but it is likely that she was also undergoing some kind of religious crisis.[16] She would later write sympathetically of conscientious questioners who found themselves trammelled by Church teaching and thwarted by its doctrines in their own pursuit of truth. Quoting Corbet's *Letters from a Mystic* (1889), in which he expresses concern about the conservatism of the Church and its refusal to accept new ideas, she writes:

> The above description will be recognised by most thoughtful people as coincident with an early chapter of their own history. Possibly it is a vivid remembrance of that painful crisis, of its loneliness, and of the condemnation of their first real struggle toward a higher life, which has embittered the minds of some (unreasonably, as it appears to us) against the Church.[17]

In such a crisis she would be able to turn neither to her father, whose own beliefs were fervent and apparently largely unexamined, nor to her strictly orthodox mother. It must have been towards the end of December of this year that she wrote instead to the retired Unitarian minister Hamilton Thom,[18] and she may have told him something of the anxiety that plagued her, and which would eventually come under medical superintendence. She had been greatly struck by his writing, and little wonder. His *Laws of Life Under the Mind of Christ*, first published in 1883, insists on the power of experience, however tragic, and the essential unity of the human spirit despite differences of worldly situation. It was a book written for the undervalued, for those who felt themselves to have failed in life, speaking to

> the disappointment which experience brings in their ideal of life. The dreams of their youth have miscarried. They are not to themselves, nor to the world, nor yet to those to whom they are most, all that was once in their purpose, perhaps in their power, to be.[19]

And yet, he insists, Christ achieved his greatest success through his apparent failure, and while all have their part to play in the world, to withdraw from it even for the seemingly highest motive is to fall into a trap:

> The *visionary*, the sentimentalist, the voluptuary of emotion ... who, instead of using such rare and beautiful gifts from God's rich power for the grace and elevation of common cares and duties and all the hard necessities of life, withdraws, for the sake of their direct indulgence, from the work and friction of the real world – has his thin being, superior as he may think it, quite apart from that way of glorified human life on which ... the divinest light and grace from Heaven is seen to rest for evermore upon the face of One who lived with common men, and knew all humiliations, and died upon a cross.[20]

If Mary felt strongly enough to write to the author, he in turn was pleased to hear that he could have 'met her religious wants, or cherished your aspirations' through his writing.[21] Now nearly eighty-two and in feeble health, he was struck, as others would be, by the young woman with the high ideals who addressed him with such candour, and wrote back to tell her that while they were unlikely ever to meet, he would often think of her. She must not, he told her, be discouraged by early disappointments; it was continuous growth that mattered. Florie recalled years later that she had been introduced to Thom's works by the warm recommendation of her sister in law.[22]

But in the meantime negotiations with Bentley continued to go badly. The original offer was doubled on condition that Sir Charles duly made his appearance in *Temple Bar*, a proposal that Mary disingenuously told Bentley she was delighted in accepting. 'I remembered your advising me ... to jump at such a chance if I was lucky enough to get it', she wrote dubiously to Richmond Ritchie, 'so I accordingly jumped. I hope I was right.'[23] But still she felt out of her depth. In London with her aunt Victoria and Victoria's second husband[24] that spring, she went to call on the firm and meet Richard Bentley face to face, but finally decided against taking anyone with her for moral support, knowing it would only make her more nervous to have a third person listening. All the same she felt in need of backup: 'I see now, that I have been unable to get anything definite out of him, although I am sure it was a good thing to have gone. I do not think I am able to cope with these men.'[25] In essence she had been thrown off balance not only by her inevitable anxiety as a woman conducting business with a successful male publisher, but also, as her account of their meeting suggests, a certain distaste for such direct dealings, in which she was placed at an unaccustomed disadvantage, with a member of the professional middle class. She reported that he was 'very civil but different to what I had expected. It seems curious one should be in the hands of a man of that kind.' She was considering joining the Society of Authors, a step she had contemplated shortly after its inception in 1884.[26] She had been talked out of it on that occasion and it seems likely that Mrs Ritchie's response to her new appeal was equally discouraging – it is only after the debacle with her bestselling book in 1899 that her correspondence with publishers makes pointed reference to having all agreements read through by the Society.[27]

But if Bentley was ambivalent about this more sober second novel, Mary was determined to impress him with her next work, which would combine a satire of London society with a series of sensational events to draw in the reader. She was not going to be trammelled by the 'bright humour' of her first novel, nor by the provincial realism of her second. In her third work she would build on these achievements to quite different ends.

It is unclear exactly when the idea came to her, but probably some time that spring someone told Mary a story about a young man of immense wealth, who was the object of a bet on his life (in a bizarre twist the young man in question actually went on to marry one of her many cousins).[28] From this dinner party gossip she began to construct a plot about inheritance, an adulterous wife and a dissolute uncle who agrees in a drunken moment to gamble on the chance of his inheriting the family estate, entailed on his nephew and subsequently on his children. It was at one level a return to the sensational fare of *The Danvers Jewels*.

Like its predecessors, *Diana Tempest* is firmly rooted in its country house setting, and its sensational plot builds on the success of the earlier novel. The debauched widower, Colonel Tempest, is the rightful heir to his wealthy brother, to whom he has not spoken since eloping with his fiancée many years earlier. The brother subsequently marries but his wife confesses on her deathbed that her son John is the result of an affair with another man. Determined to bypass the entail on his treacherous brother, the elder Tempest allows John to grow up as his son and inherit the estate. The main plot begins after Colonel Tempest is lured into placing a bet that he himself will not ultimately inherit, which would effectively mean that John must die young. While a series of apparent accidents is reported in the press, the suspense increases as Cholmondeley artfully takes the reader through Colonel Tempest's efforts to track down and pay off his confederate before his ostensible nephew can be murdered.

She wanted it to be more than simply an exciting story – running through the book is Mary's own sense of the aristocratic tradition, as John's conscientious management of the Tempest estate is contrasted with the fecklessness of his uncle and cousin Archie. Social caste is carefully drawn in the novel, and the narrator is confident enough to take it as read that money is irrelevant in this regard. With a strangely prophetic instinct, she shows her heroine moving as a matter of course among the London elite, despite living with an impoverished grandmother whose flat she helps to decorate, and it is not seen as particularly anomalous for Diana to visit the head of her family in a castle and return to cover her own furniture for the sake of saving expense.

Diana and her grandmother come, as did Mary herself, from the upper strata of the landed gentry, and the narrator makes much of the fact that generations of Tempests have turned down the titles that lesser families would have been glad to get – simply to be a Tempest is enough. However, again like Mary, they are left without the income to sustain the kind of lifestyle associated with their class. Cholmondeley herself was not of course the first author to take up this theme – one has only to think of the Deadlock family in Dickens's *Bleak House* (1853), with its array of superannuated maiden aunts living on precarious pensions and family charity. But in a society increasingly resistant to the comforting assurance of blood being better than money, Mary was well placed to confront the vulnerable position of unmarried women whose social position still precluded any form of work, even as that position began to be eroded. While her heroines tend to marry well or come into unexpected money (the former for preference), she is as quick to declaim their disadvantaged status as she is to pre-empt the pity of readers – Diana's flat is the envy of her richer acquaintance, who have no idea how she has achieved such tasteful decoration on what is known to be a limited income. The narrator has nothing but contempt for the 'millionaire cheesemongers'[29] who are buying up the ancient homes of an impoverished aristocracy, which by implication they have little idea how to furnish.

Taking up another keynote from *Sir Charles Danvers*, she would use the book to explore the question of probity in the face of temptation. John's temptation is to conceal the truth about his birth in order to protect not so much himself as the house he loves, knowing as he does that his uncle would quickly squander the enormous income and sell off the painstakingly accumulated family heirlooms.

As the plot of her new novel now began to take shape in her mind, so her completed one began its appearance before the public, beginning its run in *Temple Bar* in May. September 1889 brought good news, in the birth of a new Reginald Cholmondeley, Florie's first child.[30] But in November Hester was not well and was setting off with their mother to Torquay. From here she exchanged a series of letters with Mary, which she described as being 'what she most looked forward to and valued in the week'.[31] Mary was able to confide her anxieties and her gratifications, as well as all the news from Hodnet. Meanwhile she was receiving letters of congratulation and criticism on the newly published *Sir Charles Danvers* from her relations. James Legard was delighted with it. As he put it, 'One reads such a lot of ghastly rubbish nowadays ... that it is quite a relief to get hold of anything with ideas in it'.[32] Uncle Charles wrote to tell her that he had missed a service through sitting up the night before with the book, before spoiling the effect entirely by calling the heroine selfish and unprincipled – 'not quite so bad as some I have met with' but 'sufficiently offensive'.[33] As ever he was quick to give the highest praise to her diction and expression, a particularly annoying habit that would be taken up by another clerical figure in *Red Pottage*.

If her uncle Charles was stinting in his praise, the reviews of his namesake were pleasingly favourable, and at the end of December Mary was delighted to receive a letter from Mr Paul of the *Daily News*, comparing her to Richardson and anxious to disclaim a review in his paper written by 'some fool' who assumed her to be a male author (not the last time this would happen). He called her book 'a contribution to literature' and assured her that while he had scant respect for county families, he had a sincere respect for good work.[34] Mary in turn wrote to Hester in Torquay, 'Mr Paul is a cultivated clever man, intensely democratic, so I rather like his good opinion'. Perhaps inspired by his democratic principles, she felt able to dispense with the good opinion of Lady somebody or other, who was apparently taking a position of severe disapproval.[35] But more seriously, Mary's first suspicion that Bentley himself doubted the new book seemed justified when it transpired that there had not been enough copies printed to meet the instant demand.[36]

To add to her troubles, there was an influenza pandemic in Hodnet in the beginning of 1890. There were thirteen down at the hall, and at the rectory every member of the household was taking quinine twice daily – Mary explained to Hester, largely for her mother's benefit, that she was giving doses of thirty drops only and they meant to stop after four days on the recommendation of Dr Lyon. Meanwhile she wanted more than anything to get back to work, but there was a working party to organize, there were mission services coming up, with the necessary choir practices of new hymns, there was the usual running of the house to be got through. What with all these activities, and her project to make a paper catalogue of the library, on top of her Sunday School work, no wonder she complained, 'I hardly know how on earth the book is to be written. It has not been touched since Dec. It was simply an impossibility.'[37] It was shortly after writing this letter that she finally met George Bentley himself.

Clearly Hester was protective of her talented sister and suspicious of her publisher. It is obvious from the letter that they had discussed the embellishments Mary wanted to add to her new book as well as her relationship with the Bentley firm, but there is a teasing as well as an exultant note in Mary's letter telling her about this meeting, 'My dear Wild Cat I was received like a Princess'.[38] Bentley wanted to include *Sir Charles Danvers* in his Favourite Novels series, to come out in May. He told her that Sir Charles had increased the sales of *The Danvers Jewels*, with the result that he now wanted to bring out a new edition of that book too. He promised a place for 'Let Loose', a macabre story about a ghostly hand and a mouldy vault, in the April number of *Temple Bar*, and put Mary on the list of permanent contributors.

At what was to be their first and only meeting in an association of nearly twenty years, Bentley also gave her some shrewd advice. He told her that she had better stuff in her than she had yet shown to the world; but she must capitalize on her recent success if she wanted to make a name for herself. He was sure from what he called 'indications' that she would go on to write better books, but equally she must begin again soon, before the éclat of *Sir Charles Danvers* could be forgotten by a fickle reading public. Despite her demurral, he urged her to write an instalment of her new novel for the November number of the magazine, offering to hold a place for her until May. 'He said my next work ought to appear <u>soon</u>, and he thought it would be well worth my while to give up everything, visiting, going abroad, <u>everything</u>, for the present and get on with it.' Mary came away elated, only to be beset almost immediately by doubt: 'If only I could really work hard, and well, but it seems impossible'.[39] She particularly asked Hester to send her love to their mother, who she knew would be glad of her news from Burlington Street.

Subsequently she tried to negotiate an earlier date for the new edition of *Sir Charles Danvers*, but by March there was still no sign of it and Mary found herself writing somewhat desperately to Bentley, pointing out that her friends were unable to obtain copies from Mudie's – they were told there were none to be had until the cheap edition came out in May. Mary was getting 'seriously anxious' that the demand would die out before the cheaper one-volume edition even appeared, and urged her publisher to consider a second two-volume edition,[40] a request to which at some point he acceded. When he sent her a cheque for 10 guineas for 'Let Loose', she was appreciative, but not to be distracted.[41] Even here there were problems, when it turned out that she had inadvertently plagiarized another author's work. Or, to put it more accurately, she had naively taken on trust a story told to her as having happened to a friend of one of her cousins, only to learn from letters written to Bentley that the story was based on something he had read.[42] She was relieved when he wrote to assure her that he believed in her own good intentions, and confided in return that on her round of post Easter visits she had noticed how very cordially I have been received, and how many more friends I have than I imagined. As there is no change in myself except a new hat I put this rush of cordiality down to my story, and consequently feel sanguine for the new edition.[43]

She still had some time to wait however, and it was not until August that she was able to write, somewhat apprehensively, to the Ritchies, 'I am very glad "Danvers" is getting on to the bookstalls. I do hope it will be read, but I dont see any advertisements anywhere.'[44] In the event the book sold only 751 copies in its first four years, and generally no more than a hundred or two in any given year (it peaked at 455 in the year after *Red Pottage* appeared and sank without trace around 1912).[45]

In the spring of 1890 Mary was at least confident enough in her health to respond with something like alacrity to Bentley's demands for further work, telling him that she was already well into the second volume of a new novel, although she doubted its overtaking Sir Charles. 'I shall never have another hero like him' she told Bentley.[46] It was at about this time that Emily and Hester finally returned to Hodnet after an absence of six months.[47] Whatever their relationship otherwise, Mary had been in the habit of discussing her writing with her mother, and she also valued the opinion of her fragile youngest sister. But her optimistic mood was not to last. Bentley, keen to see the book about which he had expressed such high expectations, had offered to hold a place open for *Temple Bar* 91 until May, for publication in November. And now suddenly she could not write. As the deadline came round she was forced to write to him and explain that, given the problems of a 'larger canvas' (interestingly she still perceived her writing as a kind of painting in words) she could produce nothing that satisfied her in the least. Of course she would persevere at all costs, for nothing was achieved by giving in – and here is the authentic voice of the writer, miserable, anxious but refusing to be defeated – but still she could not write.[48] Bentley duly extended the deadline until the summer.[49]

As the summer drew to a close, Mary herself was off on a series of visits. But by now she was clearly unwell, and uneasy in mind. By July she was admitting that there was no chance of producing passable script by the time appointed, she was not working well or she would never have left home. She could only hope that her tour of Scotland might do something for her. But she goes on with barely suppressed panic, 'Imagination seems a most precarious possession. I cannot believe just now that I ever had any. I suppose it will come back if I am patient.'[50] To make matters worse she found herself 'scourged' once again by asthma, against which she had seemingly become proof over the last few years. But in her letters to friends even her own misery becomes a source of humour. As she put it to the Ritchies that August, 'I am taking a course of visits, and suppose I must be enjoying myself very much. I have been at it nearly a month.'[51] While she might bewail her fate, comparing her venture into the world to a water cure that does one good although it is not pleasant at the time, she was as ready as ever to laugh at herself and at the response she evoked in others. Of one house party she commented that:

> They were a little frightened at first, as they all knew I had perpetrated a book, which of course was <u>odd</u>: but they soon got better, and are now inclined to be curious as to 'how I did it'. The first night at dinner a young man next to me turned to me rather diffidently and said he was ashamed to say he had not read my story, 'but' he added with conscious pride 'I have bought a copy, and <u>written my name on it</u>'.[52]

However, the visits did nothing to fend off what her family feared might be a complete collapse. By the end of them Mary still found herself unable to work and was relieved when her doctor diagnosed her with 'exhaustion of the brain', if only because it explained what had been worrying her for months, her seeming inability to write a line to her own satisfaction. She wrote to thank Bentley for his consideration when she had finally had to refuse the offer of a place in *Temple Bar* 91, and then broke the news that her doctor had told her writing would be out of the question for months to come.[53] That October she was duly sent to Torquay with Hester, where she hoped the brighter air might set her up after an attack of bronchitis.[54]

In the second half of the nineteenth century Torquay had become increasingly popular as both a tourist and an invalid resort. Boasting a mild winter climate and its own bath house offering sea water medical treatments (one of Mary's literary heroines, Elizabeth Barrett Browning, took advantage of this facility between 1838 and 1841, although the original baths had since been replaced with larger ones to meet the growing demand), the town was attractively positioned looking out over the sea.[55] Crucially it was accessible by rail, although in the 1890s this would have meant a gruelling journey from Hodnet with no fewer than four changes on the way.[56] Soon after their arrival Mary wrote to Bentley again, this time seemingly determined to play down her obviously frail health. In her previous letter less than two weeks earlier she had confided her wretchedness, the constant headaches and the torture of being unable to write; now she said that the fall of the leaf is always bad for asthma, remarking with unconvincing chirpiness that 'even she' has had a touch of it in the previous month.[57]

Her response to what happened next is more characteristic. In her later tribute to her sister Hester she recalls that 'poor child, she was born under an unlucky star. As soon as I arrived at Torquay I immediately fell dangerously ill. This was the best thing possible for me, an entire breakdown was the only exit from my condition, but it was the worst thing possible for her.'[58] In fact Mary was not taken ill literally on arrival, she was in reasonable health when she wrote to Bentley on the last day of the month. But she explains her silence for the next two months by telling him that she fell ill immediately afterwards with delirium and subsequent collapse coming on the top of acute bronchitis.[59] Either way, her account is notable for two things: first, her emphasis on the suffering endured by her sister at the time of her illness; second for the seemingly extraordinary statement that a dangerous illness was the 'best thing possible' for the invalid herself. Inevitably the suffering of her elder sister from a brief but dangerous illness was 'a cruel ordeal' for the tender-hearted and sensitive Hester, but for Mary herself illness can be figured as release – she was consoled now by the doctor's assurance that a severe illness would allow her to make 'a fresh start' on her recovery, but in later life she would imbue illness with an uncanny power, as the visible and outward sign of the artistic vision.[60] The power to write is vouchsafed, in *Red Pottage*, only to the moribund Hester, named after Hester Cholmondeley, and her claim to literary genius in the novel is reinforced by her declining health.

In Torquay in the winter of 1890, Mary remembered that 'in the few minutes which she was allowed to spend in my room [Hester] was always perfectly calm and undemonstrative'. It was only on reading her diary years later that she realized the self-control her sister had exercised on these occasions.[61] But Mary recovered reasonably quickly, and by December she had no more than the weakness of the convalescent of which to complain. Frustratingly now that she felt she could work she was not allowed to, 'my doctor obliges me to pass my days in needlework and novel reading'.[62] And ironically it was now that she was forced to defend herself to Bentley, who had been understandably taken aback to read an announcement in the *Athenaeum* to the effect that her new book would be published shortly. She assured him that far from having made arrangements with another publisher, she had only written one volume of the new story, and would in any case consider it dishonourable to go elsewhere unless he had previously turned down the manuscript. What had happened was that a friend of the editor's had written to ask her whether it was not true that she was bringing out a new book, and evidently had not waited for her answer (it was perhaps in a gesture of repentance that the *Athenaeum* later wrote what Mary termed 'a pleasant review' of her new book, when it finally appeared in 1893).[63] But these were happy days nonetheless as she began to recover, talking to Hester. '[W]e understood each other', she wrote later. 'Each was interested in the other's mind.'[64]

Although she would later recast her in fictional form as a novelist, thus strengthening the link between them, it seems that Hester concentrated on poetry during this stay in Torquay. Mary's enjoyment of her sister's company was clearly reciprocated; at the end of this year Hester wrote 'Christmas Day', in which she naively – and in retrospect, poignantly – evokes her pleasure in watching the sea with a close companion by her side:

> Whence comes the glory? is it one that stands
> Beside me, pouring gladness on the day
> For me from her dear eyes? she understands,
> And as we watch the light with reverent eye
> Both our hearts know its gleam can never die.[65]

Away from the pressures and the daily routine of home life, there was time to discuss writing, but also their shared commitment to religion, and it was here too that Hester wrote the lines which Mary later used as a heading to a chapter in *Diana Tempest*, and which were much quoted in religious works in the ensuing decades :

> Still, as of old
>   Man by himself is priced.
> For thirty pieces Judas sold
>   Himself, not Christ.[66]

Later Mary would recall sitting in the schoolroom at Hodnet Rectory submitting parts of the story to the judgement of Diana and Victoria, who in turn regaled her with anecdotes from parties she had been too unwell to attend, and so provided invaluable material by proxy.[67] A few years later she would admit,

> That her books are ever written at all is in large measure due to their constant care of her weak health, their continual encouragement and sympathy, their unflagging zeal in all that relates to the story, and to their untiring unselfishness ... in saving her, whenever possible, from all irksome duties.[68]

But if Diana and Victoria would later be prepared to sacrifice their own prospects to their older sister, the less robust Hester was equally important to Mary's creative development at this stage. In particular Mary herself remembered Hester's uncompromising views and her insistence on the highest possible standard, from herself and those around her. She may even have been influenced by this intransigence herself – it was to Hester that she had confided a year earlier that an acquaintance had sent her his first attempt at essay writing and then made the mistake of coming in person to ask her what she thought of it. Mary struggled with herself and then told him the truth. It was poetical, it was well observed. But it was not well written. Made miserable by having been the one to crush his hopes, she told her sister, 'People should <u>never</u> shew me their things and ask for an opinion. I do hope no one else will do it.'[69] It was, as she knew herself, just what would happen again and again in years to come.

Early in the new year of 1891, two months after her collapse, Mary was finally deemed well enough to make a tentative effort at writing again. It meant, she recalled, a great effort for which she was not entirely ready but with her usual determination she stuck to it and two months later she was ready to try out a further two chapters on her sister, quite possibly the first she had written in almost a year.[70] These chapters seem to have related to the discovery of a lie, possibly to do with the intrigues of the older generation, and it is likely that in this initial version of the story it was the heroine who became apprised of a terrible secret affecting the hero, and decided in mercy to withhold it from him. It had been a substantial amount of work, not the sticking her toe in the water which was doubtless what her doctor had advised. But as she read these crucial scenes to her sister, Mary was confident of their effect. She waited. There was a moment of appalling silence and then Hester burst into tears. Eventually between the sobs she managed to say that she would not have done it, Diana would not have let him go on believing a falsehood. Shocked and doubtless hurt by this reaction, Mary asked was it not any good? Yes, it was 'the best you have ever written, but it won't do, because she would have told him'. There followed a silent meal, both sisters red eyed, but 'Hester suffered far the most, for she knew what a labour those two chapters had been'.[71] It is to the credit of both that Mary thought over her sister's criticism, decided she was right, and promptly destroyed the difficult work of two months. She makes no reference to this incident in a letter to her publisher that April, simply reassuring him that 'for the last 3 months I have been able, with my doctor's leave, to go on with the unfortunate book which has been half in my head, and half on paper for the last two years'. She was now, she wrote, within eight chapters of the end and feeling confident. 'I have not forgotten one of your kind and forcible words respecting the importance my next book will have on my career, and your <u>expectation</u> that I should surpass "Sir Charles". I believe I have done so.'[72] By the end of May, she assured him, she would have the first volume ready for inspection (in fact she sent him the first volume in the second week of June).[73]

At home in Hodnet that April the local papers were enthusiastically reporting on an evening of sacred song in Hodnet Church.[74] The two-hour service was attended by upwards of 700 people, and Victoria, Diana and Florie all sang in the choir, as did Regie. Meanwhile in Torquay Mary and Hester were by now back in circulation, receiving twenty-four luncheon invitations in one fortnight. Muriel Kent, who saw them while they were there, remembered after Mary's death that 'they left a lasting impression of individuality beneath their quiet bearing, reserved yet gracious ... both appeared as those with something to confer – a gift which it had cost the labour of their souls to prepare and offer to the world'. Hester she recalled as shy and dignified, 'like "Evelyn Hope" she seemed made of spirit and dew'. She unknowingly recalls Mary's own uncertainties in her comment that 'In spite of my nebulous status – neither child nor grown-up – they included me' in an afternoon party at their lodgings.[75] Mary recalled amateur dramatics at these same lodgings, for which events they made use of an additional room by permission of their landlady. As the day for one performance drew near they found to their horror that this room had been rented out as a bedroom to a visiting bachelor. The landlady did not keep her promise to change his room on the day of the theatricals, and they were only saved when he unexpectedly went out for a walk. As Mary put it, 'We hoped it would be a long one. We rushed into his bedroom and changed it into a green-room. I can see now his large evening pumps and other shoes in a line against the wall.'[76]

But this time was not wholly given over to literary discussion and theatrical parties. Mary wrote later of the friendship she and Hester formed with some of the London shop girls at a Home of Rest nearby, who had formed the most unfavourable ideas of 'ladies' as a class. Two of them would later walk several miles to pay their respects to Hester, whom they had never met.[77] In *Red Pottage*, the novel honouring her sister that she was to write a few years later, Mary allows her fictional writer to make an éclat with her first book, *An Idyll of East London*, exposing the conditions she has observed at first hand among the London working class.

In May Hester's health was considered safe and she returned home, Mary stopping in London for the season,[78] where she could remain in close contact with Bentley – in June she sent him the first volume of her new manuscript to consider for serialization in *Temple Bar*, although she could not let it out of her sight for long, constantly referring to the intricate plot of the first volume as she laboured on the third.[79] At home once again an unforeseen disaster undermined the family's hopes for Hester's recovery:

> A few days [after her return] on May 16, contrary to all precedent a heavy snow fell. It fell incessantly. It crushed all the young leaves. It weighed down the outspread apple blossom outside the schoolroom window. In spite of the utmost care it affected Hester, who lay in bed watching the flakes drift past her window.[80]

That summer as Mary exchanged slightly frantic letters with Bentley, who was ready for the remaining volumes – 'I sincerely wish they were ready for you'; 'You mention that you have not the ms with you ... which causes me some uneasiness. For, if you have not got it, and I have not, <u>where</u> is it?'[81] – there was a pandemic of Russian influenza in Hodnet, to which Hester inevitably succumbed. As this new anxiety set in there was further disappointing news from Bentley – he had not been impressed by the ending of the first volume, in which Mary had conscientiously tried to relieve her sensational story with events 'pitched in a lower key'. She was forced to admit that if the ending of the first volume had disappointed him, the second and third would be unlikely to retrieve his good opinion. But she resolutely sat down to rewrite the offending passages, for 'believe me, "Miss Cholmondeley" is sincerely anxious to "beat her last"'.[82] She was rewarded for her assiduity – in September 1892 she was again writing to Bentley to express her pleasure that the new story would appear in *Temple Bar*, which she had somehow convinced herself was not his intention.[83] Once more she combines a frank dependence on his critical opinion – she trusts his judgement, she says, and if she does not follow it, it will only be because she cannot – with a certain wariness about the terms of her contract, which she carefully compared with her previous one before asking to have a particular word explained. It is ironic in retrospect that her instinctive suspicion should have been brought out by a worry over copyright – it was later, when the firm of Bentley had been sold and she herself was forced to move on, that she would have cause to read her contracts more carefully than ever.[84] But throughout her correspondence it is her sheer determination that is most apparent – asking for honest criticism she tells Bentley that the book has cost her so much, her whole heart is in its success; she has already expended on it immense care and patience, but she is ready to expend a little more.[85] Clearly she was dedicated to writing a greater work than she had yet attempted – her response to Hester's tearful denunciation of her hard-won chapters testifies to that.

In the autumn Hester herself, still not wholly restored to health, returned to Torquay with Diana, but that winter there were further outbreaks of influenza, and as Mary sadly acknowledged, 'that refuge of invalids', Torquay, was hardly likely to escape.[86] Hester again became ill, with influenza and subsequently congestion of the lungs. It is likely that Mary herself became ill in Hodnet; certainly she remembered years later how she had 'worked so hard [and] suffered so cruelly, crouched with my head on my hands on the bed in the corner'.[87] For an asthmatic, particularly if bronchitis is causing difficulty in exhaling, this may be the only position in which it is possible to breathe.[88]

When she and her father then made the journey to be with Hester they found that she knew she was dying. 'Then ensued long, terrible weeks, which are like a lifetime to look back on, in which she tried to die and could not.' Tended by Diana and a trained nurse, there were moments when Hester shut her eyes as if for the last time, and the watchers 'performed our cruel duty of bringing her back to suffer a little longer'.[89] Diana in particular must have been exhausted by this time. It should be remembered that she alone of the family had been with Hester through the autumn and winter, and even now the task of nursing her sister – presumably also the 'cruel duty' of keeping her alive – fell mainly upon her. In these weeks the quiet room became, as Mary remembered it, a torture chamber, as Hester suffered the kind of pain that only a fellow sufferer could imagine. In her own case Mary habitually uses the euphemism 'weakness' to describe physical pain, but in her pity for her dying sister, this more palatable term slides for a moment as she identifies with the agonizing death she thought she might one day face herself, 'only those who have experienced great weakness have any conception of the cross on which Hester's fragile body was stretched, week after week: week after endless week'.[90]

It was in the intervals of consciousness that Mary told Hester that her next book would be dedicated to her. And it was now that she told her she would make a book of Hester's own best work for private circulation.[91] Essex, expecting the birth of her first child, was unable to travel (her daughter Stella, named for her young aunt and who would later become a novelist in her own right, was born shortly before Hester died). Victoria, 'her companion from childhood', stayed to sustain their mother, whom Mary describes with classic ambiguity, bearing 'with fearful courage the slow death of her youngest child at a distance from her'.[92] In her recollections Mary does not seem to consider the possibility of Hester's brothers coming to be with her at the end. It was her sisters who most naturally gathered around her. And then finally, on the morning of 7 March 1892, 'we saw that the longed-for goal was reached at last. It seemed too good to be true.'[93] Hester was twenty-two.

From a passing reference made by Lubbock, it seems that Mary wrote something at least of her feelings at her sister's death in her (now missing) journal.[94] But in her extant correspondence from the next few months there is no mention of this traumatic event. Mary would write extensively and passionately for her own relief what she would not put in a letter, and in future years she talks of her misery sustained over prolonged periods, in terms that suggest it is not even suspected by those closest to her.[95] But whatever else may have been in her mind, she kept writing, determined to finish her novel. These final chapters are concerned largely with the loss of health and vitality sustained by Diana when she believes her love for John to be unreciprocated. It is not implausible to suggest that Mary's own former lover may himself have been visiting Hodnet at the very time that she was thinking over these scenes, and they resonate with a sense of irrevocable loss that is also the realization of death itself.

On 11 July Mary wrote to Bentley from the Beaumonts' ancestral home, Whitley Beaumont, to say that she had finished her new novel, which she wanted to entitle *Nemesis*.[96] Whether or not she was aware of it, it was at this time, as she was writing the story of a family home that almost falls into the wrong hands and is saved – just – from dissipation, that the battle to hold onto Condover was being fought and lost. As a result of agricultural depression, rental income was down and the capital value of land had sunk by as much as 30 per cent.[97] Already heavily in debt, Condover did not stand a chance.

At the end of August Mary accepted £400 for the copyright of her novel.[98] If she had taken the low offer for *Sir Charles Danvers* as a reflection on her talents as a writer, she had no cause for anxiety now. *Nemesis* would fit neatly into the required three-volume format, which alone made it more marketable; more importantly, Bentley was quick to praise it as a far superior piece of writing.[99] But she was ill again,[100] worn out by the effort and the emotions of the last few months. And there was further anxiety to come – in November she was distressed to hear that her chosen title was already taken, by a serial story in a Sheffield newspaper.[101] It seems that Bentley tried and failed to persuade the more obscure writer to yield the point, and Mary had to find an alternative title, while Bentley composed an explanatory paragraph for *Temple Bar*, where the new work had already been advertised.[102] She went through a series of alternatives – *A Thousand to One* (Rhoda Broughton's preferred option), *A Halting Nemesis* and *Great Possessions* were all considered – before settling for her least favourite, *Diana Tempest*. She would have preferred to call it *John*, protesting that the heroine's role was entirely subordinate to the story, but that name too was already taken,[103] as she ruefully conceded. Then this 'stubborn awkward story'[104] of hers had to be divided into serial numbers for *Temple Bar*.

It must have been a gruelling few months, illness coming on top of her sister's death and the finishing of her novel. And in a letter from September of this year comes the first extant reference to the medication with which she combated her periodic attacks of asthma, the medication which would eventually turn on her. It is not clear when Mary was first prescribed the opium derivative morphia, but writing to Bentley with her sympathy for his own condition, she asked whether he had ever tried an injection of morphia under the skin to relieve a paroxysm? It was, she went on, the only palliative she herself found effective.[105] By the time of this letter the addictive nature of morphia and its disturbing side effects – including lethargy and a sense of mental debilitation – were well known.[106] But to set against this, it was a notoriously powerful painkiller. In 1875 one practitioner was still prepared to claim that 'those who have once experienced the rapid and unfailing relief of the subcutaneous injection are no longer content to await the action of the more uncertain remedies to which they had formerly been accustomed to resort'.[107] Prolixity aside, his words sound something like an advertising slogan. Indeed it has been said of the drug that 'Its almost magic capabilities put it in the same technological echelon as gaslight or the railway'.[108]

By the 1880s the figure of the female addict, or morphinomaniac, was a sensational and ambivalent figure in both literature and the popular and medical press. She was configured as generally upper class, weakly susceptible and essentially deceitful in the strategies she employed to conceal her illicit habit. But the medical profession continued to support the use of morphia, provided it was administered by a professional in doses not exceeding ¼ grain at a time (even this limit was sometimes exceeded in special cases).[109] Mary was almost certainly acquainted with this debate – later she would allude to having read of the symptomatic craving in books[110] – but her attitude was pragmatic. The drug relieved her pain and at this stage it must have seemed like a blessing sent for her comfort. She was never one to pretend to a moral horror she had no reason to feel.

But morphia was not her sole resource, and in January 1893 she reported less controversially to Bentley that Himrod's Powder, asthma and she had kept the Christmas festival together.[111] She was staying once again in Torquay, finalizing arrangements for the book she had been working on under such different circumstances only two years earlier. She wrote again at the end of February to say that she would shortly be returning home.[112] But by March, still battling with the proofs, she was beset by headaches and 'nervous exhaustion'.[113]

Finally she took herself off to a specialist, the celebrated neurosurgeon Victor Horseley, known for his kindness of manner as much as for his firmness with his patients. In the course of an hour's examination, he looked at her eyes, ears and hands and asked numerous questions, before diagnosing severe nervous exhaustion.[114] Then he faced her with two alternatives. If she would submit entirely to his proposed course of treatment he would cure her in two months. Or she would become a permanent invalid.

In a careful letter to her father, Mary admitted that she had not felt well for the last three years.[115] She insisted that as her treatment would be expensive, she wanted to pay for half of it and so minimize at least one aspect of the worry she felt she was causing. And she was to come home for a few weeks before the cure began. An enclosed note from Horseley himself confirmed that drugs were not equal to the case. He warned, 'I find that she is suffering from a very serious degree of nervous exhaustion. Serious not because in any way dangerous to life but because if it be not arrested it will infallibly terminate in rendering her a chronic invalid for life. And consequently totally incapacitate her. It is perfectly possible to cure her present condition but only in one way.'[116]

So at the beginning of May, threatened with a permanent breakdown of her powers, she submitted to what must have been one of the cruellest of Victorian palliatives, a 'rest cure'.[117] At its least horrifying, this prescription would involve virtual self-incarceration, with the patient ordered to prostrate themselves for a number of hours in the day, taking little or no exercise and deliberately avoiding all mental stimulation of whatever kind. At its most extreme, the treatment as refined and popularized by Silas Weir Mitchell in the United States might involve intrusive procedures (the length of the cure alone would mean that a nurse would often have to take charge of menstrual emissions some time in the course of it), and the prohibition of any movement whatsoever, even the lifting of a hand.[118] In essence the 'cure' was based on prostration and overfeeding, with the isolation of the patient from his, or more usually her, family seen as a crucial means of pre-empting the kind of collaboration thought by some medical men to be sustained by the invalid and other members of the household. The absolute control of the patient by the doctor was considered crucial to the success of the treatment, and while Horseley himself was staunchly opposed to force-feeding (a position he later defended with reference to the suffragettes),[119] the inventor of the cure was not.

It was in effect a sort of cure by boredom, with the doctor systematically breaking the patient's resistance as a key part of the process, although in England these obviously punitive overtones were less likely to be present, and the more extreme methods of Mitchell's cure found few supporters.[120] W. S. Playfair was unusual in his uncritical support for this form of treatment, when he claimed that

> The injudicious and constant nursing [in cases of hysteria], the craving for sympathy, the fact that the sickroom becomes the centre of interest for the patient and her friends, the constant discussion of feelings and symptoms, all have a most marked and prejudicial effect; and so long as these continue in operation no course of medicine or treatment, however judicious, has any reasonable prospect of success.[121]

Recommending a massage of the entire muscular system for three hours daily and the passing of an electric current through the body for ten minutes twice daily, he tellingly describes one patient under his care as deliberately 'simulating' symptoms of ill health. The case in question, he is convinced, 'is illustrative of the evil effects of over much education and mental strain, in a clever girl of highly developed nervous organization'.[122]

If this view of the matter sounds sinister, patients may well have been grateful to the doctor who supervised their care, rather than fearing him or 'resisting' their own cure, as Mitchell and Playfair assumed. It is unlikely that a patient in charge of their own treatment would consent to the rest cure unless they were desperate for help, and it derived further authority from generally persistent fears about the reckless expenditure of finite supplies of nerve force.[123] One of the main causes of diminished nervous energy, particularly in women, was thought to be overwork, and Mary was warned at the outset that she would be completely isolated for six weeks, forbidden to write or receive a letter, or to have any contact with family and friends. She would be put through a course of massage and have electricity applied to the back of her head.[124]

She wrote to George Bentley to explain her position, 'I have exhausted my powers in the production of *Diana Tempest* and nature has sent in a heavy bill'. The case notes do not survive, but Horseley was relentless in threatening that she would never write another book if she refused the rest cure. She just managed to finish correcting the proofs of *Diana Tempest* before the time agreed for this regimen of total rest was upon her.[125] After this she was not allowed to write down so much as the name of a book she wished to remember, and she did not leave her bed for 4½ weeks. Then one evening she was abruptly told to dress herself, before being permitted to sit by the window for half an hour and just as abruptly returned to bed. At the end of the fifth week she went out for half an hour, a great advance, and was permitted to receive letters from her family (although not from anyone else). She wrote at once to her father, bombarding him with questions. Where was her mother, so that she could write to her? Was he well himself? How did Victoria enjoy Lady Lewis's ball?[126] As ever she was courageous in the long hours of waiting and illness, and in what would become a familiar motif, the attending doctor, Dennis Embleton, said of her, 'I really believe I have never had a lady before who had so wonderful an influence as Miss Cholmondeley has ... I never visit her without feeling the ennobling sense of her presence'.[127]

Mary herself certainly believed that she had been cured.[128] But the possible effects of such treatment are famously portrayed by the American writer Charlotte Perkins Gilman, whose story 'The Yellow Wallpaper', first published in 1892, details the breakdown of a female patient and the rest cure that exacerbates her condition to the point where she literally goes insane. The narrator of the story is caught in a double bind – the more she resists the dictates of her loving but unimaginative doctor husband in attempting to work, the more tired and depressed her clandestine efforts cause her to feel. Meanwhile her husband enjoins constant self-control, even as he refuses to grant her 'irrational' request for another room – it is made obvious to the reader that he has placed her in a bedroom previously used to house a mental patient, and which still shows signs of its past in the barred windows and bed nailed to the floor. Gilman, who had herself been a patient of Silas Weir Mitchell and claimed that his treatment almost drove her mad, sent him a copy of the story, and he is supposed to have admitted – although never to her – that he had modified his mode of practice after reading it.[129]

A full six weeks in bed was not by any means a usual prescription in England at least, where medical experts more commonly proposed a compromise of two or three, or a month at most.[130] But even after the expiration of the six-week treatment, the restrictions on Mary were by no means removed. She was considered well enough to go to at least one country house party that summer, where she first met Sir Alfred Lyall, an essayist and veteran of the Indian Mutiny whom she would come to respect deeply over the next few years.[131] However she apparently had no contact with her publisher for another six months, until a letter in October announces her 'wonderfully' better, but dutifully reports that her doctor means to keep a pen out of her hand for a year at least.[132] Nonetheless, even as she recovered from her recent collapse and its terrifying cure, Mary was quick to pick up on a good opportunity. Apart from being a charming acquaintance, Sir Alfred reviewed for the *Nineteenth Century* and Mary lost no time in asking Bentley to send him a copy of her new novel.[133]

That month *Diana Tempest*, drawing to the end of its run in *Temple Bar*, appeared in volume form with a dedication:

> To my sister Hester.
> 'He put our lives so far apart
> We cannot hear each other speak.'[134]

Barred from writing a new novel, Mary contented herself with a long letter to Bentley, suggesting likely reviewers and others who might give her book 'a puff' or what we would now term a 'plug'. As the centre of her own literary coterie, Anne Thackeray Ritchie was not forgotten; and she suggested that Mr and Mrs Herbert Paul (she had reviewed *Sir Charles Danvers* and he was the editor of the *Daily News*) should also receive a copy. But she misjudged the mood of another reviewer, the formidable Andrew Lang.[135] Since asking to see *The Danvers Jewels* for Longman seven years earlier, Lang had praised her books to Rhoda Broughton and expressed a wish to be acquainted with their author – only his sudden illness had prevented their meeting by arrangement at a country house weekend. So Mary was stunned when he wrote what she considered a vituperative review in *Longman's*, accusing her of 'padding', an aspersion she particularly resented.[136] In fact he also praised her 'splendid plot' managed 'with much skill and some humour', before ruining the effect by telling his readers, 'you can skip the clever padding and the long sermons'.[137] She then recalled that she had been warned to conciliate Lang some time earlier (presumably at the time of *The Danvers Jewels*), and that when she failed to do so, he had eventually written her a somewhat discourteous note containing a joke at her expense. She now wondered whether this incident – he had repeated his witticism, whatever it was, in public and it had not gone down well among people who had presumably met and liked her – might explain the 'acid drop' in his pen.[138]

There was further vexation over the legal point on which the plot of the book hinges. More than one reviewer took issue with her here, suggesting that Mr Tempest left the estate to John in his will,[139] which of course was precisely what he could *not* do, as Mary thought she had made clear. And there was criticism of the bet made by Colonel Tempest – Frederic Harrison for one called this nonsensical, as it would not be legally binding. Not the point, retaliated the irritated writer, as Colonel Tempest would hardly be willing to have the incident publicized and his own part in the transaction made known.[140] But more seriously, despite having taken legal advice while she was writing the story,[141] it seemed that she had made one genuine slip. In the first edition of the story John renounces the Tempest estate because he discovers letters from his mother proving that he is illegitimate, and therefore not the rightful heir. In an interview with the cavalier Frederick Fane, his mother's cousin but also his biological father, he says bitterly 'I am – nobody'; having no claim to the Tempest name, he briefly takes the name of Fane, because it was the maiden name of his mother.[142] In the serialized version and in the first edition of the novel, he goes on to say 'and he [Colonel Tempest] is the legal heir'.[143] But as the reviewer Frederic Harrison swiftly pointed out in a letter to Bentley, as the ostensible son of Mr Tempest in wedlock, John would stand to inherit the estate whether or not his mother knew him to be the child of her lover rather than her husband. Mary was only half convinced that Harrison had not written a review in the *Saturday* making the same point, (not even a comparison to her adored George Eliot could take the sting out of this criticism).[144] After all her care in consulting a barrister, who was even asked to read the manuscript, Mary was distressed and humiliated. She made the best of the situation – too late for the second edition of December 1893, she waited till a new edition appeared in 1894, when she was able to alter the text slightly so that John's renunciation is made on wholly moral grounds. In later editions of the novel he says simply 'I am nobody'. She considered including a preface explaining the shift in emphasis, before deciding with Bentley that as so few critics were carping on this point it might be as well to leave it alone.[145] It was nonetheless irksome to have given such an easy victory to hostile critics after all her care.

But if Andrew Lang was not prepared to praise her book, and Frederic Harrison was determined to criticize her 'ladies' law',[146] other eminent figures were more appreciative. There was a long review in *The Times*,[147] and Mary confessed that she had softened towards Gladstone after hearing that he had met her sister Diana at a dinner party and immediately burst out in praise of her namesake, the eponymous heroine – indeed more than one person evidently apologized for mistakenly addressing her as 'Miss Tempest'.[148] the *Bookman* noted in May 1894 that 'that excellent novel' was passing into a third edition.[149] Meanwhile the *Academy* called Mary 'a close observer of men and manners' and would have pleased her yet more by commenting that 'The picture of Colonel Tempest's weak hankering after the money, of his shrinking from the horrible means he has used to get it, and of his vain efforts to cancel the bet, is an admirable piece of work'.[150] In America the *Dial* found John's renunciation of the estate 'absurdly quixotic' but noted 'that the author has an incisive style and handles her materials with ease'.[151]

Again Mudie's seemed to be standing in the way of the book's success. They had not bought enough copies to meet the demand and Mary was worried that after asking for it a few times, people would simply give up. One friend told her sister that at last after a very irate demand for it, a very irate answer was returned that she could not expect to get a book in so much request.[152] Such annoyances aside, Mary was justifiably pleased by the success of her new story. Despite the obstructive attitude of Mudie's it was selling well and by the new year of 1895 Mary could write to James Payn thanking him for his encouragement twelve years earlier and telling him with a certain pride that *Diana Tempest* was in its fifth edition; at the same time sales in America had hit the 9,000 mark.[153]

For now, however, her triumph in this new novel was overshadowed by anxiety, the usual lurking fear that this might yet be her last. It had been a difficult book to write, through her own seemingly perpetual illness, and her sister's untimely death. But she had not given in; she had forced herself to keep writing even in the weeks after her bereavement, desperately correcting proofs of the book to be in time before the weeks of silence in which she would be forbidden to write at all or even communicate her thoughts to anyone. She had proved herself equal to the challenge, but now that it was over she realized just what this immense effort had exacted from her in terms of health.[154] A few years later she would, in *Red Pottage*, compel herself to imagine the possible fate of a young woman whose best work remains unwritten, her health destroyed before she is out of her twenties and the kind friends who surround her fearing for her life. But she would rescue her to write 'better books',[155] as her sister Hester had not been rescued, as she must sometimes have feared she would not be rescued herself.

By the early part of 1894 she was still suffering from exhaustion brought on by overwork, worn out and miserable, wanting to start a new novel and knowing that there was no chance of doing so.[156] And yet again that February Bentley urged further efforts, reminding her that she must look to the future. It is with a sense of dull resignation that she writes to thank him, incidentally revealing the perpetual demands of her life as the rector's daughter, which continued to claim so much of her precious energy and time:

> If my health were stronger I should be greatly elated by [his kind words]. As it is, every thing reminds me of how incapable I am at present of sustained labour, or of any effort which my natural energy continually suggests. I had a tea party of farmers wives on Thursday, and had to speak to them for about 10 minutes from written notes on a parish matter. I paid for that microscopic exertion by entire exhaustion the next day. I mention this to show how far away the work in which I delight seems to recede.[157]

She might well complain that her new celebrity failed to follow her home.

But at the beginning of April she had more reassuring news – she had been promised that soon she would be allowed to write again.[158] Later that month she made an appointment to see Victor Horseley, only to find that he had been suddenly called away. She was optimistic, joking to her father about the proofs for the new edition of *Diana Tempest*, 'Truly the life of a great author has its drawbacks'. In a letter partly concerned with the upcoming bazaar in Hodnet and the interviewing of a potential curate, it is possible that she may also have wanted to remind them both that she was still more than just 'the rector's daughter'. She was finally able to see Horseley later that day and she must have discussed Bentley's importunity. In her letter home Mary stressed that the doctor was greatly pleased with her improved health. But equally he had told her to go away somewhere quietly for a while, warning that if she had a relapse she would not be so 'easy' to cure this time. She was allowed to write, but with the proviso that she would not promise anything to a publisher and not consent to be bound by any deadline. Above all, she was told that she could not be relied on to know when she was overdoing things, and she must submit to the judgement of a sensible relative on this point. 'I fear that means Di and V.' commented Mary sardonically.[159]

But while Mary herself immediately began to worry about what would happen if she could not write further books, Bentley himself was surprised by just how far she had come in the last few years.[160] As a book, *Diana Tempest* is among her best work, as she well knew; in fact she was never to feel such confidence in her writing again. The villain of the story, Colonel Tempest, was actually Mary's favourite of all the characters,[161] perhaps because, as she said, she had put so much work into him. In the horror John feels at the prospect of Overleigh falling into wasteful hands, the novel underlines Mary's own belief in the heritage and responsibilities of aristocratic families. She posits the violation of John's home as the library is broken up and the Tempest chattels sold off, only to rescue it by a strategic series of unlikely contingencies in the final pages of the last volume. In her depiction of a possible wreckage she can hardly bear to contemplate and which of course fascinates her for this very reason, Mary ironically foreshadows yet another catastrophe that would befall her own family in the next few years.

But for the moment she was concerned only to get back to work. In September she heard of the recent death of Hamilton Thom and immediately wrote to Bentley suggesting that she try writing an article.[162] He was, she wrote, a great teacher, and she was surprised later to find that she had not mentioned him in her diary that winter, during which the article had been constantly on her mind. She would be justly proud to discover that her article had increased the sale of his books – before she wrote on him she had never met anyone who had heard of him or read a line of his writing.[163]

Her later career follows an ineluctable pattern of hard work and immediate collapse, and in the event even this article would prove too much for her health. She wrote ruefully to Bentley that she was diagnosed with 'exhaustion of the nervous system from over brain work' within a week of its completion. 'I think you had better strike my name off your list if I cannot write 12 pages of *Temple Bar* after a rest of 3 years at a time when I was in perfect health apparently'.[164] But despite her deprecations, she was able to confide in Bentley because of all people outside her family, he as a fellow asthmatic knew the torture through which she had just passed. Whatever caused her collapse, it had been particularly severe and for the first twelve days she was in so much pain with combined asthma and bronchitis that she was kept constantly under morphia. When fever and congestion of the lungs set in it became necessary to discontinue the morphia, at which point 'I had to cope with increased illness plus the morphia craving of which I had read in books, but which beats all description. I daresay you have experienced it, and how it seems to break the whole body, down to the finger tips.'[165] This terrifying account – and Mary's powers of description are only too acute – is unusual in her correspondence; certainly in later life she would be reticent about her illnesses, generally talking about weakness and debility rather than distressing her correspondents by drawing attention to the accompanying pain; but this account of her craving the drug that both healed and later hurt her, confined to bed for weeks on end as she felt her whole body breaking, gives a peculiar resonance to Lubbock's description of her 'beating in solitary hours against the barriers that were round her life'.[166]

Over the next few years she would make various references in her diary to the administration of morphia during difficult illnesses, and to the yet more difficult issue of leaving it off once the illness had passed.[167] She would ascribe the habit to the mysterious woman in her short story of 1908, 'The Lowest Rung',[168] who is taken for an escaped convict but turns out to be a good Samaritan in disguise. It is even possible that Mary's battle with the drug contributed to her depression and her fears about the loss of her creative power.[169] But this constantly renewed battle with morphia lay in the future. To borrow one of her own later analogies (originally accorded to a character who loyally but catastrophically keeps her dead friend's secret):

> A wiser woman ... would perhaps have known, would at any rate have feared, that a certain small cloud on her horizon, no larger than a man's hand, meant a great storm. But until it broke she did not realise that that ever-increasing, ominous pageant had any connection with the hurricane that at last fell upon her: just as some of us see the rosary of life only as separate beads, not noticing the divine constraining thread, and are taken by surprise when we come to the cross.[170]

In the new year of 1895, still unable to work, Mary found an outlet for her frustrations in starting a parish magazine, although she joked that it would not provide serious competition to *Temple Bar*. The contents were mainly written by local clergymen and there was a serial story 'so irreproachable as to be almost unreadable'. But on writing to the appointed editor to offer her occasional services gratis, she received no answer – having been approached by half a dozen editors of national periodicals, she found herself 'Not wanted' here, as she reported to Bentley with some amusement.[171] Several aspiring writers were approaching her now explaining that they wanted to 'make their mark' in literature and asking for her recommendation to *Temple Bar* as the best place for them to start making it; one or two even wrote to Bentley himself claiming her support.[172] But still she could not write herself. In February she thanked him for another present of books, most timely for someone just recovered from an attack of pneumonia but kept indoors by 42 degrees of frost.[173] And then in March a second attack floored her again, taking with it all hope of beginning a new novel for the present. Instead she apologetically offered him another article, 'An Art in its Infancy', if it was not too light for *Temple Bar*.[174] But either circumstances intervened or Bentley doubted the suitability of the piece (the art in question is that of advertising), which finally appeared in 1901 in the *Monthly Review*.[175] It would be some time before Mary again had anything 'flippant' for which to apologize. In the next two months, she lost two more figures central to her life, one she closely resembled and against whose memory she would continue to struggle until she herself died well into the next century; one she had met only once but whose support for her writing had helped to rescue her from the 'quiet country life' to which she had thought herself permanently condemned.

On 11 April Emily Cholmondeley suffered a blackout and died at Condover.[176] As Mary retold the event, 'My dear mother had a poets' death. The enjoyment of hearing some very beautiful sacred music was too much for her, and snapped the very slender thread she had on this world.'[177] There were initial fears that the shock might be too much for her father, who had been with her when she died, but the family rallied round to protect him, as his daughters in particular were to do for the rest of his life. It may have been some consolation to Mary at the time that her mother was reading one of her books – for the third time – when she died.[178] Whatever darkness had descended on her over the years of her illness, Emily had clearly retained her appreciation of literature and her pride in the achievements of her talented daughter. All of which makes it all the more extraordinary that Mary later claimed in *Under One Roof* that her mother had had no love of the beautiful.[179] In these first weeks she was emphasizing not the estrangement that had grown between them over the difficult years since she had been forced to adopt something of her mother's role and responsibilities, but precisely the shared aesthetic sense that she would later try to deny.

As time passed she became more remote, an attitude she seemingly made no attempt to disguise. As early as the following month she was staying in London with her aunt Victoria when Sir Alfred Lyall came to pay his respects. She waited in all afternoon only to learn that by some accident he had not been let in. And when he returned the next day, it came out that he had already written her a letter of condolence, which Bentley had failed to pass on. Mary was evidently more preoccupied with her own apparent neglect in failing to answer the letter than in the tragedy that had called it forth in the first place. She was frankly relieved that he had not taken offence and withdrawn his overtures towards friendship, telling her father in Hodnet, 'He has the name of being the cleverest man in London and all the beautiful fashionable women are devoted to him. I dont wonder. There may be other people as interesting as he, but I have never met them.'[180] Whatever her relationship with her mother had come to, this letter written a few weeks after her death makes uncomfortable reading. In fact Sir Alfred Lyall would remain one of the friends of whom she was most proud, including a sketch of him in her next novel, *A Devotee: An Episode in the Life of a Butterfly*. It was also on this visit that she first met another man who would profoundly influence her, the writer Hamilton Aidi. 'He praised my book very highly and said repeatedly how glad he was to meet me, and should I be in London again soon? and he hoped to see me again. I am not proof against such blandishments. I thought him most agreeable.'[181]

On 29 May her publisher and mentor George Bentley died of angina pectoris.[182] She told his son Richard, who now took over the firm, that she felt that she had lost not only one who she had hoped might in the future become a personal friend, but one who in the past had the rare power of inciting her to do her best. She always felt towards him as a pupil, and also to a degree that might seem unnatural when put into words, a conviction that he was the one person who understood her capacities and her failings, and would help her to make the best of the first and to avoid the second. In addition to the loss of her mentor, she would lose a publisher in 1898, when Richard Bentley sold out to Macmillan.[183]

If she did record either of these calamities more fully in her diary, it was in the volume that has since disappeared. But in the third volume, begun in early June, she simply notes that she is returning home after seven months' absence, and preparing to take up 'the new page of home life' to begin with the return of the others the following week. She is depressed and obviously weary, 'I can do no good thing. It is true. I cant. But I suppose I shall be strengthened, through failure, and depression, and minor jealousies, and disappointment, and weak health.'[184] The reference to doing 'no good thing' sounds suspiciously like a comment on her new book, which she was finally working on at about this time. As at the time of Hester's death, she may have found some consolation in writing. Or it may simply not have occurred to her that personal distress should be allowed to influence the work on which she was set. By 7 June she had finished the rough copy of what she intended to be a one-volume story. She wondered if it was any good, thought it was probably not, but decided that unless Diana and Victoria thought it very bad it would most probably be published.

In fact *A Devotee* has a claim to be Cholmondeley's most unjustly neglected work. It proffers a careful outline of the triangle between a shallow woman, the young man who loves her, and his elderly cousin who marries her out of pity when his first refusal leaves her ill. Written shortly after the sale of Condover, it also has something to say about the new inheritance tax, the agricultural depression and 'The new aristocracy of the ironmaster and the cheesemonger and the brewer', noting bitterly that 'the old must give way before the power of their money'. Loftus, whose quixotic action lays him open to widespread disapproval because his estate is on the verge of having to be sold and his new wife is rich as well as young – 'Miss Carruthers was called beautiful. Perhaps she was beautiful for an heiress' – was by her own account a portrait of Mary's friend Sir Alfred Lyall (whose work she quotes directly in the heading of chapter fourteen).[185]

Loftus is distinguished and courteous, and the narrator notes approvingly that after the romantic disappointments of his youth, 'All intimacy was alien to his solitary nature. It was alien while it was courteously welcomed.' On finding that his confidence in others has been misplaced, he simply makes a quiet withdrawal, leaving the friend in whom he has been disappointed to make the discovery perhaps years later that he has been shut out of the inner circle. His reticence and kindness making him a natural confidant, 'He confided in no one, for he was burdened with many confidences, and those on whom others lean can seldom find a hand to lean on in their greater weakness and their deeper troubles'.[186] The theme of the reserved confidant of others who has no one to whom they in turn can confide would resurface in her next novel, as would the significant theme of silently withdrawing from those who have proved themselves unworthy. But Mary may not have noticed that in this character, with his noble bearing and dignified restraint, his close scrutiny of characters who have no idea how much he hides from them and how little they understand his inner thoughts, she had also drawn a picture of herself.

A more direct approach to the reader's understanding comes in her comment on the night watches of the ill, who see nothing but pain in the coming of dawn:

> For those who do not sleep, life has two sides – the side of night as well as day ... Those who sleep at night, for whom each day is not divided by a gulf of pain, who look upon the darkness as a time of rest, and the morning as a time of waking, know one side of life, perhaps, as the passers-by in the street know one side of the hospital as they skirt it – the outside wall.[187]

The story was serialized in *Temple Bar* (Richard Bentley gave her £100 for the serial rights, twice what the much longer *Sir Charles Danvers* had won for her). It was the last story of hers that would appear in the journal. The one-volume story of old versus new money, when it later appeared – although not with the Bentley firm, as she might have expected – was dedicated to her sister-in-law Florie, 'upon whose strong hand I have so often leant' (and who was incidentally descended from weavers, the child of a family who had themselves taken advantage of changing times to buy large aristocratic estates).[188]

But Mary was once again exhausted, and looking forward she felt only that she could not go on with all that she had to do for much longer, let alone for years, without being 'engulfed in fatigue'.[189] On Trinity Sunday she was singing in the church choir, her mind full of 'small parish things'.[190] And two days later she was writing of Elizabeth Barrett Browning's haunting elegy to love lost, 'You See we are Tired my Heart and I':

> How tired we feel, my heart and I!
> We seem of no use in the world;
> Our fancies hang gray and uncurl'd
> About men's eyes indifferently[191]

'I wonder whether she felt it to be <u>hers</u>, she who wrote it, as intensely as I know it to be <u>mine</u> who only read it',[192] a comment that incidentally tells us a lot about Mary's troubled response to her own writing in later years. She would come to feel that when she wrote she was in some sense making over something of herself to others, and this anxiety became so pressing that even in middle age there are passages in her diary where she uses ellipses to conceal a name or literally refuses to write what is in her mind.[193]

But she was not to be inactive for long. Shortly after writing this entry she learned that her father and Victoria were seriously ill at the Great Western Hotel in London, where they had been staying. She promptly rushed to London to be with them, only to fall ill herself almost as soon as she arrived, 'as I always do if there is anything useful on hand'. And there they remained, with a hired nurse who also became ill, Dick joining them in the midst of the confusion on a visit from Australia.[194] When Victoria was able to move she was removed to Condover, with Mary to nurse her. There was an initial fear that her lungs would be affected, but over the next two months she steadily improved. It was Mary who once again succumbed to asthma on her return home. And again she was anxious about her writing; reading *A Devotee* to Victoria and Dick, she felt again that it lacked incident, that it was not good. In these days of illness she would remember her brother singing a somewhat trite popular song about suffering:

> Before I had looked at [the words], as one may look at a map of India, believing the map entirely, and that Calcutta and the Ganges are rightly placed; and perhaps able to speak glibly about them. It was like looking at the same map on the return from the country. The thin lines of the rivers and little dots for the towns looked quite different, because <u>I had been there.</u>[195]

As she had written only a few months earlier, 'One meets young people who are positive spendthrifts of affection. They ... think there is plenty more where that came from, and they fling it from them with both hands.'[196] Now her health continued to decline and she was eventually carried off to Condover in her dressing gown, where she immediately perked up under the care of Regie and Florie and with the luxury of a room for writing off her bedroom.[197] It would be one of her last opportunities to go there. Despite the struggles of the last few years to hold onto what she undoubtedly saw as the family home, Mary herself seems not to have known that a deed of sale had been executed only a few weeks earlier;[198] perhaps she was considered too ill to be told the grim details, but the estate had already been conveyed to her father and her brother Tom in order to allow them to sell it and pay off its debts.

Still her father's health was causing concern and it became obvious that Victoria could not spend the winter in Hodnet. So on 16 November, with parting injunctions to their father to stay in good health – 'or I shall send one of those

piercing glances across from Madina which you are so frightened of'[199] – Mary
and Victoria took ship for 'Madina', most likely Medina Sidonia, in southern
Spain, about 30 km east of Cádiz. It must have been a sad, if not an anxious
parting, on the father's side at least. He had lost his wife of forty years only a few
months earlier, and now two of his daughters were leaving him for the uncertainties of a protracted sea voyage. Each of them would come close to death before
he saw them again.

It is from this point, when Mary begins the third volume of her journal, that
the devotion between her and Victoria becomes obvious. Victoria had been
particularly close to Hester, the nearest to her in age, and Mary too had shared
a deep bond with her youngest sister as each worked towards a writing career.
Despite the eleven-year age gap, Mary now came increasingly to depend on her
more resilient sister. They had a similar sense of humour, lived together for the
rest of their lives, and were often linked together in their friends' minds in ways
that suggest they may even have taken on something of each other's personalities.
Now in 1895 they both suffered from acute seasickness and felt at least a few
hours of regret that they had ever left England, but as the weather worsened in
the aftermath of a storm in the Bay of Biscay, their spirits rose, and Mary wrote
home in elation:

> all I can say is that I would not have missed it for worlds. The sea was very high, and
> I cant tell you the pleasure it was to us to sit in our chairs lashed to the deck and see
> the great wall of black water rise up like a hill over us, and then topple over, while the
> other side there seemed to be nothing but a chasm below our feet.[200]

Otherwise the outward passage was uneventful, until Mary was attacked by
asthma yet again – 'To gasp and gasp, and then at last to suffocate. Will that
be the end'[201] she wrote bitterly in her diary – and was ill almost constantly
in the succeeding weeks. On 11 December she was writing to her father from
Reid's Hotel in Medina that she had not reckoned on a week's illness followed
by another week to reach her present stage of convalescence, 'I have begun to
go downstairs, being carried up and down, as I have no legs'.[202] She had left off
the morphia, and a few days later Victoria was writing to say that her sister had
captured the heart of a German lieutenant some fourteen years her junior, who
had confided to a mutual acquaintance that she had such 'lofely eyes' and was
constantly flying forward with shawls and cushions.[203]

Perhaps a week after this reassuring letter was dispatched, Mary had another
relapse, beginning the new year in bed, dosed up with morphia and almost too
weak to cross the room. It was at this point, in a hotel room hundreds of miles
from their family and with Mary heavily drugged and more or less prostrate,
that Victoria fell dangerously ill with an attack of pleurisy.[204] It must have been
a terrifying experience for both of them, and all too reminiscent of that winter

in Torquay when a bedridden Mary had to be looked after by the increasingly frail Hester. After his prolonged stay in England, their brother Dick set sail for Australia on 16 January,[205] and it is therefore likely that he only learned some time later of Victoria's illness.

Life and death were, as Mary put it, pretty evenly balanced, in these first days of 1896.[206] In this emergency once again her immense force of will was brought to bear as she struggled to overcome her own illness for the sake of her sister. Judging from her earlier letter to George Bentley where she details the horrors of abrupt withdrawal from morphia, she must have been in immense pain, but in her diary she focuses entirely on her weakness and the divine assistance that somehow enabled her to save her sister.

> When I understood I left off the morphia for I knew it would break what little nerve I had left, and I remember thinking as I felt my own great weakness, 'I shall not be able to be with her or help in this illness. Nothing short of a miracle could enable me to do it.' Nevertheless I was enabled to do it. Let me record it here. What I honestly thought impossible I was strengthened to do. ... I was with her sometimes as much as 10 hours a day. I was cheerful and calm while I was with her, tho' I broke down at other times. I longed for some of my own people but I did not send for any one, for I knew no one could arrive in time. And at last dear V after going down to the edge of the valley took up her life again.[207]

Very little of this horror is tangible in the letter Mary wrote to her father at the time, in which Victoria gets on wonderfully well although the nurse is still by her bedside all night. Dr Grabham comes in for some stick, for failing to take Mary seriously when she herself collapsed again a few days later. He told her it was 'all nerves' and two days running made her dress and go outside, until eventually she had to be helped into bed with bronchitis and what she describes as a 'pluretic rut' in her side. He was, she admitted as she lay being 'poulticed and painted and dosed', devoted in a crisis but completely unsympathetic to anything less.[208] Now, warned that her illness might turn to consumption in the unpropitious climate of Medina, she and Victoria agreed to set sail once again for Tenerife.

But her thoughts were not entirely on her own or Victoria's illness. A year after joking to Bentley that she was not planning to upstage *Temple Bar*, she wrote a contrite letter to her father about the parish magazine, regretting her 'undue reserve' and wishing she had been more open-hearted with him. From her letter it appears that only now had he learned of his eldest daughter's involvement – touchingly his response was to order a number of extra copies.[209] But, approaching seventy, his days as rector of Hodnet were coming to an end. He had evidently asked Mary and Victoria to discuss the matter between themselves, and when Victoria was found to have pleurisy in her good side,[210] the writing was clearly on the wall. She would need to be carefully looked after for a year at least, and should not be exposed to the harsh winters of Hodnet. Mary was apprehensive about her father's resignation, which would inevitably entail a move of house, but she was definite nonetheless. While he was better after his illness of the autumn before, still he could no longer be at the centre of the parish as he had always been, and she told him now:

> It has been your personal influence, work and intercourse among the people that has been the pivot of everything so far, and has been the means of bringing about so much for which we have all been thankful. My pride in you has often made me long that your work being completed you should lay it down before your inability to do as you <u>have</u> done is felt in the parish.[211]

An argument that may have weighed more with him was the precarious health of his youngest surviving daughter. Unlike her oldest sister, Victoria seemed to take a genuine interest in the affairs of the parish, the choir and the Sunday school, and Mary warned that it would be all but impossible to prevent her overexerting herself if she were to remain in the village.[212] For Mary herself, the prospect of leaving her childhood home may have been daunting, but she knew that it was also the opportunity she had been waiting for ever since she published her first book. She was probably not aware that a leading specialist on asthma, Henry Hyde Salter, conveniently recommended London as a palliative for the condition, claiming that by far the majority would be cured by going to live there.[213] But she was not taking any chances when she now wrote 'V. and I have no doubt that a flat in London is <u>the</u> thing. If we move I do trust there is no doubt it will be London.'[214]

Having made her case, Mary prepared for a less critical move, to the island of Tenerife. She had reason to be glad of the change, writing indignantly to her father at the beginning of March about the 'heartless' way in which the travel companies concealed the outbreaks of illness at the health resorts – there was a serious outbreak of typhoid at Medina (including one at Reid's Hotel) and yet unsuspecting invalids from home were hurrying out there to be cured. Tenerife was, she suspected, too low down for her, but she could not go higher up with her asthma. It was while they were staying here that news reached Mary and Victoria of the death of their uncle Regie on 10 February, the second bereavement their father had sustained in less than a year. 'I wish I had never spoken hardly of him. <u>He</u> never spoke unkindly of anyone' was as far as Mary was prepared to go in her letter home.[215]

By March she was feeling restless and bored of Tenerife,[216] but she remembered it fondly enough to give one of her most interesting heroines, Annette in *Notwithstanding*, a convalescence there. She paints an idyllic picture in 'A Day in Teneriffe', although even here, despite her renewed protests against the constraints that shut out independent thought, she is ambiguous about certain aspects of the women's rights question, commenting on a stout woman in trousers carrying a tray of tomatoes on her head, 'Surely the most advanced of our "new women" only needs to see a few of these fat Spanish women in trousers, in order to be convinced that we cannot in all things imitate man with advantage'.[217] This joke about women in trousers is not necessarily intended as a political statement, but it is worth noting in passing how casually she jumps from the idea of unfamiliar female costume to the women's rights movement in general. She herself would be the victim of just such sweeping assumptions before the end of the century.

Now, however, she had a familiar reason for her malaise. She was not fully restored to health, and on the orders of Dr Grabham she had had a morphia needle sent out from England.[218] Only Victoria had been taught how to use it, to save Mary herself from possible temptation, a reminder that morphia was a notoriously addictive drug as well as an essential form of pain relief. Mary's response to this event tells us something of the relationship an unmarried woman approaching middle age might be expected to have with her father (in a letter from London the previous spring she had assured him that no one but Tom should be allowed to read the consignment of French novels she had been promised by a friend).[219] This latest letter, not dissimilar in its assumptions, is notable also for its honesty, and its underlying fear:

> I hope that V. will keep it while I am at Hodnet, and Florie while I am at Condover. I quite see, with all my <u>present</u> horror of morphia that it would be wiser for me not to have possession of it. I was given such quantities of it at Madina, and also of chloroform the latter quite pure <u>that I hope I may never see them in this world again</u>. How shocked Di would have been had she known that I had a bottle of chloroform by my bedside at night, and poured some on my handkerchief several times a night. Dr Grabham told me to use it freely, but it never was any real relief. I think it right to tell you I have got the needle, as I ought not to have one without your knowledge.[220]

Mary's correspondence from Tenerife, as so often from home, shows the contradictoriness of her relations with the world; a dutiful Victorian spinster, virtually asking her father's permission before following the orders of her doctor, yet she makes no pretence of consulting him, as she would have done her mother, about her writing or her business arrangements.

It was in the same month that Mary wrote to her father about having a morphia needle that Richard Bentley's offer of £100 for the serial rights to *A Devotee* was received and 'cheerfully accepted'. She suggested that he send the proofs for correction while she was there and in possession of health and leisure, 'two valuable commodities of which I enjoy only too little in England'.[221] She remained uncertain about the merits of the book, fearful that it did not live up to *Diana Tempest*, but it contained two characters, Mr and Mrs Gresley, in whom she felt a particular interest and who would resurface in the much better known *Red Pottage* a few years later. Although it went into a second edition, *A Devotee* would remain one of her least read books.[222] But in her diary she recorded the despondency and the resurgent hope that she would not share with Richard Bentley. She remembered George Eliot, who like her had doubted herself, had suffered dark hours and ill health, but who had not lived in vain. She saw clearly the contradictoriness of her own personality:

> why do I envy people on the road, when all the time I know that the twin hedgerows which keep out 'dangerous views' would have choked me, while they protected others. It seems I want two opposite things. To be happy, and at ease, and live without effort, to be liked by the majority, to offend none, to attempt nothing. And I want as well to express the thoughts which press upon me, to work out at whatever cost that which only years of labour, of patient effort, of sustained thought can work out; which I am ready to give, which I am quite ready to give.[223]

And yet she admitted she was sometimes lonely in her art, 'Why do the very qualities which bring me love and admiration from my fellow creatures place at the same time a barrier between me and them?'[224] And so over the next few months she and Victoria convalesced on the island. From her later accounts this seems, despite a level of boredom, to have been a restful period, in which they could refresh themselves away from the demands of home life, after the tragedies and crises of the last few years.[225] For a little while longer they could put off the complications and worry of a move from Hodnet and the search for somewhere to live in London.

By 9 April they were planning their return home. Now Mary wrote to her father, 'My mind cannot grasp such a large subject as that of our leaving Hodnet'.[226] She made no mention of it to her father but, two days later, on the anniversary of her mother's death, she wrote in her diary,

> She was often lonely, and I know she must have felt acutely how no one would go by her urgent advice. We could not, but that of course it was not possible for her to see. Poor Mother. I do trust she is happier now.[227]

The sisters remained in Tenerife for another month before setting off for home and, after a crossing of nine days, Mary and Victoria reached England on 9 May. Afraid of the now unfamiliar climate, they made a slow journey home, paying visits to their friend Mrs Margesson at Finden Place in Sussex, and her aunt Victoria in London, before returning to Hodnet.[228]

In July Mary was able to escape to London again for a week, where she met other women writers. It may well have been Rhoda Broughton who introduced her to her own friends and acquaintance, such as the feminist Ethel Arnold, author of *Platonics* (1894), a novella about a female friendship that just about survives the marriage of one woman to the man her friend loves; and her sister the prolific Mrs Humphry (Mary) Ward, known both for her philanthropy and her marked anti-feminism; she had signed the notorious Appeal against Female Suffrage in 1889 and Mary never could take to her altogether, remarking that she gave 'the impression of great intellectual power, but little humour'.[229] She also enjoyed the company of distinguished men such as Sir Alfred Lyall. She admitted to herself this trip had made her feel something of a 'distinguished personage', widely complimented as she had been on *Diana Tempest*. But if all the praise had gone to her head, returning to Hodnet provided the cure, 'I always find my own county where no one attaches the least value to what I write, has a very wholesome effect on me if I am inclined to be vain, as I always am after living in London'.[230]

It must have been with mixed feelings then that she had to record the latest disaster to overtake her family. Her father retired in July, evidently accepting that he was simply too old and too frail to discharge his duties effectively.[231] Uncle Charles had suffered a paralytic stroke earlier in the year and this warning may have acted as a catalyst for his own retirement from office.[232] Before handing over the living to his nephew Henry Heber-Percy, Richard was presented by the parishioners with a silver vase, and the parish magazine published his farewell letter. Taking leave of the people of Hodnet, he wrote characteristically,

> I cannot but regret that you should have given me such a very costly present which was not needed to keep dear Hodnet and its people in my remembrance. I do rejoice, however, at this additional token of your affection towards me ... Your gift and address are especially pleasing to me as coming from all denominations and bearing the signatures on your behalf of those I regard so highly.[233]

This resignation of the living of course meant the loss of Hodnet Rectory where he himself as well as his children had grown up. There would under normal circumstances have been Condover to fall back on, had it not been for the complicated nature of Regie's affairs. But, as Mary put it, 'the two houses fall at the same moment like card houses'.[234] In his later account Lubbock follows Mary's own example in *Under One Roof* and passes speedily over this incident – he tells his readers glibly that he has already told them how the family came to live in London when the rector retired from his work. For Condover, worth about £4,000 a year thirty years previously when her uncle Regie came into possession, was now so heavily in debt that when it had to be sold to a rich merchant a few months after his death, it only left about £2,000–3,000 after expenses. It must have seemed like the fulfilment of her nightmare in *Diana Tempest*, and this time there would be no benign intervention by the author in the final chapters: 'Well it is sold, and presently all the pictures and cabinets and the pretty things which many generations have accumulated will be sold too, and we shall belong to the vagrant class'.[235] For it was taken as read that Mary and her two unmarried sisters would continue to live with their father; in leaving the genteel Hodnet Rectory, they would simply reassemble the traditional family structure in the rather less genteel confines of a London flat. The Condover library alone was splendid enough for its sale to appear as an item in *The Times*.[236]

In the space of a few weeks, Mary had lost her own home, the more impressive family home where she would have expected to be a welcome guest for the rest of her life, and her entire connection with the parish in which she had grown up. But the trauma of yet another loss notwithstanding, there must have been something liberating for her in this enforced move from Hodnet. There would be no more charity bazaars to organize, no farmers' wives to entertain and no insular county society to accuse her of siding with 'snobs' and 'outsiders' when she tried to talk to them about her writing.[237] It was not just her father whose parochial duties had come to an end.

Soon Mary would have constant access to the kind of society she craved, that of other literary men and women – over the next two decades she would turn the family domicile into a kind of informal literary salon, entertaining eminent authors and younger writers such as Percy Lubbock to tea and luncheon parties, and ultimately inaugurating a highly formalized women-only club, which met weekly to discuss books and ideas.[238] In July and August 1896 she was busy looking for new accommodation in London and finally the family found a flat in Knightsbridge. This 'flat, commonplace pile', as Lubbock witheringly described Albert Gate Mansions,[239] was a world away from the genteel country houses they had left behind. For the last thirty years of her life Mary, like Diana Tempest, would regularly leave London to spend weeks or months travelling between large country houses, and then she would return to the set of rooms in 62 Albert Gate Mansions. But surely there is more than a resolution to make the best of things in her fairly sprightly comment, 'It is hard to leave Hodnet, but the right time has come, and, once the wrench is over I think we shall be very happy together in London'.[240]

By September the family were paying their farewell visits. Mary was sorrowful at leaving their old friends Rowland Corbet and his wife, and had a long talk with them at their house when she went to say goodbye; 'I warmed myself by them, as I did by their fire', she wrote afterwards.[241] According to a critical member of the younger generation, Rowland Corbet would eventually become garrulous and self-satisfied – 'I'm sure he is sincere in his belief in himself' – pampered by his adoring wife, herself considered unworthy of him by his even more devoted lady admirers.[242] But this was years later. It was he who now preached a farewell sermon on behalf of his old friend, and he would remain close to the Cholmondeleys for the rest of his life, being nursed through his final illness by Essex (whose daughter Stella it was who found him so unimpressive) in 1919.

With the exception of her cousins Algy and Alice, Mary was less distraught about taking leave of the Heber-Percy family – 'We have lived near them for more than 20 years always on happy affectionate terms, but we have discovered in that time that friendship with them is impossible. They <u>cannot</u> care for any one outside their own family.'[243] And did she herself alienate those around her, as she sometimes felt she did?

> God intends me to comfort others, to cheer others, and my miserable depression, a jealous temper, an irritable pride, comes between me and those who might lean on me. God means me to be a helper, and His will is not accomplished in me.[244]

Just before they left there was some consolation for the disappointed Tom, who had once expected to inherit Condover, and who now engaged himself to Lady Margaret Herbert. Then, having destroyed two manuscript novels in a bonfire in the garden – early efforts, she told Richard Bentley, which had reached their proper destination and he should be grateful that she had never tried do palm them off on him – finally, on 10 October 1896, Mary left her home in Shropshire for the last time.[245]

There would have been much in the London of the 1890s to fascinate Mary, much to inspire and perhaps to perplex her. George Gissing had just published his New Woman novel centring on middle-class female employment, *The Odd Women*, in 1893. In 1895 Hardy's *Jude the Obscure*, with its unmarried lovers and its criticism of traditional values, had appeared to a mixed reception of acclamation and howls of protest. In the same year Oscar Wilde had been sentenced to two years' hard labour for homosexual acts, signalling a blow to the flamboyant Aesthetic movement he had helped to popularize.

But Mary was in no condition to take it all in. Immediately on her arrival in London she fell prey to acute bronchitis for five weeks, and once up from her sickbed her thoughts turned immediately to work.[246] She wanted to begin a new book, but she was still weak. On 23 November, 'full of despair', she wrote a list of characters on the first page of a blank book.[247] By the beginning of December she had outlined the plot and written part of the first chapter.[248] Such was the genesis of the novel that would make her more famous than she had ever imagined; the first she would publish without the reassuring medium of *Temple Bar*; and which would prove financially disastrous to its author. Now in her small bedroom in the new flat in Knightsbridge, beginning work on her first long piece of fiction in over three years, she wrote, 'It becomes more impossible every day'.[249]

5 'STRUMMING ON TWO PIANOS AT ONCE': LONDON AND THE WRITING OF *RED POTTAGE*

The Mary Cholmondeley myth would never become a cultural industry in the way that the myth of the Brontës did. But such as it was, it could be said to have begun with *Red Pottage*. In the writing of *Diana Tempest*, her first important book, she had been concerned mainly with staying one step ahead of the reviewers, knowing they would be quick to pounce on any weakness or 'ladies' law'[1] (as indeed had proved the case, despite her care). And she was consciously establishing a position for herself in the literary marketplace, determined to surpass *The Danvers Jewels* and *Sir Charles Danvers*, even as she capitalized on their success. She had learned a lot from George Bentley in the ten years of their association.

But in the writing of *Tomorrow We Die*, which she would later rename less dramatically *Red Pottage*, she had no amenable publisher with whom to discuss her anxieties or who could give her trusted advice on the marketing of literary fiction. In fact with this book, her most autobiographical to date, she was more concerned with the personal revelations she felt she was making to a curious public.[2] And her sense of herself as a public figure, with the concomitant need to control what would now be termed her 'image', would develop in response to the success of this last novel. She was notoriously reluctant to give interviews,[3] but, as a bestselling writer, she would find her background and personality increasingly discussed in the press.

But for now she was intent simply on writing her new novel. Finally she was established in London, as she had always wanted to be. She wrote nothing in her diary for several months after beginning *Red Pottage*, and so there is no reference to the death of her uncle Charles in January 1897. He had been laid in state in front of the high altar of St Lawrence's Church, Birkenhead, before being buried at Flaybrick Hill Cemetery, with Mary's brothers Tom and Regie, and her uncle Algernon Heber-Percy as chief mourners.[4] It is not clear why her father did not go, but there is no evidence to suggest any rift with his older brother, and it is likely that he was simply too frail to make the journey from London. Charles's obituary in *The Times* notes his capability as a preacher,[5] in which he differs markedly from the High Church Revd Gresley, who had first appeared with his adoring wife in a sort of walk-on part in *A Devotee*, and now perhaps seemed too good to have wasted in this cavalier fashion. But whether or not she had his expressed opinions in mind (and she would always deny that her most controversial character had any one original or even that he was a composite portrait),[6] still a few months after her uncle's death Mary would satirize Gresley's suspicion of female novelists, and she has a field day with his manner of praising Hester's grammar rather than acknowledging her gift for language. It is also interesting that Charles had devoted some time to writing religious tracts that never found the large readership he desired – Gresley spends much of his time in *Red Pottage* working on tracts attacking dissent, which no one ever reads.

Of course the central aim of the novel was not to take potshots at deceased relations or anyone else. Despite her misgivings about her ability to execute it, Mary, like her writer heroine, knew that her idea was worth the sacrifice of her time, energy and what little health she possessed. But she was arriving in London as a writer without the support of her long-term publisher, and she had in fact published her last book with the firm of Bentley. It was in 1898 that the company was officially taken over by Macmillan, but already in 1897 Bentley's authors must have been feeling a level of suspense, as they waited to hear whether or not their next work would be commissioned. Mary waited for three months and then, having ascertained that other writers had already received encouraging letters while she had not,[7] she assumed that *A Devotee* was not wanted and sold it to Edward Arnold for £50. It was an unlikely choice, Arnold specializing in educational and general titles rather than fiction (by 1900 he had still only published 20 novels as against 250 educational titles). Her next novel, as it turned out, would be his only bestseller.[8]

It must have been an unsettling change in many ways, although Mary was beginning her new life with such security as an assured social network could provide. On her previous visits to London she had already made acquaintance with influential figures in both politics and literature, and with the recent success of *Diana Tempest* behind her, she could claim an unquestioned place among her literary peers when she returned to take up permanent residence. Despite their essential failure to get on, she continued to see the controversial writer and anti-suffrage campaigner Mrs Humphry Ward; she had already been introduced to her more advanced sister the New Woman writer and suffragist Ethel Arnold. Like Cholmondeley herself, Ethel Arnold had been responsible for the care of an invalid mother for several years, and, again like her, she would become addicted to morphia prescribed for her own damaged health.[9] A few years later, in 1900, the unsympathetic Mary Ward caricatured her sister as a mad hypochondriac in *Eleanor*, Cholmondeley's least favourite of her books.[10] But, however similar

their circumstances, there is no evidence to suggest that the two became intimate. It is Ethel's sister Mary who features repeatedly in extant letters and diary
entries,[11] largely because Cholmondeley (again presumably like Ethel) found her
deeply annoying. She would, however, become firm friends with another namesake, the sensation writer Mary Braddon (Mrs Maxwell) and her son William.
For now at least Rhoda Broughton was also on hand, living near the Maxwells
in Richmond (even after her move to Oxford in 1900 she continued to come to
London when she could). At some point she almost certainly met Edith Wharton,[12] with whom she had several friends in common, including Percy Lubbock
and A. C. Benson. It was probably in these first years in London that she first
became acquainted with two others, Henry James and Howard Sturgis.

Sturgis would become a close friend and merciless critic of Cholmondeley's
work, as Lubbock remembered after the deaths of both. More than that, he was
the one person who could persuade Mary into self-forgetfulness: 'neither Mary
nor I cared at all if the needle [of his wit] pierced us, for his mere company gave
us a holiday from ourselves, a treat that we didn't often enjoy elsewhere'.[13] In her
autobiography *A Backward Glance*, Edith Wharton confirms that Sturgis was
'one of the most amusing and lovable of companions ... Indolent and unambi-
tious as he was, his social gifts were irresistible'. Further on she comments that

> In Howard Sturgis's case, even more than in that of James, the lack of a Boswell is to
> be deplored, for in his talk there was the same odd blending of the whimsical and the
> shrewd, of scepticism and emotion, as in his character, and the chosen friends who
> frequented [his house in Windsor] were always at their best in his company.[14]

It was Sturgis who exhorted Mary to write more satire and less dramatic incident into her novels, insisting that she was made for comedy not tragedy. She
in turn did her best to take his advice, although as Lubbock acutely observed,
'Was her hand lighter and her mind brighter in the refreshment of Howard's
society than when she was left alone? Very likely: but it is when we are left alone
that our books are to be written.'[15] Given Lubbock's account of Mary's and his
own despair when they failed to write up to Sturgis's exacting standards, it is
interesting to learn that even as he ruthlessly critiqued the work of his friends, he
himself was the victim of equally disheartening treatment at the hands of Henry
James. *Belchamber*, the novel for which he is chiefly remembered, is a satire of
the fashionable society of 1890s London. Published by Archibald Constable &
Co. in 1904, it failed to achieve a wide readership (James privately called it 'feebly Thackerayan', while reviewers censured its openness about 'painful' facts).[16]
Sturgis was apparently particularly upset by James's criticism that he had failed
to make good his central effect, and subsequently, in the words of Wharton,
'relapsed into knitting and embroidery'.[17] But these events lay some years in the
future. In 1896 Mary was still taking stock of her new environment, planning

how to make the most of her new opportunities, and beginning her first long novel in three years.

Within a few years of her arrival she would be congratulated on her books by cabinet ministers, and make critical assessments of the young Winston Churchill, whom she met at an evening party.[18] Already in late 1897 she was writing to the Secretary of the Colonial Defence Committee, Captain Matthew Nathan, to remind him of an earlier meeting, and inviting him to dine at the flat in Knightsbridge. Nathan, who soon afterwards left for a post in Sierra Leone, and who would spend much of his time abroad during Mary's own lifetime, would nonetheless become one of her closest and most valued friends over the next quarter of a century.[19] He also became a sounding board for her ideas on emigration and the woman question, and it was to him that she expressed her increasing anxiety over particular government policies.

All of this was a world away from the insular society of Hodnet. As the debate over the nature and status of the New Woman raged on in the press, Mary now found herself part of a more congenial culture, in which single women travelled unescorted on the London underground, and a female writer could 'perpetrate a book' without being considered 'odd'.[20] But Mary's response to the question of the New Woman remains problematic. She was clearly no friend to rational dress, as her derogatory comment about the 'fat Spanish women' in trousers, whom she had observed in Tenerife, makes clear.[21] In her anxiety to satirize women's meetings in her writing, her usual refined irony gives way to a rather shoddy sarcasm, as when one of her characters says that it has been raining cats and dogs, only to be met with the response, 'Surely only cats at a women's meeting'.[22]

But it is important to remember that the debate over women's rights was more complex than it may appear in the wake of later events, and after the lapse of over a century. As recent work on the New Woman phenomenon makes clear, it is a mistake to assume some kind of consistent and homogenous agenda put forward by the female intelligentsia of the late nineteenth century. The term itself was used in the press alternately as a rallying cry and as a term of abuse.[23] It could conceivably refer to women in very different circumstances, holding substantially different views. The young unmarried girl who used her own latchkey while living with her parents; the middle aged copy typist venturing onto masculine terrain in the new offices of the 1880s and 1890s; the aristocratic novelist and the professional orator all could be described and conveniently grouped together through the unifying stereotype provided by this new catchphrase. Many professed New Women deliberately distanced themselves from media representations of the mannish or desexed woman whose unnatural intellect failed to make up for her lack of attractiveness. Mindful of the scathing attacks in *Punch* and other periodicals, the most determined exponents of women's rights were quick to insist that they were not neurotic and hysterical, nor carelessly dressed and unlovable.[24]

Furthermore it was still possible at the turn of the century for successful women writers and journalists, whose own lives testified to the possibilities of female emancipation, to berate other women who did not conform to the ideal of willing dependence. Such a strategy could, apart from anything else, neutralize the threat posed by individuals by focusing attack on those who might seek to emulate them. Eliza Lyn Linton, a successful journalist who had come to live alone in London as a young woman, and who was separated from her husband, had made her name with a notorious series of articles in the 1860s, excoriating girls who would not admit marriage as their natural goal, and the superiority of men as their safeguard against the storms of life.[25]

If the New Woman herself was essentially a fictional construct, given the repository of hostile stereotypes ranging from the forward young girl to the mannish platform orator described as a threat by Mrs Fenwick Miller in an article describing her own first speech (in 1873), it is hardly surprising that she should be so hard to pin down.[26] In fiction she can be identified by any one of the conspicuous traits variously associated with her: she may hold a Cambridge degree, as does Vivie Warren, in George Bernard Shaw's *Mrs Warren's Profession* (1894); or simply ride a bicycle, as Cholmondeley's own Rachel West does; she may be introspective, tortured and creative, like Sue Bridhead in Hardy's *Jude the Obscure* (1896); or simply tied to a profession by financial constraints, like many of the characters in Gissing's *The Odd Women* (1893); again, she may be sexually emancipated like Grant Allen's *Woman Who Did* (1895), Herminia Barton, who rejects marriage to her lover on grounds of social principle; but equally she may be a purist, as in Sarah Grand's *Ideala* (1888). In the first decade of the twentieth century Cholmondeley would respond to many of the questions so widely circulated ten years earlier – her references to the 'brawling brotherhood', the question of the million odd 'superflous women' who could find no one to marry, show that she had been listening.[27] Her novels feature women who are, if not emancipated in the modern sense, nonetheless independent in their thinking. Diana Tempest, realizing that her legal cousin will never propose to her, finally asks him to marry her instead, a feat matched by few if any Victorian heroines outside the pages of Wilkie Collins.[28] And if Mary's own struggle as a talented female writer does not of itself make her a New Woman, her recasting of the battle in fictional terms makes *Red Pottage* identifiably a New Woman novel. But equally noteworthy, as her own letters to friends make clear, is Cholmondeley's own guarded investment in the very patriarchal culture she is attacking – there is nothing straightforward about her satire of traditional values.

Of course its melodramatic plot places it, with its forerunner *Diana Tempest*, firmly in the sensation genre inaugurated by Wilkie Collins in the late 1850s and

'60s. But if the masterfully handled psychodrama helped to make *Red Pottage* the most successful of Mary's novels, it is also the most autobiographical. Most obviously her characterization leans heavily on family members – it is not difficult to trace her brother Richard Vernon Cholmondeley in the engaging Dick Vernon, who begins life by sowing mustard seed on his parents' billiard table and ends as a successful vintner in Australia. 'There really was not room for him in England', as one character wryly comments.[29] Another favourite brother, Regie, makes his appearance as the lovingly observed small boy of the Gresley house, who swallows Dick's 'magic' halfpenny and has to be shaken vigorously by the heels. In the novel Regie and his aunt Hester, the writer, have a particularly close bond – it is she who inculcates moral values in him and shares his imaginative susceptibility, and she will later sit with him throughout a dangerous illness. Even a small niece, the later to be famous writer Stella Benson, makes a shadowy appearance as the youngest of the Gresley children. More puzzling is the characterization of the oldest child, a sensible but tediously literal girl called Mary, who has little part to play in the unfolding of the narrative and who alone fails to capture the affection of her creative and talented aunt.

But in its exploration of the lives of Victorian women, the book is at once more personal and more widely political than these castings would suggest. While it does not contain a recognizable manifesto for women, it is determinedly female-centred in its focus on two single women, both of whom struggle in a male-dominated environment. The ironmaster's daughter Rachel West has been brought up in luxury and is ill equipped to fend for herself when her father dies unexpectedly in debt. Her experience immediately raises two of Mary's central preoccupations – the lack of value attaching to female members of the household and the inadequacy of their education:

> She ate the bread of carefulness in the houses of poor relations not of high degree, with whom her parents had quarrelled when they had made their money ... She learned what it was to be the person of least importance in families of no importance. She essayed to teach and failed. She had no real education. She made desperate struggles for independence, and learned how others failed besides herself.[30]

Eventually she succeeds in earning a bare subsistence in London by copy writing, only to be upbraided by a half-starved fellow lodger, who shouts up at her, 'He always employed me until you came ... and now he gives it all to you because you're younger and better looking'. It is this experience that leads her to reflect on the ruthlessness of Victorian economics, 'I might have known that I had only got on to the raft by pushing someone else off it.'[31] But Mary Cholmondeley was not George Gissing and *Red Pottage* is not an account of the female struggle for survival in the East End of London. Rachel is reinstated in 'society' when her father's partner dies and leaves her a new fortune. Instantly she is beset by fortune-hunting suitors, but she is reluctant to relinquish her independence by this point and lives alone, a discreet but resolute example of the New Woman that Cholmondeley herself never managed to become.

Rachel's counterpart Hester Gresley is a strong-willed literary genius, who has refused at a young age to marry her most obvious match in the novel, Lord Newhaven; his narrative punishment for replacing her within the year is to find himself disastrously married to the vapid and posturing, if superficially attractive Violet, who fails to value his attachment and, losing it, begins a series of flirtations ultimately leading to adultery with Hugh Scarlett. But if she breaks with tradition by refusing to marry, in one sense Hester lacks Rachel's resolute independence, passively agreeing to go and live with her brother in the country on the death of the aunt who has brought her up, rather than living alone or accepting Rachel's more congenial offer of a home with her.

In the limited choices open to its central characters, *Red Pottage* stands as a damning indictment of received tradition, according to which women must marry or fail. As Lord Newhaven cynically puts it:

> It is the blessed custom of piling everything on to the eldest son, and leaving the women of the family almost penniless, which provides half of us with wives without any trouble to ourselves ... The average dancing young woman living in luxury in her father's house is between the devil and the deep sea. We are frequently the devil, but it is not surprising that she can't face the alternative, a poverty to which she was not brought up, and in which she has seen her old spinster aunts.[32]

No wonder that, as Elaine Showalter comments in her introduction to the most recent published edition of 1985, 'In several of the scenes ... Cholmondeley's anger and passion express themselves in violent images which shatter the urbane epigrammatic sophistication of her usual prose'.[33]

But Mary was not a feminist writer in any straightforward sense, and while her most heavily satirized figure dismisses the cause of women's rights with 'a jocose allusion to the woman following the plough, while the man sat and home and rocked the cradle', she has little time for another male character who tries to enlist Rachel's support in an organized campaign – her crushing, if rather optimistic response, is 'I thought the new woman had effected her own emancipation'.[34] This response is significant not only for its wishfulness, but also in its implicit class focus – if the 'new woman' was a middle- or possibly upper-class phenomenon, the working-class women Rachel has so recently left behind can hardly be said to have effected their own emancipation. It is possible that Cholmondeley is referring here to the recent opening of higher education to women. London University had allowed women to take a degree from 1878, Cambridge had followed suit in 1881, with Oxford finally giving way in 1884. But it is otherwise difficult to ascertain precisely *what* rights she wants for women – she cites the dilemma faced by upper class-spinsters not so much as an argument in favour of their entering a profession as to attack the tradition of leaving the estate in its entirety to an eldest son. Pulling together the few scattered comments in her writing from this period, it is clear that Mary passionately endorsed certain items on the feminist agenda, while remaining sceptical about others. She had very personal reasons for decrying the convention which would attempt to bar women from most kinds of work; she satirized as a matter of course Gresley's glib joke dismissing women's rights with references to female plough-hands and cradle-rocking men.

But while she approved of liberated women effecting their own emancipation, it never gets much clearer what she means to convey by the term itself. As she moved towards the first years of the twentieth century, she was suspicious of organized women's movements, which she insisted on characterizing through stereotype – it is Rachel who in the 1900 play of *Red Pottage* assumes that the audience are all cats, and the bishop's sister attends them in between busybodying on her numerous and eclectic committees. Not until 1909 would she publicly address the question of female suffrage,[35] and it comes as something of a surprise to see how well she recalled the debates of late Victorian England, that she had skated over so matter of factly at the time. Indeed one of the anomalies of *Red Pottage* is that the bishop of Southminster, the moral barometer of the novel, concurs with – even more surprisingly – Hester's own account of the best women's failure to behave honourably, using the familiar terms of Victorian patriarchy, 'it is owing to that difference of code that women clash so hopelessly with men when they attempt to compete or work with them'.[36] This arbitrary statement is contradicted neither by Hester nor by Rachel, although it inevitably raises the question, of relevance to both of them, what kind of work should be open to women if they are not fit to work with men?

Nonetheless *Red Pottage* is largely concerned with the predicament of unmarried women who do attempt to work, while remaining within the conventional family setup. In the ordeal Mary imposes on her fictional writer, she gives an intimate account of what it means to be a visionary but strong-willed and ambitious woman, trapped by one's own participation in a culture that routinely sacrificed its daughters to the wider needs of the family. Not surprisingly she is sympathetic to the internalized self-doubt which discourages women from pursuing their ambition in the first place. Like many another writer, she has trouble reconciling these two imperatives of personal ambition and creative vision, later insisting through Hester that the side of her which loves success has had no part in the writing of the book. In fact she makes no attempt to justify female ambition in itself, dwelling instead on the divine purposes of literary genius and the difficulty for a woman in particular of meeting those aims, 'To some of us Christ comes in the dawn of the spiritual life walking upon the troubled waves of art.

And we recognize Him and would fain go to meet Him. But our companions and our own fears dissuade us.'[37] In this meditation Cholmondeley artfully side-steps the question of feminine self-assertion, making her fictional writer – and by extension, others like her, including Cholmondeley herself – a disciple of a difficult and sacred vocation, rather than a competitor in the literary market-place. That she herself did feel a sense of responsibility in her writing is obvious from her journals and the recollections of friends.[38] But there is another side to her quest for literary fame, presented in her letters to Bentley and other writers such as Anne Thackeray Ritchie and Rhoda Broughton. From the beginning she was conscious of her standing in the literary world, she went carefully over her contracts,[39] and she was determined to succeed. The yearning after an ideal, the feeling for the writer's almost sacred vocation, is genuine. What she keeps out of *Red Pottage*, and so away from Hester Gresley, is the determination to win over an uncertain readership whose tastes and education were not necessarily her own, the anxiety over production and the timing of new editions, and the perpetual surveillance kept over Mudie's and the reviewers.

But it is wholly appropriate that in her most celebrated novel she should recall the frustrations of her own youth, as the fey Hester Gresley, already a rising literary star, attempts to find time to write in the household of her wholly unimpressed brother, the sincere but narrow-minded vicar of Warpington. James Gresley is as unable to appreciate his sister's abilities as he is to understand her personally, as the narrator makes clear, 'both fanatic and saint were fighting for predominance in the kingdom of that pinched brain ... He looked as if he would fling himself as hard against a truth without perceiving it, as a hunted hare against a stone wall.'[40] This is clearly demonstrated when he burns his sister's masterpiece, believing it to be immoral. In Mary's original plan the manuscript was to have been accepted by a publisher but returned for minor revisions – stepping up the irony, the final version has Hester sending for it herself to remove the very passages that cause her brother to destroy it. But the narrator spares him the final indignity of a further confrontation with Hester. Again in the original scheme, the Gresleys were to have berated her for her 'vindictiveness' in refusing to live with them afterwards,[41] but in the event Mary decided to spare them the inevitable satire that such a scene must have entailed.

Of course Gresley is consistently satirized but, with her experience of the country clergy, Cholmondeley has more sympathy for him than most of her readers have been able to muster. He faces the familiar dilemma of an expanding family and a poor living, and his jealous wife recalls in condemning Hester's absence from church that she herself has often attended early morning services shortly before giving birth to another child. But if the narrator is willing to make allowances for Gresley personally, she is merciless towards his denunciatory pamphlet, 'Modern Dissent', in which he mixes metaphors and disregards salient facts with ruthless enthusiasm. This pamphlet, which allows Gresley to appear as a local author himself while holding forth on his favourite topic, usurps the time Hester should be spending on her own novel, as he selfishly demands her assistance with its composition. At the same time he makes light of her superior abilities, claiming that she is better than he is at 'grammar and spelling'.[42] Hester's novel on the contrary is something on which she will expend her very being, seeing herself in quasi-religious terms simply as the instrument that helps to bring it into being. While she describes it passionately as her own 'child',[43] it is itself parasitic, a drain on her health and strength, as the narrator constantly points out even as she looks to its completion as to a moment of transformation. This giving of the self to a work of value is seen as ennobling and itself helps to mark the genuine work of art. But the mutilation of female genius as perpetrated by Gresley was a theme that provoked Mary's most biting satire, and she would return to it in one of her most accomplished stories, 'The Goldfish', over twenty years later.

In London Hester has become noteworthy with the success of her first novel. But, like the writer of another successful novel, *Diana Tempest*, she finds that such celebrity does not necessarily filter down to the provinces. In her brother's house Hester, like Rachel before her, suddenly finds herself the least regarded member of the household. She faces constant interruptions from importunate neighbours, as well as other members of the household who regard her request for solitude and time in which to write as 'self-important and silly',[44] and spends much of her time in housekeeping matters to relieve her frail and overburdened sister-in-law. Finally she is reduced to working literally with the first light of dawn and ultimately through the night, rather than try to accommodate her need for solitude in her writing to the incessant demands of the daily routine. The character is of course partly based on Mary's youngest sister, who died too young to fulfil her potential, and whose work was in a sense lost, as Hester Gresley's masterpiece will be destroyed. Like Hester Cholmondeley, the fictional writer of *Husks* (one of Mary's ideas for the title of *Red Pottage*)[45] is extreme in her feelings and opinions, a trait the narrator associates with the artistic temperament. As a child the original draft describes her as 'delicate, excitable, passionate, imaginative',[46] linking her directly to the sensitive and emotionally volatile Hester Cholmondeley, who demanded stories from her older sister and cried bitterly when they were not satisfactory. If Mary gives her own name to the least attractive of the Gresley children, she gives her sister a vicarious chance to write a novel, as she was never able to do in life. The narrator comments:

> The unbalanced joys and sorrows of emotional natures are apt to arouse the pity of the narrow-hearted, and the mild contempt of the obtuse of their fellow creatures. But perhaps it is a mistake to feel compassion for persons like Hester, for if they have many evil days and weeks in their usually short lives, they have also moments of sheer bliss, hours of awed contemplation and of exquisite rapture which possibly in the

long run equal the more solid joys of a good income and a good digestion, nay, even the perennial glow of that happiest of happy temperaments which limits the nature of others by its own ... and believes it can measure life with the same admirable accuracy with which it measures its drawing-room curtains.[47]

In *Under One Roof* Cholmondeley describes her sister as 'a free lance and a rebel', and more tellingly she uses a description borrowed from her own novel in describing her as having a neatness and finish about her appearance, 'as if she had been cut out with a very sharp pair of scissors'.[48] But if Hester inevitably recalls the lost promise of Mary's dead sister, she is also Mary herself, wrestling with the gap between her passion for writing, her uncertainty about her own ability and her dubious health. Observing the evident change in her friend, Rachel comments uneasily to herself that

> Hester, always delicate, was making an enormous effort under conditions which would be certain to entail disastrous effects on her health. The book was sapping her strength like a vampire, and the Gresleys were evidently exhausting it still further by unconsciously strewing her path with difficulties.[49]

But Hester insists on remaining with her brother until her book is finished, and the bishop agrees that the repression of her life there is somehow necessary to her writing. Mary had not forgotten how she herself had been 'turned back, quietly ... to the silence of a country life, without interest in country life' and how 'these I know in my own heart are the conditions in which I can (at times) work'.[50] Like her creator, Hester believes that she must sacrifice her health and even her happiness in order to write her best work. The allurements of London are left to the fatuous dilettante Harvey with his *Unashamed*, so much admired by society hostesses such as Sybell Loftus. A woman writer, it seems, is not true to her art if she will not risk dying for it. This valorization of illness would surely be her final answer to any suggestion that Miss Cholmondeley should rest before she was destroyed by her own work. Hester determinedly 'spends her health' on her novel, as the act of writing itself both demands and ultimately destroys vast reserves of energy, gaining force as the physical resistance of the writer visibly ebbs away.

It is by a similar exercise of will that Hester is able to save Regie from what it is feared may be a fatal illness. Like Mary rousing herself from her own sickbed to nurse Victoria in a foreign country, Hester is somehow able to sit up all night resting Regie's head on her knee. Only when Regie is moved and Hester tells the doctor that she will have to scream in another moment, does it become obvious what an effort she has been making. The doctor tells a bewildered Gresley that she has been sitting still with cramp since the end of the first hour. This immense act of will in suppressing the need to scream is quickly passed over in the narrative, but it is a crucial and suggestive moment that gestures far beyond the immediate context of Regie's illness, in its glancing critique of the female role in general.

By the time she began this account of a woman writer's passionate self-suppression and fixed resolution, Mary knew that she would never return to the life of a country spinster, ordered by the endless round of parochial work and feminine visiting. As Linda Peterson has observed, her father's retirement was crucial to her genesis as a New Woman writer, in that it 'released her from a sense of family responsibility, and allowed her to move from Hodnet ... to London, a relocation that put her in touch with a more advanced literary coterie, including Henry James, Howard Sturgis, and the Findlater sisters'.[51]

But after two months in the more congenial atmosphere of London her own health showed no signs of improving, and in December of that year she and Victoria were again trying the effects of the clearer air of the south coast; the winter of 1896 saw them installed in the popular health resort of Bournemouth.[52] As Mary knew, to leave London was still to leave her fame behind her – the sisters make no appearance in the local Dorset papers, nor are their names in the Visitors' Directory for the time.

Nonetheless it should have been a time of recuperation, conducive even to the writing of a novel about the strain of becoming an author in poor health and with limited time. Such were the judicious effects of the town's mild climate that many asthmatics who went there for their condition ended by taking up permanent residence. Victoria at least rapidly regained health and strength. In an attempt to recover her own health Mary learned to ride a bicycle (a standard motif of the New Woman that she would later use to characterize her heroine Rachel West). But she was not impressed by the curative properties of the town and subsequently recalled with horror her struggle to write the new novel 'between asthma, and the strumming on two pianos at once by other lodgers ... 9 chapters in 4 months, and much of that inferior'.[53] These are the chapters that set up the dual plot of the novel. The dissolute Hugh Scarlett decides to break off his intrigue with frivolous Lady Newhaven as he travels to meet her at an evening party, and on the same night finds himself drawn to the superficially less attractive Rachel West. Leaving the scene he is summoned to a *tête-à-tête* with Lord Newhaven, who insists that each of them must draw a lighter, or strip of paper. Whoever draws the short lighter must kill himself by a given time. Hugh loses, and as he finds himself increasingly attracted to Rachel and determines to change, she is told of his past and of the lighters by Lady Newhaven, who was listening at the door of her husband's study. What neither woman knows is which of the men drew the short lighter, having nothing to go on but a short laugh from Lord Newhaven as each man inspects his lighter without speaking.

It is by a slight wrenching of the narrative that Rachel is made the dearest friend of Hester Gresley, who has recently gone to live with her brother, near the country seat of the Newhavens. In the original manuscript Mary wrote that 'Few women are capable of friendship and those few not seldom attract each other.

This faith is given to those who value it. Till a more exciting emotion comes their way.'[54] But in revising the script, she modified the rather unfortunate last phrase, remarking simply that, 'The passing judgement of the majority of men on such devotion might be summed up in the words, "Occupy till I come." It does occupy till they do come.'[55] Rachel and Hester, however, are to prove the exception:

> here and there among its numberless counterfeits a friendship rises up between two women which sustains the life of both, which is still young when life is waning, which man's love and motherhood cannot displace nor death annihilate; a friendship which is not the solitary affection of an empty heart nor the deepest affection of a full one, but which nevertheless lightens the burdens of this world and lays its pure hand upon the next.[56]

Both of these characters will be involved in a separate plot that tests her endurance and leads to a serious illness. The apparent lack of structure in this dual plot was noted by reviewers at once and is often perceived as the major flaw of the novel. But the parallel plots are necessary to Cholmondeley's purpose. She cannot allow her fictional writer to marry and so endanger her writing, but Hester's bond with Rachel will supersede every other relationship in the book; Rachel herself is capable of sustained happiness precisely *because* she lacks Hester's imagination, but she is unequal to the demands placed upon her by the unfolding of the melodramatic suicide plot. She maintains a reserve that astonishes an admiring Newhaven when he realizes that she is the confidante of his wife; but her failure to intervene before the expiry of the five months agreed upon arguably contributes to the tragic ending, and she is unable to empathize with the unfortunate Hugh until the bishop has been castigating her for several pages. In exploring the limitations of each figure, and their lack of opportunities, Cholmondeley powerfully probes and undermines the roles available to women at the time. Each is necessary to complete the other and it is wholly appropriate that on hearing of Hugh's entanglement with another woman, Rachel should abruptly leave London to visit friends in the country, near Hester.

With rather less faith in the influence of provincial air on a troubled mind, Mary was dissatisfied with her novel and desperate to escape the strumming lodgers. As soon as she was able to travel after a combined attack of asthma and influenza, she fled back to her aunt Victoria in London, where, she noted with satisfaction, 'I soon picked up'.[57] But she had spoken too soon. Almost immediately asthma laid hold of her again and when she next turned to her diary it was only to record that 'Constant morphia has made writing difficult for the last 6 weeks. I cannot see what I am writing now, so must stop. I am thirty eight today, and I have achieved almost nothing, almost nothing.'[58]

This assessment of course says rather more about Mary's state of mind than it does about her achievements. In the last twenty years she had, against all the odds, published four novels, as well as a number of stories in national magazines. Her depression may have been brought on by the comparative failure of the last to date. After its run in *Temple Bar* in 1896, *A Devotee*, which first featured the character of Sybell Loftus as well as the Gresleys, had of course been left stranded when George Bentley's son sold the family business to Macmillan and the new head of the firm showed no apparent interest in keeping her on. It was at this point that she entered into negotiations with Edward Arnold instead. In losing Bentley's support, Linda Peterson has argued, she was able to pull herself out of a literary rut and experiment with more daring fiction, but at the cost of losing her place in a magazine that could have consolidated her reputation over the decades: as Peterson comments,

> With ... *Temple Bar* Cholmondeley had formed an association with a long-lived periodical, one in which she could learn the house style, count on a regular outlet for her work, and establish her reputation. After she lost Bentley as her publisher, she was never able to establish another such ongoing relationship.[59]

A Devotee had in fact enjoyed a run in *Temple Bar* shortly before the sale of the firm to Macmillan. But on its appearance in volume form, the story was barely noticed by the press and Mary herself seems not to have set much store by it. Nonetheless it was the first significant step towards what would prove the most ruinous association of her career. She would later note with classic understatement, 'It is a great shame'.[60]

Ironically, this was the year in which she noted that 130 people, many of them new acquaintances, had been to tea parties at the flat in Knightsbridge.[61] In April, anxious to protect her increasingly frail father from worry, Mary was forced to answer questions put in 'a very urgent manner' by Mrs Heber-Percy relating to the running of the Hodnet boys' school prior to their departure. Was the school always considered to be Church of England or was it not? Who paid the expenses over and above the £15 endowment and the government grant? Were the curates able to give religious instruction when they wished? Unwilling to cope directly with this onslaught of questions, Mary wrote an affectionate but weary letter to her cousin Algy, remarking on the tendency of religious minds to assume that anyone not attacking the dissenters must secretly be one of their number.[62] Sadly, from the extant manuscript it seems that Gresley's assertion, 'I have no belief in holding out our hands to the enemies of Christ',[63] actually predates this eruption from Mrs Heber-Percy.

Eventually the constant whirl of social engagements became too much, and at the end of June Mary wrote to an admirer of *Diana Tempest* that she had been unable to accept any invitations for the last two months.[64] She had not been out socially after a dinner party at the Lyalls' prostrated her for ten days. By July she was still too ill to work and had to decline 'capital seats at the Treasury' for the

Jubilee procession. She rallied herself for an evening, as one of the givers of the 'Distinguished Women of England for the Distinguished Men dinner'.[65]

But the end of July found her alone 'except for dear old Ninny', at her brother Regie's house in Hertfordshire. It was to be 'the scene of a great struggle for me, and thank God, a victory'. After three months of constant morphia, two grains a day at one point (the maximum dose usually advised at the time being a more cautious ¼ grain), she set herself to repay the patient support of her family by forcing herself to leave it off. 'And it is done. And the dreadful days and nights are over, days when I lay in the open air, hardly able to move, crying from misery, and nights worse than the days. Thank God it is done, it is over.' As she began to recover Mary forced herself to walk, to take bicycle exercise, and even subjected herself to a daily sluicing in cold water. For the first time in years she found herself able to enjoy food, and she was eating and sleeping better. Finally she began to write again, hopeful that the improvement in her health would make it easier in the future.[66] By October she was ready to return to London.[67]

She came back looking 'ridiculously young' and with renewed confidence, bicycling in the park after breakfast, writing until lunch and then enjoying idle afternoons in the mild autumn weather.[68] It must have seemed as if the novel begun under such unpromising circumstances was going to be easily written after all. Mary herself was wholly unable to account for what happened next. On one day in the space of a few hours the familiar 'sore throat, suffocation, fear, asthma, morphia' returned. Over the next ten days her temperature shot up to 105.[69] She would later ask after one of these attacks, 'Does any one who has not experienced it realize what it is to go for two days and nights never sitting up, leaning forward, unable to lean against anything, much less lean back against pillows[?]'[70] But she forced herself once again to leave off the morphia, in itself 'like a second illness'.[71] She would use this horror as a metaphor for Hugh's waking realization that he is to die by his own hand:

> For a few seconds he lay like one emerging from the influence of morphia, who feels his racked body still painlessly afloat on a sea of rest, but is conscious that it is drifting back to the bitter shores of pain, and who stirs neither hand nor foot for fear of hastening the touch of the encircling sands on which he is so soon to be cast in agony once more.[72]

The comparison of morphia to alcohol as a form of corruption by James Gresley during Hester's near-fatal illness is one of his more asinine pronouncements. Of herself Mary wrote at this time 'I have often been weaker, but my real strength is gone, and the <u>look</u> of health[,] and life is a burden once more. How well I know the oppressed pale face, aged and lined which I have just looked at in the glass.' But even as she wrote this, another thought was struggling for utterance, a thought to set against this 'great catastrophe' of her life. The diary goes on:

If God set before me two lives, one gifted with perfect health, and a slow conventional mind, and the other – the life I have now, a failure in nearly all directions owing to ill health and long periods of pain, disappointment, renunciation, but having this one decided talent permeating it – if God set these two lives before me, health and a conventional mind. Ill health and pain and a talent. <u>Which should I choose?</u> I am only just up after illness. Nevertheless I should not hesitate one second. I should answer instantly the only possible answer. Ill health and talent ...

Talent stands upon my little six foot of earth, casting his black shadow all over it, the shadow which I call pain. In that shadow all my little flowers die. But shall I ask Talent to stand further away, and let the light fall on my slip of earth? God forbid. Let him come nearer if that may be. But the flowers? Let them go.[73]

This is precisely the choice made by Hester in *Red Pottage*, and her clear-sighted heroism is rewarded by ethereal visions. When she finally finishes the book, it is to an awestruck burst of rhetoric from the narrator, who ascribes to her an atmosphere momentarily perceived even by the considerably less sensitive James Gresley:

A ray of sunlight, faint as an echo, stole through the lingering mist, parting it on either hand, and fell on Hester.

Hester, standing in a white gown under the veiled trees in a glade of silver and trembling opal, which surely mortal foot had never trod, seemed infinitely removed from him. Dimly he felt that she was at one with this mysterious morning world, and that he, the owner, was an alien and a trespasser in his own garden.

But a glimpse of his cucumber frames in the background reassured him. He advanced with a firmer step, as one among allies.[74]

Just a few weeks after her last entry Mary was rereading her old diary, containing the 'fragments' of the seven years in her youth when she had been in love and believed herself to be loved in return. It was here, when she realized that she was not to marry the man she loved, that she had 'buried her grief like an ugly bulb', wondering whether it would come up in 'beautiful resurrection' as flowers do.[75] At this point she seems to have had no doubt that she had done right in remaining silent in the face of her lover's unaccountable anger, all those years ago. A conversation between Hester, Rachel and the bishop that she wrote in Bournemouth outlines her own philosophy. Rachel and the bishop maintain that if good and evil co-exist in everyone, there is no need to take notice of the evil. Passionately rejecting this view as hypocrisy, Hester answers:

'I think we ought to believe the best of people until they prove themselves unworthy, and then – '

'Then what?' said the Bishop, settling himself in his chair.

'Then leave them in silence.'[76]

Now, looking back on the moment when she had parted in silence from the man she loved, Mary resolutely tried to draw on the comfort and the 'added powers' that God had brought out of that traumatic time, and she claimed, 'I would not alter one hour of it now'.[77] Less serenely Hester defends her uncompromising silence by insisting:

> It is my own fault if I idealise a thistle until the thistle and I both think it is a vine. But if people appear to love and honour certain truths which they know are every-thing to me ... and then desert when the pinch comes, as it always does come, and act from worldly motives, then I know that they have never really cared for what they professed to love[78]

Mary would claim, on behalf of both herself and Hester, that 'repression is posi-tively necessary to her to enable her ... to get up steam'.[79] Her own repression and misery, she would later claim, were the crucial factors in her success – the suf-fering of her youth, in other words, had been worthwhile, because it had indeed come up as a flower. Determined that everything had turned out for the best, she may even have missed the irony of her own repeated metaphor. If her suffering came up like a flower, still all her little flowers died.

That December Mary was ill again, 'laid up for the hundredth time' as she resignedly put it. Depressed in spirits, she again started to doubt her talent, con-vincing herself that 'the new book which illness has once more interrupted will be as mediocre as everything I am and feel'. By her own reckoning she had not written a hundred words a day during the last year. Her one hope on the last day of the year, and it was a faint and intermittent one, was for a stronger faith, 'a further step in the religious life'.[80]

But 1898 began better than Mary might have anticipated. By early March she had been well and morphia-free for two months, half the book was written and she was beginning to dine out again, even going skating with Rhoda Broughton.[81] By now the sisters were holding regular Thursday luncheon parties,[82] entertain-ing old friends as well as the ever increasing circle of new acquaintance. Always in her mind was the 'further step in the religious life' that she had been long-ing for on New Year's Eve. It seemed to her that she was drawing closer to God and, as she was fully aware, her calmer nerves were surely helping to improve her health. She and her sisters had their first dinner party at the flat, she dined out with the Ritchies and Sir Alfred Lyall, noting with understandable complacency that, 'Times have changed since I used to dread dinner parties: because I was sure to be left out'.[83]

But Mary herself had changed. She was no longer the shy young girl blushing uncontrollably at her first Hunt Ball or hoping only to appear creditable when she visited her brother at Cambridge.[84] Always able to laugh at herself even in her most serious moments, she gives Hester the authorship of a crucial passage in the book, but allows the reader access to it only through an uncomprehending James Gresley:

'When we look back at what we were seven years ago, five years ago, and perceive the difference in ourselves, a difference amounting almost to change of identity; when we look back and see in how many characters we have lived and loved and suffered and died before we reached the character that momentarily clothes us, and from which our soul is struggling out to clothe itself anew; when we feel how the sympathy even of those who love us best is always with our last expression, never with our present feeling, always with the last dead self on which our climbing feet are set – '

'She is hopelessly confused', said Mr Gresley without reading to the end of the sentence, and substituting the word *ladder* for *dead self*.[85]

But the satire gives way to a feeling of foreboding, as Gresley slowly comprehends that the clerical character he has been favouring does not come well out of the book. Having read to the end, he consults with his wife, who deliberately goads him by pointing out that Hester will publish her work with or without his consent. Cholmondeley keeps the reader in suspense for several pages, but there is a feeling of inevitability as the manuscript is consigned to a bonfire in the garden shortly before Hester's return from a visit to Southminster.

Of course Mary herself had burned two of her own manuscripts on leaving Hodnet, a link she acknowledged in a later interview with the *Bookman*. But this catastrophic moment in *Red Pottage* may be indebted as much to a literary as to a personal source. In 1894 her friend Rhoda Broughton had satirized 'lady novelists' in her novel *A Beginner*. The heroine spends much of her time trying to conceal her authorship of a first novel in which she nonetheless takes considerable pride. *Miching Machello*, intended to be read as a moral homily on the unrestrained exercise of passion, shocks the genteel but parochial world in which Emma lives by its supposed enthusiasm for questionable love scenes. Nonetheless it is greeted with some half-hearted praise in the provincial press, before being killed off entirely by the ridicule of a prestigious London paper. When it transpires that this review has been written by the very man who has just proposed marriage to her, and in whom she has been planning to confide her literary ambitions, Emma allows her aunt to buy back every available copy of the book and consign them to a bonfire. Mary wrote twice to Bentley, her and Broughton's publisher, once in January as it began its run in *Temple Bar* to say that she and her family had been laughing over it; but in thanking him for her personal copy on its publication that summer, she confessed to a more personal response. The book had appealed to her particularly,

> because not long ago I was a beginner, and the little world in which I live is so little, so very like Emma's, with its one word for an author 'a little scribbler' and its amazement at what can induce me to join the ranks of literary persons: generally designated as 'snobs' and 'outsiders'.[86]

Now Mary was beyond the reach of that 'little world' and in the process of writing her own masterpiece. But in the destruction of Hester's manuscript, she may well be recalling the thoughtless arrogance of that parochial world, where the figures she most aspired to follow had been designated 'scribblers', or 'dabblers with the pen' as Gresley says to Hester. In *Red Pottage* the burning of a woman's most personal work is not a subject for amusement, but an unspeakable act of cruelty.

Indeed the climax of this plot is reached as a distraught Hester demands of her brother, 'I did not let your child die. Why have you killed mine?' Just at this moment Gresley's son Regie comes in and Hester pushes him out of the way as she runs distractedly out of the house. She goes straight to the bishop and tells him 'I don't know what I did, but I think I killed Regie. I know I meant to.'[87] This is an uncomfortable moment to say the least, and it is meant to be. The plot in manuscript specifically talks about Hester's 'murderous instinct',[88] and the writing reinforces this intention, despite the bishop's later comparison of Hester's behaviour to a dog who finds himself caught in a trap and simply has to bite something in his agony. Hester's illness is partly brought on by her horror at what she has done, but the murderous rage against masculine intervention inspires a revenge that is conscious and – while instantly regretted – quite deliberate. In a later novel (*Moth and Rust*) we will see one of the characters reading the *novels* of Hester Gresley, confirming that Hester will write 'better books', as the doctor and bishop assure her. But as she herself points out, the writing of any number of books will be no consolation for the loss of this one.

Mary could not know that in writing *Red Pottage* she herself had reached the height of her powers. Nor could she know at this point that it would be one of the most read and perhaps the most controversial novel of the last year of the century.[89] But, as Percy Lubbock later remarked, the literary world was by now receiving her as one of its own.[90] Old acquaintances were beginning to treat her differently. As she bitterly observed, she was 'dear Mary' now to the Shropshire set who had ignored her or treated her with 'kindly tolerance'[91] when she was an aspiring young writer living in her father's rectory. Her diary from this time is full of her engagements and the people she has met.[92] Lubbock notes approvingly in his memoir that she became the natural confidante of her friends.[93] Not altogether pleased by the role herself, Mary noted in *Red Pottage* 'Those in whom others confide early learn that their own engagements, their own pleasures and troubles are liable to be set aside at any moment. Rachel was a punctual, exact person, but she missed many trains.'[94] By Easter she was so exhausted that she was planning a visit to Tolmers, so often a place of refuge when the pressures of London became too much.[95]

Eventually she determined to cut down her social engagements while she concentrated on the book, and by June she was nearly at the end, writing steadily and feeling younger than she had done.[96] But still her anxiety over her abilities persisted. At about this time she met John Cross, the widower of her literary hero George Eliot whose genius always inspired in her both awe and something like despair. Her doubts about her own writing took the form of a misplaced belief that *Red Pottage* would never be as good as her most well received novel to date, *Diana Tempest*. She would place her own frustrations almost verbatim in the mouth of her fictional writer, the talented and suffering Hester Gresley. As she wrote in her diary, 'The sad part is that it is so feeble compared to the reality which I try to describe. It is all so splendid and beautiful in my mind. When I try to write it down it is nothing.' Worst of all, 'when I forget what it should have been, will I admire it?'[97]

Hester utters 'the old, old lament of those who worship art', confiding to a sympathetic but uncomprehending Rachel that she labours day by day, and spends hours sitting silently outside until inspiration comes, only to find:

> I cannot reach up to it. I cannot get near it ... when I try to write it is like drawing an angel with spread wings with a bit of charcoal ... But there are no words, or if there are I cannot find them, and at last I fall back on some coarse simile, and in my despair I write it down. And Oh! Rachel, the worst is that presently, when I have forgotten what it ought to have been, when the vision fades, I know I shall *admire* what I have written. It is that that breaks my heart.[98]

In her novel Mary as controlling narrator could identify with what she makes clear to her readers is Hester's genius, acknowledging the long tradition of writers who have felt inadequate in the face of their own expectations. But in the pages of her diary she had no external critic to contradict her when she once began to doubt the value of her work. Like the fictionalized Hester, she was subject to both her own doubts and the dubious assessments of those around her. If *Red Pottage* routinely satirizes both Gresley and the local families who would admire Hester so much more if she would only write 'goody goody books',[99] it is important to remember that it is the reader alone who can derive satisfaction from this satire – in the context of the novel, Hester is ineluctably trammelled by these figures, just as Mary herself had been in her youth by the kindly but unimaginative families of Shropshire.

Now Mary was determined to concentrate on her writing, but she did manage to attend a dinner at the House of Commons at about this time,[100] and it may have been here that she began one of the most important friendships of her life. Percy Lubbock would claim that by the time he met Miss Mary Cholmondeley she was intimidating to younger writers as the already renowned author of *Red Pottage*; in fact he has embellished the facts slightly for the sake of artistic effect – 'Mr Lubbock' makes his first appearance in Mary's diary after she met him at this very dinner.[101] In the course of her engagements she also met the American writer Bret Harte and got into a debate with him about the English class system, commenting tartly that 'If a man calls a girl "gurl" and a brougham a "brewham," I may like and admire him, but I know for all that what society he is <u>not</u> in.'[102] The dilettante author who belittles Hester's work in *Red Pottage* is shown up by his talk of the young English 'gurl', which rather suggests that the young lady from a county family who had once argued with John Nettleship about the status of actors had not changed in every respect. Also in June Mary was at a Women Writers' Dinner as one of the committee, with 150 writers and journalists present. One woman told her that her books had been the first link that led to a very happy marriage, but she was not pleased by this 'outrageous' compliment. And she was still insecure enough to deprecate the link between literary women and 'dowdiness'

> What an assembly of ill bred ill dressed slovenly looking women. And these as my confrères with whom I ought to feel 'ésprit de corps!' There were a few women who looked nice, and attractive ... But my heart sank as I looked round at 'all of us'. Why should literary women be so unattractive, and surely if one can be nothing else one can look <u>clean</u>[103]

More conducive was Sarah Bernhardt in *La Dame aux Caméllias* a week or two later – Mary was so impressed she promptly reread the book. She was less impressed by Mrs Humphry Ward's latest, *Helbeck of Bannisdale*: 'not a book that takes any hold of one'. And when would her own book be finished? She thought that two months solid effort would be enough for the remaining ten chapters, those chapters as she noted, that would contain 'all the meaning of the book'.[104] It is at this point that Rachel accepts Hugh's proposal, only to reject him when she learns that he is in some sense responsible for Lord Newhaven's supposed accident – in fact when Hugh refuses to fulfil their compact, Newhaven kills himself in a gesture of both honour and revenge. It is only Rachel's serious illness – she forgives Hugh too late to stop him crashing through the ice of a nearby lake and subsequently dying of his injuries – that rouses Hester from a dangerous torpor, wondering whether to live or die.

In the original schema of the novel Mary had no intention of sparing Hugh in any sense. Lady Newhaven was to have threatened him with exposure, having received a posthumous letter from her husband telling her that he had not in fact drawn the short lighter as his death would lead her to suppose. When Hugh refused to break with Rachel, Lady Newhaven would show her this letter, and he would kill himself in despair at Rachel's rejection, having been too 'cowardly' to fulfil the compact before. The bishop would 'soften' Rachel towards him too late to save his life. Even in the published version Rachel's reaction is problematic, as she claims that Newhaven's taking of his own life two days after Hugh was due to die was the honourable thing to do, and she claims moreover that Hugh is at fault for not foreseeing this eventuality. But the scene as it stands is more palatable than the original plan – in the final version Lady Newhaven confronts Hugh and Rachel together, and Hugh burns the letter unread before finally confessing to a disbelieving Rachel. This belated admission that he has withheld the truth from her is what prompts her to reject him, leaving the reader free to skim her pronouncements on Hugh's inadequacy in still being alive at all.[105]

But the 'meaning' of the book lies not so much in the suspense of these last episodes, intensely dramatic as they are, as in Hester's words of despair when she realizes her book is lost:

> It was part of myself. But it was the better part. The side of me which loves success ... had no hand in it. My one prayer was that I might be worthy to write it, that it might not suffer by contact with me ... I knew what I was doing. I joyfully spent my health, my eyesight, my very life upon it. I was impelled to do it[106]

Mary later acknowledged that she put many of her own ideas about writing into Hester's mouth,[107] and this passionate defence of the literary vocation is surely her own. But it was not to be written that summer. With the rest of the family abroad – her father was in Brittany with Diana and Victoria – the timing would have been ideal. But, unable to face the heat of a London summer by herself, she was about to set off for a summer of country house visits.[108] Before she left she was fascinated by her meeting with the poet Aubrey de Vere, describing him as 'A gentle tall old man, with a refined face and charming manners'.[109] Then to Shrewsbury to stay with Tom and Margaret, then to the Rowland Corbets at Stoke, finding time to pay a duty visit to Hodnet Hall. Revisiting the old church she simply felt oppressed, 'I felt we had <u>escaped</u>. The time had indeed come for us to leave Hodnet. Yet this visit was painful too. Now I have been once I need never go again. There is no link with the place.'[110] Then more visits, to the Gaskells at Wenlock Abbey, to Tatton, where there were sixteen to dinner on the first night, to the Leightons at Tabley, with its old house in the moat untouched for 150 years. If life in a flat in Kensington seemed something of a come down after these visits, the diary remains silent on that point.

But back in London Mary could reflect on her return to Shropshire with all the security that a safe distance brings. For the rest of her life she would use the example of Gresley as a means of protesting that her characters were not taken from the life – despite the stream of accusations that began with the book's publication, she had categorically *not* based him on a real clergyman.[111] All of which makes it even more intriguing that the text pinned up in his church porch, 'How dreadful is this place. This is none other than the house of God', was spotted by Mary herself on one of these Shropshire visits (she would have preferred an early twenty-first-century poster outside Shrewsbury Abbey, with the words 'Don't worry about tomorrow. God is already there' in large print).[112] As the *Bookman* pointed out in an exclusive interview,

> if there is one class more than another of which Miss Cholmondeley is competent to write, it is the country clergy ... And positive proof that Miss Cholmondeley has not

exaggerated her type is to be found in the fact that quite a large number of persons have written to her declaring that they see in Mr Gresley an exact portrait of their own vicar.[113]

A carefully included note in the published text of *Red Pottage* mentions that she saw Gresley's chosen passage displayed in a country church in August 1898, about fifteen months before the book was published and therefore easily within recent memory. Speculation can be a dangerous thing, but it is tempting to wonder if she is suggesting a parallel between her fictional vicar and one of those Shropshire worthies who viewed dissenters as worms, and anyone who stayed on good terms with them, such as Rowland Corbet, as a traitor to the cause. She would not be the first writer to make a claim for authenticity in her story,[114] but by deliberately drawing attention to the date of her discovery, she makes sure that the church in question will be recognized by its parishioners – and perhaps more importantly, its vicar – if not by Ernest Hodder Williams of the *Bookman*.

In September she was back in London, with the flat in horrible disarray, and planning to fly to Tolmers before the painters came in on the 16th. Inevitably one recalls her exuberant account of the recalcitrant stove of that first winter in Hodnet Rectory. Now Mary is very tired, choosing wallpaper, packing china and making 'countless small arrangements'.[115] She would spend three weeks ill in lodgings before returning to the flat, and it was another month before everything was straight again.[116] But by the end of the year the family was comfortably installed, and Mary could say looking back that it had been the happiest year she remembered. Her greater security in her religious faith had in turn brought better health and spirits and she had been able to work. She was enjoying life more as a result, although there is a note of stoic resignation in her question, 'Why did I not learn these beginnings of wisdom earlier in life [?]'[117]

So began 1899, 'under happier auspices than usual', despite the inevitable colds.[118] Her brother Dick was home on a visit from Australia and when Mary was once again stricken with asthma she might well say that she was 'not much disheartened' by this latest attack. She had taken virtually no morphia (it was this experience that prompted her harrowing description of being unable to lean back for two days and nights) and had turned down all dinner party invitations, remaining at home for a fortnight.[119] One of her stories, 'Dick's Ordeal', appeared this year in an anthology published by Mowbray.[120] But it was in February of this year also that she sold her new book to Edward Arnold. She let him read only one chapter, apparently telling him that the rest was not copied out and was therefore illegible. In fact she had a cool half dozen chapters left to write and a deadline of 31 August by which the manuscript was to be in his hands for publication in the autumn.[121] At this point Mary was jubilant when he offered her £1,000 for the copyright, assuring her that the American market was virtually worthless – accordingly American sales were not separately covered in the contract as she had requested.[122]

The retelling of this transaction by the literary agent Curtis Brown, who later represented Mary in both England and America, tellingly focuses on her naivety and essentially unworldly nature, while deprecating the short-sightedness of a publisher who could so offend one of the bestselling authors of the decade that she never had dealings with him again. She was 'that gentle and gracious lady' who would not allow her next publisher, John Murray, to pay more for *Moth and Rust* than she thought he could afford.[123] In another article he claims that she got a mere £100 for the copyright of *Red Pottage*.[124] When the book shot to the top of the bestsellers list, an 'astonished' Arnold 'could not turn out editions fast enough' and aspiring authors poured in on him believing he could work a similar 'miracle' for them.[125] Brown's account suggests a familiar, and carefully constructed, myth about the Victorian woman who is herself unable to account for her phenomenal success. While Mary may have connived at this sort of mythmaking, in fact she was already famous by 1899, with no fewer than four novels to her credit – at least one critic rated *Diana Tempest* more highly than the admittedly better selling *Red Pottage*.[126] What Brown must also have known better than most was that this 'gentle' middle-aged woman was notable not just for her powers of storytelling, but for her unflinching will and ambition.

That Easter Mary was looking forward to a visit to her brother Regie's house in Hertfordshire, after six months of the heavy London atmosphere. But, forced to put off her visit when the servants became ill, she found herself in sole possession of the flat while her father and Diana went to visit Tom and Victoria enjoyed a boating holiday with friends. She relished these few days alone more than she could have imagined, taking tea in the open air at Kew and admiring George Eliot and Elizabeth Barrett Browning in the National Portrait Gallery ('I do not think Mrs Browning has influenced me at all, but no one except Emerson has influenced me as much as George Eliot').[127] Looking at Millais's picture of Carlyle, she wondered ruefully how much the nation had paid for it – her family, she remembered, had only got a few hundred when it had fallen in the wreck of the Condover estate. And she was working solidly on the book, noting that she had done more in three days under these circumstances than she generally managed in a week. If she could have three such weeks, she thought, she would be able to do it. But she was committed to a round of dinner parties and was also forced to admit that there was more housework to be got through in Victoria's absence.

Finally on a hot day in June, three days before her fortieth birthday, she was able to write:

> It seems quite incredible but nevertheless today I finished 'Red Pottage'. Diana Tempest was finished in great cold. This book in greater heat, in my burning hot south bedroom, over a kitchen, beside a kitchen, and with a kitchen flu running up the

wall at my elbow. Poor book, how often interrupted, how often forcibly laid aside, how feeble compared to what it should have been. Poor book. But at any rate you are finished at last. I say it, but I dont believe it.[128]

Understandably Mary sympathizes with the conditions in which her fictional author is obliged to write. 'Hester's attic', she notes with meaning, 'was blisteringly hot. It was over the kitchen, and through the open window came the penetrating aroma of roast mutton newly wedded to boiled cabbage.'[129]

On 8 July Mary left London and boiled cabbage for her promised visit to Regie and Florie in Hertfordshire. While staying with them she was able to work for five hours a day rewriting her book, until on 13 August she decided that now it was really finished. She read the final chapters of the book to them in the billiard room, 'in an ever increasing excitement', one sitting on either side of her. As she finished they got up with tears in their eyes and kissed her. The next day she sent the manuscript to Edward Arnold. On 15 August she found herself in the throes of yet another asthma attack.[130]

Still recovering in October and hardly able to leave the flat, Mary thanked God for the love of her family throughout these times, remembering how Diana, at first alone and later assisted by Victoria, had nursed her through her long illness. This last attack was one which she had almost certainly anticipated, in the account of Hester's decline as she writes and her final collapse and near death following the burning of her book. But again Mary's exceptional determination somehow kept her to the task she had set herself, even in the face of physical collapse:

> I dont remember much about it except the exhaustion, the hand round my head, the morphia, and the horror which it throws on everything, the long depression of convalescence, not wholly gone yet. I was delirious for many nights. And by day proof sheets after proof sheets arrived. All these while she nursed me dear Di read, and the hours in the day when my head was clear; whenever there were any such hours were spent in consulting these many sheets. I did not care, but I remembered that I had cared about the book, and I forced myself to do them. I corrected them twice over. I could not do it again in such illness, but I did it, Di helping me. And now I remain like a sort of stupid animal. I can do nothing more. My body is gradually recovering. I drag it out into the sun on these soft October days, and sit, and look at the dogs and the children and think of nothing.[131]

She would instantly admit to Rhoda Broughton that her own ideas about writing permeated the book, while disclaiming any obvious relationship between herself and Hester Gresley. 'I suppose there is a good deal of me in Hester', she acknowledged, 'tho' I had hardly realized it. I think the character is entirely opposed to mine.'[132] But what she did not tell her friend was how anxious she had been at the threat to her privacy implied by the act of publishing the book in the first place. Uncertain of its reception, Mary asked herself in her diary how she *could* have put in it so much that she hardly told her most intimate friends. She found herself dreading the day of publication as if it had been 'a hated wedding day'. As often as she could she said to herself, 'It will be all right'.[133]

The first letters to come in were from Regie and Florie – Regie began with an eight-page effusion, which he burned before starting again in more sober vein. Reading the book for himself, he worried about Dick, that he should not have fallen in love with a woman who could have preferred the second-rate Hugh. But he was grateful that he had 'eyesight to read it & ears to have heard you read it' and he was discerning enough to call it her best yet. He promptly began reading it aloud to his daughter Mary, who he suspected did not understand very much of it (likely enough, as she was about nine at the time) but thought it beautiful nonetheless.[134] Meanwhile Florie was so struck by it on this second reading that she wrote independently on the same day, saying all the right things:

> I feel now that much as I admired it when I first heard it I did not half appreciate it. I wish I could find words to tell you just what it is to me. Since I first read Hamilton Thom's book which you recommended to me, nothing I have read has struck me so much as full of really valuable teaching & suggestion as this book of yours. I find I can't say really what I want to, only I must thank you for what I feel is & will be a continual help.[135]

And the public confirmed her opinion. Despite the disasters of the Boer War, which according to one reviewer had all but destroyed public interest in most novels of that year, the book was an instant sensation, its very name inspiring the latest catchphrase of the London season. As Percy Lubbock gleefully remembered, it became the fashion for young men of letters to ask each other, 'Have you read Pottage?'[136] Eleven days after publication Mary was correcting misprints for the second edition, and she had already been asked to put it on the stage.[137] By December it had reached its third edition. The press reported with some excitement that Queen Victoria was having the book read to her in instalments.[138] At home her father in particular was delighted with her success, bestowing a beautiful diamond pendant on her ('Dear kind Father. It overwhelmed me to think of how I had sometimes been impatient of what seemed unnecessary economy, and all the time he had perhaps this beautiful gift in his mind. I dare not think what it cost him').[139] Meanwhile Rhoda Broughton wrote 'a delightful letter' of congratulation, meeting even the expectations of the original Dick Vernon in its praise of the book. Mary wrote gleefully to thank her, telling her that her brother had requested several readings of the letter over his after-dinner cigarette, while informing her at intervals that she was 'a very gifted person!'[140] These congratulations safely delivered, Rhoda was soon was teasing her about what she called her 'Mess of Pottage'.[141] No letters were received from anyone of the name of Percy or Beaumont, but that, Mary commented somewhat tartly, one must not expect.[142] She would complain that none of her relatives had congratulated her on the book, but on the other side of the world her New Zealand cousins were zealously hoarding reviews and pasting them into a scrapbook.[143]

Indeed the reviews on both sides of the Atlantic were almost all reasonably flattering (she later estimated that there had been about 150 of them, compared to the one known review of *A Devotee*)[144] but many reworked the criticisms launched against her precursor in the sensation genre, Wilkie Collins, in the 1860s. She was allowed to be a storyteller *par excellence*, but prone to exaggeration, and a populist rather than a 'serious' writer. *The Times* would only allow her protagonists 'just enough character for the purposes of the tale', although it conceded, 'So far, however, they are extremely well done. Miss Cholmondeley has a pretty gift of satire and the book is full of entertainment. All who read novels for recreation ought to be grateful for [*Red Pottage*].'[145] The American *Critic* began by saying 'I have carried away from the reading of "Red Pottage" two distinct impressions. The first is, that Miss Cholmondeley is immensely clever; the other, that a short upper lip is the earmark, so to speak, of the British aristocracy.' It continued regretfully, '[Gresley] will not recognize himself in this carefully executed portrait, and that is a pity; but men of his type are past praying for – they can only be knocked on the head'.[146] The *Nation* in New York was unusual in complaining that she did nothing more than 'throw conventions overboard' in reversing the moral stature of her male and female characters, allowing all the rectitude to the women and denigrating the men.[147]

Other reviews, however, did take her more seriously, even where this meant censure as well as praise. Adding insult to his previous injury, Andrew Lang now decided that her previous books had been 'very good indeed', before taking issue with the melodramatic duel plot in this one (bizarrely his criticism was not so much of the pact itself, more that no rational man of the modern day would have consented to kill himself when pistols or even swords were to hand).[148] The *Academy* took issue with her lack of construction and claimed – this must have horrified her – that she had 'little ear for the music of words, or feeling for the dignity of the English tongue'; nor it claimed was *Red Pottage* quite comparable to the earlier *Diana Tempest*. Nonetheless,

> Gifted with plenty of invention, plenty of wit, some humour, some imagination, and a fresh touch of originality which lends allurement to everything she writes, Miss Cholmondeley has an excellent chance of taking rank with the novelists whose work is worthy of serious consideration and praise.[149]

The *Athenaeum* thought the group in Warpington, where Gresley lives, made the most impressive part of the book and the *Saturday Review* allowed it to be, despite some strained plotting, 'worth more than a wilderness of ordinary novels'.[150] Echoing the *Athenaeum*'s appreciation of Gresley and the Warpington group, the London-based *Literature* enthused, 'The genuinely religious, untiringly zealous, intolerably bumptious parish priest with his dull and devoted, hopelessly narrow-minded, and heroically unselfish wife have seldom been drawn in literature with more absolute sureness of touch'.[151]

The American *Dial* admitted to having failed to understand for the first half of the novel just why it was so popular in England, but by the end of the book the reviewer is quite ready to admit its powerful writing as well as the force of its characterization. This reviewer was perceptive enough to comment that, 'There is something impressive in the tragic irony that invests the life of the clergyman who figures so largely in this story, and makes him the instrument of a tragedy he can never even remotely comprehend'.[152] Surprisingly another American paper thought the novel inferior to *Sir Charles Danvers* as well as *Diana Tempest* (the novel to which it is more usually compared to this day), while conceding that it 'holds the attention to the last word of the last chapter, and when you say this of any novel you have said almost the best thing you can say'.[153] In Australia the *Sydney Daily Telegraph* described the novel, despite its 'occasional disjointedness' as 'a thoroughly honest, as well as a fascinating piece of work'.[154] The *Edinburgh Review* noted:

> Her chief concern is plot and dramatic or melodramatic psychology. But in so far as she is a satirist ... she is making her contribution to the novel of manners, setting down as she sees them certain contemporary types, fashions, and societies.[155]

But among the most gratifying reviews was that of the *Spectator*, which covered all bases by admitting that her handling of plot disarmed criticism, while her characterization showed an understanding of her art. It finished by hailing *Red Pottage* as a 'brilliant and exhilarating novel, by far the most exciting and original of the present season. In addition to such praise, it was one of the only reviews to comment on Hester, calling her 'a most fascinating specimen of the intellectually emancipated modern woman', and also one of the few to notice that if Cholmondeley is ruthless in her treatment of Gresley, her approving characterization of the bishop should render her above suspicion of being antagonistic to the Church itself.[156] In 1910, eleven years after its publication, one enthusiastic reviewer in the *Edinburgh Review* was proclaiming that '"Red Pottage" is a book to be read by candidates for Orders. Examining chaplains would do well to set papers on it; it should be discussed at Church Congresses and in Clergy Retreats'.[157] This last comment was particularly ironic given the scandal Mary's satire had caused in certain quarters at the time. While Hester was apparently a universal favourite with readers, the character of Gresley provoked a literary storm in a teacup. Mary received numerous letters from people claiming that she must have modelled Gresley on some particular clergyman of their acquaintance, while others assumed that she had some grudge against the clergy in general. One reader of the *Guardian* suggested that 'The poor feeble creature is described with an appetite' and that 'Mr Gresleys certainly exist, but only a woman in a (perhaps wholly justified) tantrum would speak of them as the type of the clergy in general'. She was denounced by name from a London pulpit, although 'when a witty bishop wrote to me that he had enjoined on his clergy the study of Mr Gresley as a Lenten penance it was not possible for me to remain permanently depressed'. Other readers wrote to her with the favourite platitudes of their own local vicars, imploring her to come down and see them for herself. One wrote with a description of a vicar who had begun – he would have said *commenced* – his last sermon with the words '"God is love" as the Archbishop of Canterbury remarked last week in Westminster Abbey'. Mary was left wringing her hands that such gems had come too late for use in the book.[158]

But some of her public proved less conspiratorial in their tone. Mary later recalled her vain efforts to pacify two old ladies who had taken particular exception to Gresley and were thoroughly offended by the 'profanity' of the book. She took the trouble to send them a copy of a sermon preached in its favour by no less a person than the bishop of Stepney, in St Paul's – only to receive 'a dignified answer that they had both been deeply distressed by my information, as it would prevent their ever going to hear the Bishop of Stepney again'.[159] More extreme yet was the anonymous letter, 'which I am convinced was written by Mr Gresley himself' claimed an amused Mary, informing her that as he was faithfully religious he had felt obliged to destroy at least one copy of *Red Pottage*.[160] The debate over Gresley would continue to rage well into 1900. The *Bookman* sympathetically recalled this 'ridiculous controversy' some years later, commenting 'he was meant to be hated by the reader, and the reader certainly did hate the Rev. Mr Gresley with the hate of long acquaintance in the flesh. To this degree he was, artistically, a triumph.' But, inevitably, 'So soon as a writer hits off human nature, especially a disagreeable aspect of it, there is a hot chase for the specific purpose he had in view'.[161] Gresley was seen as a satire on the Anglican Church, an attack on sacred institutions, even a clergyman who had injudiciously 'jilted' the author. Notwithstanding her professed amusement, such attacks must sometimes have hurt. Many years later a much younger friend would claim that, 'It perplexed Mary Cholmondeley that certain passages in her novels were considered flippant, or taken as evidence of an irreligious mind'. She is supposed to have retorted, 'How could I speak lightly of that which I hold most dear?'[162] Somewhat extraordinarily, the central dilemma of the woman writer who struggles so single-mindedly in *Red Pottage* just to find the time to write seems to have excited little comment. As any female writer of the time would have been only too aware, it is in the story of Hester and her lost manuscript that the real message of the book is contained.

But what Mary did notice in those first weeks was that the readers of *Red Pottage* felt a greater sense of personal relationship with her than *Diana Tem-*

pest had evoked. Like Regie and Florie, people seemed to draw nearer to her, and she noted with a certain humility, 'God has been very good to me, if this is so'.[163] For all that, she was cautious about giving too much away to a newly fascinated public. In the spring of 1900 she would consent to an interview with The *Bookman* – her first in an English periodical – on the strict understanding that she saw the proofs, and she was quite particular about the accompanying photograph (unhappy with the two that had already gone the rounds of English and American papers, she agreed to sit for another especially for the purpose of this interview).[164] In his article Ernest Hodder Williams reminds the reader that his subject has always refused publicity, before setting to work with a notably accurate account of her early life. He lingers fondly over her aristocratic line-age, before detailing her (what is to a modern reader somewhat intimidating) childhood reading of Charles Dickens, Walter Scott, William Paley and Dean Stanley. But in some ways the article is surprisingly revealing, alluding to Mary's having taken over the household at sixteen, her own ill health and the forced sale of Condover.[165] In everything but the last detail, which would later disappear from her account, it was in that sense a rehearsal for *Under One Roof*, in which she would offer a vivid account of her early life as she recalled it.

Like the heroine of *Red Pottage*, she had been able to speak to a wide audience with such apparent intimacy only because she was removed from them person-ally – the novel makes it very clear that Hester's powers are not compatible with the exigencies of married life. Despite the feeling of closeness, there was no one with whom she could count on coming first, reflecting stoically 'I shall perhaps not even be second some day in my Victoria's heart, if as I hope she marries and has children'.[166] In fact, like all of the Cholmondeley sisters bar Essex, Victoria was to remain unmarried until she died.

6 'NOT MINE TO KEEP': *MOTH AND RUST* (1902) AND *PRISONERS* (1906)

What thou doest do quickly, for even while we speak those to whom we feel tenderly grow old and gray, and slip beyond the reach of human comfort. Even while we dream of love, those whom we love are parted from us in an early hour when we think not, without so much as a rose to take with them out of the garden of roses that was planted and fostered for them alone. And even while we tardily forgive our friend, lo! the page is turned, and we see that there was no injury, as now there is no compensation for our lack of trust.[1]

The last year of the century ended in triumph, with the spectacular success of the book begun three years earlier, the book that had seemed 'more impossible every day'.[2] Mary still kept by her the diary in which she had written, twenty-two years earlier, 'what a great pleasure and interest it would be to me in life to write books'.[3] Now an exhausted Mary was turning down offers from Tillotson's and John Murray, opportunities that would have seemed unimaginable as she worked on *Her Evil Genius*, wrenching the time from parish visiting and choir practice in Hodnet Church.[4] She had begun life in the year when Darwin's theories were set, as many believed, to tear the Church from its foundations – now, aged forty-one, she herself was at the centre of a religious controversy of sorts, her satire of the Revd Gresley ricocheting around literary London and attracting notice as far away as America.

To those living through them, the last days of a century are a time of uncertainty, but also a time for reminiscence and, inevitably, evaluation of what has gone before. Like her contemporaries, Mary must have spent time in these last weeks of the century reflecting on her life to date, on what she had achieved and what she had missed. On a summer day in 1877 she had confessed that 'I grow anxious now and then to know what my life is to be, forgetting how disappointed I should be, were I to know'.[5] Was she disappointed, despite the phenomenal success of her novel? Whatever she thought in these last days of the century, she did not see fit to record.

Throughout the following year tributes continued to come in from across the board (many years later she would receive a letter from J. M. Barrie telling her that he 'had always loved' *Red Pottage*).[6] And there was a further deluge of tempting offers from publishers keen to secure one of the most popular writers of the day, all of which Mary refused.[7] She was exhausted, confiding to John Murray in March, when he too made another offer she felt bound to turn down, 'People who write ought to be made of cast iron!'[8] He was wise enough to keep the offer open without putting undue pressure on her. But Mary had other reasons, beyond her damaged health, for being wary of committing herself to a publisher so soon. For one thing the theatrical world was not slow to realize the potential of the dramatic scenarios in *Red Pottage*, and for the first time since leaving Shropshire, Mary was indulging her love of play writing.

With the help of Kinsey Peile, she was working on a script for the actor-manager George Alexander, of the St James's Theatre, having set her heart on him for the part of Hugh Scarlett.[9] Alexander, or George Alexander Gibb Samson to give him his full name, had a reputation for hunting out new talent. It was he who had asked the then unknown playwright Oscar Wilde for *Lady Windermere's Fan* in 1892, and after his death it was discovered that he had paid out as much as £7,000 by way of encouragement to writers for scripts he never actually used. These writers, as a friend recalled years later, were always made to feel welcome when they went to discuss their ideas with Alexander, and it may have been his idea that Mary collaborate with the more experienced Peile.[10] Mary seems not to have enjoyed this partnership, however, commenting darkly when the script was finished that she would not be working with him again.[11] Nor did she find Alexander himself easy to deal with – there seems to have been some dispute over business arrangements, and, greatly as she admired him as an artist, she professed herself ready to withdraw altogether rather than yield to pressure.[12] In the event she was paid £200 in advance, with a clause built into the contract stipulating for the reversion of rights if the play had not been produced by April 1902.[13]

She was in any case unwell for the first few months of the new century, and the play had to be written in the uncertain intervals of health – in March she was lamenting that she had been unable to work on it since the beginning of the year.[14] But once again Regie and Florie stepped in to help, having her to stay in March and then offering their empty house for her to write in over Whitsuntide. Reluctantly Mary put off a visit to the bishop of Stepney, who had so publicly defended the seriousness of her convictions, and in May she set off again for Hertfordshire.[15] She had once derived bitter amusement from the idea that *The Danvers Jewels* might have been written 'at a white heat', wishing that the enthusiastic reader who supposed so could have seen her 'plodding wearily from chapter to chapter'.[16] Now her play of *Red Pottage*, like the novel that inspired it, was eventually finished 'in burning heat' on 26 July and sent off to America, where Daniel Frohman of the Lyceum was as keen as everyone else to cash in on the success of the book.[17] Following the debacle with Edward Arnold, Mary had been careful to hang onto the American rights.[18]

For its part, the book of *Red Pottage* continued to sell at an impressive rate throughout the two years after its publication. By March 1900 it had sold somewhere in the region of 31,000 copies in England and the colonies alone and, five months after Harper Brothers reached an agreement with Arnold for the American rights, the head of the firm told Cholmondeley with a bow that he had just paid £2,100 into her account.[19] But of course it was not into her account that the money was paid. For this was the book she had sold outright for £1,000 to Edward Arnold. She had requested a royalty of 25 per cent and a separate agreement for the American rights, but she had been elated enough at getting the one-off payment, to be put off with his assurance that the American rights were worth 'almost nothing'.[20]

Ironically, that June Mary found herself exchanging a series of letters with Macmillan, who were making the best of their loss and bringing out a new cheap edition of *Diana Tempest* on the back of the *Red Pottage* craze. Despite her request, they had failed to print the names of her other books on the title page – she was still on polite enough terms with Arnold to ask him to reciprocate – and only now was she told that the firm had written to ask her for her next book when they first took over from Bentley. Either this letter was a judicious fabrication on the part of the head of the firm, or she had never received it, but she pointed out ruefully that by the time she had received a note from him after waiting for several months, she was already in talks with Arnold for the rights to *A Devotee*. She now told him with a certain bitter satisfaction that her modesty had in those days been in robust health – it was now quite extinct, and she refused to commit herself to a new novel which she had no immediate plans to begin.[21]

By this time *Red Pottage* was in its fourth edition, and she calculated that October that if she had been given the 25 per cent she had originally requested, she would have made £6,000 already, with a further £5,000 on the American sales based on just 20 per cent of the profits.[22] Arnold himself was making 30c. on each copy of the book sold in America, which it continued to do at a comfortable rate for some time. At its peak it was selling to the American market at the rate of 1,000 copies a day, and at the latest reckoning, it was still being bought at the rate of 2,500 copies a week, while as far away as Australia it came in second only to Ellen Thorneycroft Fowler's *A Double Thread* by the end of 1900.[23] As late as 1904 in America Harper's were selling the serial rights to the *Louisville Herald* for $300 on Arnold's behalf, and copies of the novel were still being sold into 1913.[24]

In retelling the story years later Curtis Brown deprecated Arnold's short-sightedness in the way he handled Mary's complaint – in one account, Brown claims that the publisher had only given £100 for the copyright, with a further

£100–200 honorarium, 'and felt that he had done a noble deed'.[25] In his book of reminiscences, he sets the initial figure more accurately at £1,000, and claims a further £1,000 honorarium.[26]

A recently discovered letter from Arnold himself throws further light on the story – in 1900 he wrote to the unfortunate author to congratulate her on the sales figures, blithely offering her £500 so that she might enjoy a share in the unexpected profits.[27] Her personal record gives a figure of £2,000 for her profits on the book, suggesting a response to Arnold's letter that is a sad loss indeed. Either way, what is interesting is that Brown himself describes Edward Arnold as 'an amiable and eminently honest man ... But he lacked imagination'.[28] Mary's feelings about this transaction are obliquely suggested in Brown's account – he says that naturally she left her former publisher as soon as she could. Her own comment on the occasion was understandably less elegant. Railing against the injustice of Arnold's taking the entire American profits when he had told her they were not worth a separate agreement, she told herself furiously that, 'I should like to see into his mind. I should rather be myself than him.' But she admitted to herself that these feelings of bitterness came over her at moments of depression, and she told herself resolutely that the whole business was in the past, while the book itself had brought her 'much that money can't buy'.[29]

The reception of her masterpiece, then, had proved a mixed experience for Mary. Initially jubilant, her delight in her success was soured by her acrimonious parting from Arnold, and she was horrified by the reports filtering back from the Boer War begun in October of the year before, as English troops were sent out to relieve the colonial forces in the Transvaal.[30] But even here there was a consolation to be found in the enjoyment of the troops in reading her work. Convalescent officers were encouraged to discuss *Red Pottage* to relieve the tedium of their days – to her surprise Hester was a universal favourite with the officers, but one patient was found flushed, saying he must get out of bed and kick Gresley. Mary was clearly moved by this response. An imperialist like others of her class, she had, she confided to her diary, felt that she could do nothing for these men who were giving their lives.[31] She could hardly go and nurse them, knowing that she would instantly become ill herself. And now she learned that for many of them her book was not only interesting or a means of passing the time, it was actually 'a comfort'. After her frustration at not being able to help these men, now it seemed

> that I did go out to them after all. My best self, which never is exhausted, which never has asthma went softly out to them to amuse and interest them, as I could not have done if I had been there in person.[32]

And she was justifiably proud of her success, admitting in her diary,

That such a wave of success should have reached <u>me</u> was and still is a constant source
of astonishment to me. ... I took a large bite of a certain gilt apple, and tho' it may
have been very bad for my constitution – it was very sweet – and I dont see that it has
done me much harm.

But inevitably this very success brought with it anxiety, the concomitant fear of
future failure:

One thing I do notice in myself, a sort of change in one thing. In old days when no
one thought anything of me I always had in the very depths of my mind a stubborn
feeling that I was worth something after all. I thought more of myself when others
thought little of me. Now, when – ahem! when things are as they are I think less of
myself than I did. The sense of resistance is gone, and I miss it.[33]

Equally hard to come to terms with was the reaction of those close to her, who
were too sincere to flatter but seemed only now to apprehend a side of her character that they should have known was there. They were:

drawn towards me, <u>really</u> drawn by the book. But they had known me before. I was
the book before it was written ... That is what puzzles me. It looks as if some people
only recognize the most elementary things in one's own character when the crowd
is cheering on under one's windows. But they saw one slowly making that which the
mob cheer. But I don't understand it.[34]

Contained in this bewildered lament is Hester's unvoiced appeal to Rachel,
'"Love knows the secret of grief." But can Love claim that knowledge if he is
asked how he came by it by one who should have known?'[35] In middle age and in
the wake of the stunning success of her most important novel, Mary could still
find herself anxious, even angry, as she wondered why her family never understood her as instinctively as she felt she understood them. Why they should be
so suddenly moved by the picture of her as she saw herself, that was also the picture of the daughter and sister they had lost. They should have known her secret
without having to be told.

'Love knows the secret of grief.' It is not surprising that the summer of 1900
should have been a time of such anguished emotion for Mary, such emphasis on
the human failure to perceive a secret grief that should have been no secret. No
wonder either that in June of this year she wrote, 'My only real peace is in good
work'.[36] For it was in this month that she saw her old lover again, and she was
soon to learn the real reason why he had left her some fifteen years before. It is
likely that they had met since the Cholmondeleys came to London in 1896, in
the crowd of a party or even less formally, through visits paid to the entire family.
In her fictional reworking of their relationship, written a few years later, she pictures an old lover feeling disgusted by the passage of time on the rare occasions
when he meets the woman he used to love.

He had met Magdalen once or twice in London of late years, and had felt dismayed anger at the change in her – an offended anger not wholly unlike that with which he surveyed himself at his tailor's, and inspected at unbecoming angles, through painfully frank mirrors, a thick back and a stout neck and jaw which cruelly misrepresented his fastidious artistic personality.[37]

But this encounter came at a time when Mary was feeling particularly vulnerable. She was still recovering from a severe bout of whooping cough, which somehow remained undiagnosed for the first seven weeks. As she recalled afterwards, 'How I managed to go about with it, to dine out with it, to write my play with it I cant imagine, for I was really very ill with it'.[38] In the same month, her brother Dick was married to Hilda Leyland of Haggerston Castle in Northumberland,[39] which may well have left her comparing the happy ending enjoyed by her brother and his fictional namesake, to her own unhappy affair, which she had never forgotten. Later she would quote Rochefoucauld to explain the predicament of her heroine Magdalen in *Prisoners*, 'On garde longtemps son premier amant quand on n'en prend point de second'.[40]

It was while she was in this state of mind that her old lover – even in her diary his name is simply expressed as a dash – came to call at the flat. Mary observed that he looked 'haggard and nervous'. That night, in a moment that could have come from the pages of *Jane Eyre*, Mary was sitting with her family, reading Stevenson's letters to herself, when she became aware of a voice:

> some one spoke to me, not with an outer voice. It was an appeal, most urgent, most insistent. I could distinguish no words, but I understood perfectly. I knew it was —. I answered calmly. I was not the least surprised or shaken. The appeal and agitation seemed to surround me entirely. Then it gradually withdrew and went quite away.[41]

Over the next few days Mary began to question, not that she had heard a voice, but whose voice it had been. On an undated page opposite this passage she continued to question her first impression, writing, 'I have since come to the conclusion that tho' some one did undoubtedly come to me and appeal to me I have no real knowledge who it was'. But the real tragedy of the whole affair lies in that persistent lack of confidence that made her conclude in the original entry, 'at the moment I was sure. I shall never know if I was right because I shall never dare to ask.'[42] Many years before in Hodnet she had parted from her lover in silence rather than request an explanation. Now she lacked the courage to approach him. A year later she would hear an explanation from someone else entirely, only to realize that it had come too late.[43]

But in the summer of 1900 she was busy, as far as the outside world could see, finishing her play of *Red Pottage*, entertaining at the flat and paying numerous visits: to Howard Sturgis, whom Lubbock would later remember as having been so critical of his and Mary's writing; to Bishop Creigton, who had praised her book and in whom she had hoped to find a friend ('He is a common minded man … I am much disappointed'); to Hamilton Aide, who gave her useful advice on the play; and there were no fewer than twenty or thirty invitations for country visits – characteristically Mary relished the prospect of a stay in the country now she was no longer expected to live there.[44] In the event she became ill and had to return to London after ten days, but she had managed to see the Gaskells of Wenlock Abbey, the Rowland Corbets, Sir Alfred Lyall and the Acton Reynold Corbets, all old friends whose conversation must have come as welcome reassurance at this time when she was doubting her vision in more than one sense.[45]

Back in London that autumn her father was ill with sciatica and Mary herself was struggling with further disappointments. Her play, so eagerly sought by managers on both sides of the Atlantic, had been turned down. First George Alexander rejected the script, and then Frohman, who had hurried her for its delivery, began to hesitate.[46] It is not easy to say why Alexander changed his mind. Earlier in the year Mary had experienced a certain amount of stress over the business side of their negotiations, but this was apparently settled by April and as late as August she was confident that he would accept the script.[47] The play of *Red Pottage* focuses entirely on the Newhaven / Scarlett plot, retaining some of the original dialogue with only minor revisions. The critics might well have been pleased by the tightening of the plot in several ways. For instance, Dick Vernon is linked to Hugh Scarlett as his former fag at Eton and confides to him his own love for Rachel. Modifying her original stance on Hugh's failure to destroy himself in the name of honour, Mary allows the bishop to tell Rachel that Hugh wanted to tell her the whole story but that he enjoined silence on him; further, that he was right not to fulfil the contract and that she therefore has nothing to forgive. In another twist, when Hugh steps onto the ice in a bid to take his own life, it is Dick who wrestles with him, and restores him to life and to a happy marriage with Rachel.[48] Admittedly the play is marred by some fairly appalling moments, notably the ending line, 'Is this possible? We will never part again.'[49] But there are also moments of real suspense, as when Rachel breaks her silence and implores Newhaven not to go to London for his son Teddy's sake. Teddy entering at that moment, she tells him to persist in asking his father to stay at home until he gives in – which he is of course about to do when his wife bursts on the scene and sends the child to bed.

Perhaps the real reason Alexander felt unsafe is to be found in the crisis brought on him by another writer, Syndey Grundy, whose *A Debt of Honour* was met with groans and hisses on its opening night on 1 September. Worse, there were public charges of plagiarism over parallels with Mrs Clifford's *The Likeness of the Night*.[50] Both feature an adulterous husband and a female suicide (in *A Debt of Honour* the mistress takes poison while in Clifford's play the wife drowns herself). Perhaps a replacement that also featured adultery and suicide by drowning just seemed too much of a risk. But the problem may simply have been that, notwithstanding her early love of theatricals, Mary's talent was for writing prose rather than drama. Undeterred by initial rejection, and despite the effect on her always precarious health, she embarked on a complete rewrite, only to be told by an experienced critic that her play was a failure. The play was admirably written, he said, it was true to life – but it would not 'act'. After eighteen months' hard work, the disappointed author resolved to 'creep back into my own little mud hut, instead of building card houses'.[51] In 1902, when it became available under the terms of the contract with George Alexander, another actor-manager was asking for the script, but Mary seems not to have expected much from this. Despite repeated attempts and even a second complete rewrite,[52] the play was never to be put on an English stage. Meanwhile, to add to the humiliation, Frohman was apparently keeping it in reserve for the New York Lyceum 'in case one of his other plays fail'.[53] In the event it was left to the Ideal Film Company to produce a silent movie based on the book in 1918, which at least resolved the problem of the unworkable script, even if it did mean handing over half the profits to Edward Arnold.[54]

Nonetheless she was working – she sold the serial rights for a 5,000-word story for £40 at about this time – and by the spring of 1901 she was hopeful that 'the lean years' had come to an end.[55] She was also still enjoying her celebrity as the author of *Red Pottage*. She met Winston Churchill at an evening party, later describing him as 'one of the two most promising young men of the day',[56] although on this occasion she noted

> I found him brilliant, almost too brilliant. He expressed himself with such ease and such power over language that one felt his very facility would be against him later on ... He appeared to me a very able man, but not a first class one.[57]

The Duke of Wellington asked to be introduced to her, and Mary was clearly pleased by the attention she continued to receive in these circles.[58] But she had not for one moment forgotten the source or the cost of her success. Like Dickens before her she might have said that her early trials had worked together to make her what she was. What she actually said was this:

> I was quite delighted and I suppose if the truth must be said somewhat elated by my evening there – and it seemed to me on thinking it over afterwards that the interest in me, and this popularity which I receive now (whether for a moment only of course I cant tell) would never have been mine if all my early life had not been cruelly destitute of any interest and popularity. I was nothing, a plain, silent country girl, an invalid whom no one cared a straw about. I dont know why they should. But in all those early years, those enormously long years a sort of dull smouldering fire of passion seemed to be gradually kindling in me, a determination which I can liken to nothing but a slow fire to overcome all these dreadful obstacles of illness and ugliness and incompetence. If I had been a pretty graceful girl who had danced myself into

a fairly happy entirely commonplace marriage, if I had had any degree of popularity then when oh! how I should have valued it, I should never, I <u>could</u> never have arrived where I am today. It is not my talent which has placed me where I am, but the repression of my youth, my unhappy love affair[,] the having to confront a hard dull life devoid of anything I cared for intellectually, and being hampered at every turn I feebly made by constant constant illness. What I have thought, what I have felt, what I have suffered in those past years have been the kindling that year after year fed the flame which kept me alive. It is this flame which throws light upon what little talent I have. My talent is the least part of me. Where God has given me strength is in <u>how I am to use my talent</u>.[59]

It is interesting that as a girl Mary would have chosen marriage over anything else. And now? There is a sorrow and indeed a tough realism in her reflections on this period of her life – that 'I dont know why they should' suggests a complete lack of self-pity – that hardly fits with Lubbock's comment, 'The weight [of her past] was wonderfully lifted now',[60] as he well knew from what he would have read just a few pages later.

But in the meantime there were visits to Winden to see Howard Sturgis, tea with Arthur Benson, son of the famous archbishop, whom at this stage it is worth remembering she liked 'more and more'.[61] His brother, the writer E. F. Benson, gives a compelling picture of Mary Cholmondeley at the turn of the century. Tellingly he notes that although she was the eldest daughter, 'no material cares of house-keeping fell on her shoulders, all was managed for her'.[62] Clearly Diana and Victoria were protective of their creative and frail sister. He and Mary got on well enough for him to send her a series of mock love letters after she had made a joke about wishing to receive a love letter every day – in the end she had to beg him to desist, and he retorted that she had missed a great deal in stopping him.[63]

On a more serious note, Benson confirms Lubbock's account of Mary's sympathetic qualities, for which she was sought out as much as for her recognized celebrity. He also notes with just a shade of kindly irony that she was 'conscious, though without the slightest priggishness, of her responsibilities'.[64] That Mary took her responsibilities seriously, and expected others to do likewise, is illustrated by her entertainments at about this time. The sisters, Benson recalls, were 'At Home' to a few select friends in the evening at half past ten. Victoria would despatch cards with a tea pot and tea cup drawn on them, while Mary would take responsibility for the guest list. The twenty-five or so guests would then be given tea and steered towards Mary for conversation, before being dexterously removed to make way for others at the appropriate moment. These tea parties – Benson notes in accounting for their ultimate decline that people who have left their firesides at ten at night are 'difficult to animate' over a cup of tea[65] – were intended to confer an honour on the chosen ones, and after a couple of refusals one would not be invited again. Anne Thackeray Ritchie later recalled the difficulty of disposing of tea cups with no table to put them on.[66] But always Mary's more 'sybilline' qualities – the term Benson uses – were redeemed by her self-awareness and her sudden flashes of humour. As he points out, no 'undiluted Sibyl' would have written that

> If I have not lost my temper during the day, or been sarcastic to my sister because my throat hurts me, or cross to my maid because I had got my feet wet, I lie down at night feeling that there are not many people as saint-like as myself.[67]

So life in the flat in Kensington went on. In June the *Living Age* published Mary's article 'An Art in its Infancy' on the advertising industry.

Some time over the summer came the explanation for which she had always been waiting. A year after that evening when she thought she heard an appeal while reading quietly in the flat in Knightsbridge, she finally learned the reason for her lover's apparent desertion, which had so altered the course of her life. It was October before she felt able to write down the barest details. When she did it was in a controlled, almost matter of fact tone that suggests considerable mental preparation. If 'all diarists are involved in a process, even if largely unconscious, of selecting details to create a persona', then Mary is also aware that even the persona, or the pose as Stella Benson would later put it, was too intimate to be carelessly conveyed.[68] The moment when she learned the truth must have been one of the saddest of her life, and she was not prepared to share her reaction even with her own diary. The explanation was after all a simple one, and Mary's account is equally bald, 'he had been told that his attentions bored me. I was told so by the person who had mentioned that fact to him.'[69]

It is tempting to try and 'pin the tail on the donkey', guessing from Mary's carefully guarded prose exactly whom she is trying to protect or cannot bring herself to name. The very fact that her lover so easily believed her to be indifferent, based entirely on a conversation with someone else, is itself suggestive. One obvious supposition is that his informant was a member of Mary's or even his own immediate family – who else's mere word would carry such immediate conviction? But equally, Mary's reserve was such that she would later complain of those closest to her not actually *seeing* her, without an elaborate fictional portrayal to guide them – it is possible that while she loved the unnamed man, as she put it, 'unwisely and devotedly', she was too reticent to make this obvious.[70] The flaw in this theory is that the relationship lasted in some form or other for no less than seven years, although there is no evidence that he was an acknowledged suitor for all of this time – on the contrary, while there was clearly some understanding between them, he seems likely also to have been regarded as a friend of the family in general.[71]

Whatever the reasons for the unnamed person's intervention, and it is possible that Mary herself was not given a further explanation, the moment of crisis was one that she would continue to rework over the next few years. In coming to terms with the event, she was able to construct it as fiction, but a fiction based on verifiable sources. It has been astutely argued that unlike a novel or memoir, which controls its relation of events from a fixed perspective, a diary 'is created in and represents a continuous present. And ... many diarists reread previous entries before writing a current one, creating a complexly layered present to which a version of the past is immediately available.'[72] Implicitly Mary was relying both on her own memory and also on the now missing entries in her diary of 1878–95 (which she mentions having read a few years before this belated denouement)[73] to substantiate her view of events. In the novel that she would begin two years later, she made it clear where she still placed the blame:

> he never cared enough for me to make an effort on my behalf. That was not his fault. He mistook a romantic admiration for love, and naturally found it would not work. How could it? it was not necessary to turn heaven and earth to gain me. But it *was* necessary to turn a few small stones. He would not turn them.[74]

Characteristically guarded is the provisional thought attributed to this character, who loses and then – in a fantasy fulfilment – redeems her half-hearted lover. Amazed by the (as it happens, misplaced) trust her brother-in-law expresses in his wife, she 'may have thought' of the difference to her own life 'If only once long ago I had met with one little shred of such tender faith'.[75] Mary would return to this theme twice more in her fiction, as she tried to make sense of her loss by blaming first her lover, then herself, and finally achieving some kind of serenity, on paper at least. In 'The Understudy' a middle-aged woman meets her lover after a separation of years, when he takes the lead in the play she has written about their affair and his treachery; he uses the part to make an oblique appeal to her, even adding his own words of justification. In this version the woman denounces herself for her failure to forgive, 'Your love was only pretty words and pride and self-seeking, and a miserable streak of passion' she tells herself.[76] By 1907 Mary had schooled herself to see only the tragicomedy of a middle-aged woman who still defines herself through her youthful love. When Emily's lover in 'St Luke's Summer' is banished by – and here the temptation to make guesses has to give way before Mary's loving remembrance towards the end of her life, of her 'kindest and most generous of brothers' – her father Thomas and her brother Tom, she is exactly the age at which Mary may well have met her own lover.[77] In this version the young man goes to Australia, where he spends twenty years preparing a home for the woman he loves, only to find when he returns to claim her that she is too old to adapt to a new life. The story ends with his decision to return alone and put off a reunion with regular, affectionate letters and tales of pecuniary disasters.

It is impossible to say exactly when Mary learned the truth about her lover. But in late July 1901 she records a conversation that was to prove an unlikely source of comfort, and it is likely that she is thinking of this revelation about her past in what she writes. On 25 July a non-conformist minister came to see her. He had recently lost his wife and was, like most of the clergy, 'more of a talker than a listener'. Mary sat out the visit patiently, thinking like her own Rachel West how many men and women had thanked her afterwards for what they called conversation with her in which she had not said anything. But the conversation turned to suffering and how Mary herself had the power to reach people through her work. She would surely have agreed that the words 'love' and 'pain' are lightly used until 'our own crucifixion', until 'At last it dawned on me that that meeting was not so much for his consolation, as for my benefit. When he went away I felt I had been helped in spite of my impatient patience of the first hour.'[78]

She would have time to reflect on this meeting in the weeks that followed. Weak in health, she was banned from visiting by the family doctor, and after a few days with Hamilton Aide at his cottage in Ascot she locked herself away in the flat for three weeks of solitude. Used to the company and support of her family, she was unsettled by the idea of being left suddenly alone, but in the event these weeks gave her time to think and to prepare for the battle with herself that she knew would come. She realized to her surprise that she had not been so happy in years, discerning only now that she had been living at a terrific strain, a strain she felt slowly being released in the silence of the empty flat. And then comes the cryptic comment, 'A great difficulty seems moving towards me. I do not know what I am going to do, or what I ought to do, or how I am to meet it. but I <u>shall</u> meet it. and I shall not be left without counsel.' On 20 August, the day of this entry, Regie was coming to take her down to Preshaw (the manor house to which he had moved a few weeks earlier) with him. 'Good bye strengthening merciful solitude', she wrote, 'I will come to you again.'[79]

By the autumn she was as busy as ever. In October she was sending one of her best stories, 'The Pitfall', to Henry Newbolt for the *Monthly Review*. This story, in which a jealous woman encourages her rival to elope with another man rather than honour her engagement, was as controversial as anything she had written, and she noted with some satisfaction that it had already 'raised a blister on a sensitive mind to which I have privately administered it'.[80]

At the same time she was working on *Moth and Rust*, with a twist on her trademark dilemma of the guilty secret that one character must reveal in order to be redeemed – in this version the heroine must keep another's secret even at the cost of incriminating herself. In this first story to be written after the secret Mary herself had so painfully learned, the girl keeps her integrity only to lose a mistrustful lover. The original intention was for her to be transfigured and ennobled by this experience[81] – but Mary's own feeling would not allow her to present this as a plausible outcome, and the narrative shows Janet as an embittered and lonely woman; she finally marries a far more romantic figure than her lost fiancé, the talented painter who has fallen in love with her at first sight and trusted her throughout. But the evident smoothness of this ending is instantly destroyed in the narrative comment that Janet does not love her husband. In Mary's next novel she would return to the figure of the serene accepting heroine who is elevated by her youthful trials. It was this radiant serenity to which Mary herself desperately aspired after all. But not yet.

Mary's diary for the next few years is somewhat cryptic, not least because she seems to have thought better of any explanation it contained – a number of pages have been cut out that might have helped to explain her remaining, opaque references to some great trouble. But from the few traces she does leave the reader, it is possible to put together a tentative – if speculative – account of what happened next. In the autumn of 1901 she is writing *Moth and Rust*, but unable to give it her best because some anxiety is constantly with her.[82] During the following spring she is staying at Preshaw, where she manages to finish the novel. It is a happy time but overshadowed by some bitterness. Still waiting for an end to 'this tyranny', she writes in the summer of 1902 'I am too old to be broken on the wheel again. Surely surely I shall be permitted to regain my peace of mind. I feel my culpable weakness in having lost it.'[83] Some time over that summer she receives a letter from her old lover 'after months of silence'.[84] Unless we are to accept that they were in the habit of regular correspondence, this implies that she has been expecting a significant letter from him for some time, and most probably in response to one she has written him. Whatever this letter contains is sufficient to distract Mary from the writing of her new novel, *Prisoners*.

These fragmentary diary entries seem designed both to suggest and at least partly to conceal the outline of a narrative too personal to be fully revealed and too painful to be kept to herself. Some time between October 1901 and spring 1902 did Mary write to her old lover to tell him that he had been wrong all those years ago in assuming that 'his attentions bored her'? Did she wait anxiously for a response to her letter until she finally received a discouraging answer that summer? And if so, was she forced to admit, as she would soon make her new heroine comment, 'A new edition of that old story now that my hair is grey would be, I think, a little out of place'?[85] In retrospect she certainly placed the beginning of her problems some time in 1900 (the year of the ghostly voice), and further trouble culminated in a period of complete breakdown from 1903 (six months or so after the arrival of the letter while she was beginning *Prisoners*). She would later question how such days and nights could be endurable at all, stretching from weeks to months and years. During this time she appears to have suffered physical pain, and was subjected to the torment of mental visions.[86] It seems possible that she had been plagued by these mental intrusions for some time. In

Red Pottage Hester is able to see frost and snow writing messages to her on the window pane, and asks Rachel if this is simply a hallucination. However:

> Rachel did not answer. She had long since realised that Hester, when in her normal condition, saw things which she herself did not see ... But, fortunately for herself, she saw that most ladders possessed more than the one rung on which she was standing.[87]

Perhaps significantly, this was the novel in which Mary felt she had revealed something terrifyingly personal, that she rarely communicated to her closest friends. And disturbingly, in an undated diary entry from 1902 or 1903 she claimed that her own visitants – 'They know where I met them first' – who had initially destroyed her peace, but now 'came in power' and smiled at her, were showing her how to write, how to live, and how to appear to others.[88] Despite the consolation she now finds in the thought of these visitations, 1903 is 'this darkest year' and by the end of 1904 she is still undergoing what she later terms a 'burial alive'.[89]

While it is not clear what form her illness took in 1903 and 1904, she said later that much of her subsequent life had been 'crippled' by the same cause.[90] Whatever the physical manifestation of her illness, and whether or not it was attended by further battles against morphia, Mary herself certainly had no doubt that it was traceable to the events of 1902, the year in which she received her old lover's letter after the months of silence. It is possible that a second abandonment quite literally made her ill. Afterwards she would ask herself,

> Was it of such importance after all that I should be distressed? If I had been humble, and simple, and less egotistic I should have suffered much less. Oh! If I might but have met this trouble with the knowledge I seem to have now of how to bear it.[91]

This note of determined resignation comes in an entry from October 1905. By the end of 1906 she is able to say that she has been grateful for the last year, when she has had less unhappiness to conceal.[92] Mary kept a diary for a further five years, until 1911, but the subject of her two years' 'burial alive' is never mentioned again.

Of course in the autumn of 1901 these anxieties were only just beginning, and Mary was determinedly pushing herself on to work. In September 'A Day in Teneriffe' appeared in *Chatauquan* and she agreed to sell the book rights of her new story, *Moth and Rust*, to John Murray,[93] whose forbearance in not trying to impose an immediate agreement on her had so impressed her at the time of her first success with *Red Pottage*. Again it is interesting to compare the agent's account with the extant letters. Brown recalls that when he made terms with Murray for a generous stake in the profits, he was expecting Miss Cholmondeley to be as pleased as he and the publisher had been, only to be met with a horrified refusal – not, as he initially thought, because she had become suddenly rapacious, but because she was aghast at the thought of 'dear Mr Murray' losing money by her.[94] But Mary's letter of acceptance to Murray himself is notably more assertive than her correspondence with Bentley fifteen years earlier. In an oblique allusion to her previous disaster with the contract for *Red Pottage*, she tells him that any agreement will have to be approved by Mr Thring of the 'Authors' Society'.[95] Her next letter accepts his terms with modifications, and she is quite particular about the overseas rights.[96] She would later ask him to negotiate £50 for the Tauchnitz edition – she remembers that Tauchnitz only gave £50 for the much longer *Red Pottage* but the value of her work has gone up since then.[97] By 1904, when she wants the story to appear in half a dozen newspapers before agreeing the second serial rights, she feels sure he will want to extend 'every courtesy' to her on this matter.[98] Brown's picture of a gentle spinster trying to make terms against herself is hardly met by the facts. Whatever her personal distress, Mary was not going to make any more mistakes in the literary marketplace.

Mary seems to have got on well with her new publisher, and she must have enjoyed the greater feeling of control so evident in her letters – writing to Newbolt she is diffident about 'The Pitfall' and admits that it would offend the uneducated or less 'cultivated' reader; to Murray she states simply that it 'will find a place' in the volume of which *Moth and Rust* was to form the greater part.[99] The main story involves the determination of Janet Black, an otherwise commonplace middle-class girl, to protect the secret of her dead friend's adultery whatever the cost to herself. When she burns incriminating letters it is supposed that she has deliberately destroyed an outstanding IOU from her brother that goes missing at the same time. Her aristocratic fiancé breaks off their engagement, to the great relief of his mother, and the missing IOU resurfaces too late to prevent him marrying someone else. She initially included her ghost story 'Let Loose', first published in *Temple Bar* some years before, as well as 'Geoffrey's Wife' and 'The Pitfall', to boost the word count, before deciding that this was a story she would prefer not to have read on the grounds that it was 'stupid' and 'inferior'.[100] The *Monthly Review* called it 'a remarkable study of character'.[101] 'This novel is uninteresting' was the damning verdict of the hitherto friendly *Athenaeum*, whose reviewer was far more taken with the accompanying stories, where 'instead of feebly approaching a dimly descried situation, [the author] appears to hold it in the hollow of her hand'.[102]

1902 was to be a year of contrasts. While Mary wrote in her diary that she had not been able to concentrate on *Moth and Rust* because of the anxiety attending its composition, her other books were doing well.[103] Macmillan brought out further imprints of *The Danvers Jewels* and *Sir Charles Danvers*; less gratifyingly, Mary was forced to watch a fifth edition of *Red Pottage* go through the press with Edward Arnold. She even contributed a poem to *The Book of Beauty – Era King Edward VII*. Despite the rather unpromising title of the book, Mary's only pub-

lished poem, 'We Twain', would be not a piece of society frippery, but a lament
for lost opportunities and the passing of time:

> We twain have wandered divers ways,
> Apart have earned both blame and praise;
> Apart have weathered stormy days.
>   Apart, apart!
> Yet thou hadst ever need of me,
> And greater need had I of thee,
> 'Tis weary bondage to be free.
>   And dwell apart.[104]

By March anxiety had left her with such a heavy cough and cold that she was
unable to speak.[105] In the spring of 1903 she compared the first stages of writing
Prisoners to 'loving again'.[106] Again she instinctively compares the act of writing to a kind of surrender of the soul, making this a reason for withholding the
details of her personal life from an implied reader of the diaries:

> So much of me belongs by a kind of right to other people. The result of what I have
> felt during this year especially will not remain mine. It will turn in some way I don't
> understand into thought and closer knowledge of things I have never experienced.
> All I have felt will live again in another form, a form as different as the seed differs
> from the flower. Then it will cease to be my own. It will be as it were to love again, and
> will be mine to give – not mine to keep.[107]

Again the analogy of the flower transforms suffering into greater knowledge,
greater books. But she was still able to write amusingly to Edmund Gosse; in a
letter that shows no trace whatsoever of the distress that was so constantly with
her, she regrets that the new King's coronation may have to manage without her
– an especially painful thought as she has a new gown for it. His superficial sym-
pathies, she goes on, cannot reach down to a woman's deepest feelings – namely
those about dress.[108] It is not altogether likely that pique at being unable to wear
a new dress was among her deepest feeling at the time. But by August she was
moving about again, paying another series of visits.[109] By now *Moth and Rust* had
safely come out (on 4 November), and letters of congratulation were pouring
in from her friends.[110] During this period she continued to socialize with other
writers and artists of different ages.

   In these early years of the twentieth century she was asked by Mary Creighton
to address the Friday Club, an exhibiting group of young British painters set up
by Vanessa Bell in 1905. Modestly or disingenuously denying that she knew anything at all about art, she nonetheless managed an entertaining speech, regaling
her audience with an account of how she had once been invited in the most flattering language to speak at a prestigious gathering in Edinburgh, greatly to the
surprise of her family and not at all to her own. Unfortunately she had been sent

the rough copy of the letter by mistake, on the back of which someone had written, 'Is she any good on a platform?' The invitation was not accepted.[111]

She also received comic letters from Philip Burne-Jones, son of the more famous Pre-Raphaelite painter Edward Burne-Jones, and from W. B. Maxwell, the son of her friend Mary Braddon.[112] Her letters in their turn may give the impression of healthy enjoyment. In fact she was in the middle of the nervous breakdown that would later seem to her to have been all but unendurable. Her diary for 1903 contains only the one December entry, and that is tantalizingly vague.[113] Of course she had been ill, but the sketchiness of her entries in these years, taken with her use of ellipsis and indirection to signify her former lover, points to a more personal reason for her silence. The written word *as a form* is specifically meant to be apprehended and interpreted by others, even in the absence of the writer. Mary's reluctance to put certain things into words, even if in theory no one will see what she has written, is part of a deeper resistance to being appropriated and interpreted by others. So much of what she wrote, so much even of herself, became public property – as she said herself, so much of her belonged by a kind of right to other people.[114] One means of retaining her sense of a private self lay in this refusal to communicate. And so she remains largely silent about the things that trouble her most. In June she told Henry Newbolt that she had been working solidly since February.[115] In September she returned to Cromer. But despite the frantic activity – months of uninterrupted work, repeated visits to family and friends – 1903 remains 'this darkest year'.[116]

The following year would be a year of work, punctuated by further stress. In March 1904 the weekly magazine *Sunday Stories* published a story by one Sophie Gardner called 'To her Own Hurt', which clearly plagiarized *Moth and Rust*.[117] Murray 'kindly and yet firmly' intervened, and an apology by the unfortunate Sophie appeared in the 13 August edition.[118] But the whole business had caused Mary great distress. She may well have felt for the humiliated Sophie, but again her words were being misappropriated and a part of her private self taken from her.

The following month she was again at Preshaw, busy with *Prisoners*[119] (her brother's house was in fact used as a model for the Bellairs family home), but she was soon to discover the benefits of a country residence under her 'own' roof. That August for the first time she took Flora Lugard's cottage in the Abinger Forest for a month, writing delightedly to Matthew Nathan about the 'wortleberry just beginning to turn russet and gold like a miniature autumn forest under one's foot'.[120] Mary always appreciated flowers and plants – she would later become a keen gardener – and clearly she loved being among the pine and mossy paths of the forest. She hints also at another boon, what she would call in her diary 'the wonderful power of solitude, its blessing and comfort'.[121] It was, she candidly wrote to Nathan, the first time in her life when she had 'played at' having anything of her own. In a burst of enthusiasm she invited Diana to come and stay for a few days before she began writing, only to dismiss her with something like exasperation despite her sister's evident enjoyment of the place. She was, Mary complained only half jokingly, so independent, so oblivious of their changed positions towards each other. For Diana to contradict her at home was one thing, but she quickly found it was unsuitable that she should continue to do so in her own (for the time) house, while actually drinking her claret and eating her cutlet. 'I had never experienced these territorial feelings, these old manorial rights before. Now I quite understand them.'[122] Their niece Stella Benson's diary confirms the impression of Diana by this time as well meaning but somewhat difficult to be around. While she took an interest in Stella's writing and even took her to the theatre, still 'She always somehow manages to greet one with a rebuke' and increasingly her deafness became a problem. The young Stella felt understandably irritated that Diana would mishear what she said and then repeat what she thought she had heard as a great joke at her niece's expense.[123] This feeling of irritation was one of the many things that Stella seems never to have realized she had in common with her aunt Mary.

Now, having hurried her sister's own return to London, Mary caught herself wondering how she herself could bear to return to the usual round of what Nathan had once termed 'leg of mutton duties'.[124] Having despatched the unfortunate Diana, Mary invited Percy Lubbock for a few days' visit, writing to the editor Henry Newbolt that she envied Lubbock his 'clear acute mind, humble and so serene' (again that desire for a serenity that continued to elude her). Tellingly, she describes herself in the same letter as living 'on the fringe' of the literary world.[125] She had joked to Matthew Nathan that her new work was a subject of worldwide interest, but already she was starting to feel her celebrity slipping away.[126]

The book itself was not going according to plan. She had been implored by more than one woman not to denigrate her own sex, as some felt she had done in previous books.[127] In this new novel her ostensible aim was to highlight the sin of egotism in the male character Wentworth – and now his counterpart Fay was turning out to be far worse even than this least likeable character. The entire plot hinges on this character's refusal to vindicate her old lover's innocence when he is caught in the grounds of her Italian villa, where a murder has just been committed. In fact Michael, who has not seen Fay since her marriage, has been to see her at her own urgent request, but although her husband dies urging her to tell the truth, she allows Michael to face a lifetime in prison rather than compromise her own reputation. While the psychological imprisonment of several characters, including the unmarried daughter wearing away at home, is carefully depicted, *Prisoners* is not Mary's most successful book, and the *Bookman* was unusual in comparing it favourably to *Red Pottage*.[128]

But her market value was still high, despite the disappointing sales of *Moth and Rust*, which it was now clear would come nowhere near its predecessor. In October she regretfully declined an offer from John Murray for her new book, on the grounds that Curtis Brown had arranged a serialization deal with another firm, Hutchinsons, and she was advised to sell the English book rights and the serial rights together.[129] By December the book was nearing its end, and Mary was complaining piteously through a London smog to the absent Matthew Nathan, now governor of Hong Kong:

> My book is drawing to a close and the hero and heroine must shed tears of blood amidst the bluebells. But are there really such things as bluebells? Is there any <u>clean</u> air anywhere, or any light beyond this hideous electric light with its once white shade? It seems so horribly natural to wriggle on in the dark day by day, and to knock up against people in the streets that I shall very soon believe life always was like this, and that is only a hallucination that sunshine and heather scented air exist. I am learning how moles look at life[130]

These letters sparkle with enjoyment and give the merest suggestion of the frustration she often felt. 'A dark year but not quite as dark as the last', she wrote in her diary on the last day of December.[131]

The next year, 1905, would prove less traumatic than the two years 'in outer darkness'[132] through which Mary had just passed. In January 1905 she finished the draft of *Prisoners* at Flora Lugard's cottage. For this saddest of all her books she got £5,000 from Hutchinson, considerably more than she had been able to get for *Red Pottage*. In February Mary returned to London, where she and Victoria received over 500 people over the next two months. Something of the energy Victoria must have expended on her family is evident from Mary's explanation as to why these entertainments came to a temporary end later in the year – Victoria was on a painting trip, travelling to Rome and Florence, and she herself was remaining quietly at home with her father and Diana, taking up her work again.[133]

In May she escaped once more to Preshaw, where she spent the next three months, bar three days visiting her family in London. Thanks to Regie (by now a Justice of the Peace) and Florie, she was able to work solidly, and finished the final version of the book in August, when she was obliged to change the name, for reasons that are not clear, from *Misery and Hope* to *Prisoners: Fast Bound in Misery and Iron*.[134] In a rare flash of optimism Mary wondered whether it was in some respects an advance on *Red Pottage*. But she admitted her personal interest in its worth,

> It is a very faulty book but it has cost me so much that I hope and almost believe it is worth something. Now of course is my dark time about it now that it is finished and its failures and faults become more and more apparent to me.[135]

Once again her current achievements would be inextricably mixed up with the shadow of *Red Pottage* – by the end of the year Arnold was cheerfully advertising a new edition (its thirteenth impression).[136]

The remainder of the summer and autumn were largely taken up with visits, to Colonel Margesson and his family at Finden (Stella Benson would later comment witheringly that Mrs Margesson believed herself to have been reincarnated and to have psychic abilities); to the Locker Lampsons; to Barlborough; and to the Bensons.[137] At the end of the year Mary met Lord Tennyson, a descendant of the poet, whom she liked, and attended a dull dinner with the Humphry Wards. Again she turned to her diary to confront her continuing depression, determinedly chivvying herself, 'I find the social life more and more of a strain. But I must continue to make a persistent effort about it. There is no safety for me in living too much alone. I should become difficult, exageratid [*sic*], morbid.'[138] But if solitude was dangerous, even a close and supportive family could be a source of constant strain. The comments that follow are revealing, not only in the sense of claustrophobia they so honestly disclose, but in their implications for Mary's earlier life and the resentment of her mother that would resurface in the next few years. As her friends were aware, Mary was simply not designed to be the mainstay of a household. Her social life, she concluded,

> makes a kind of balance to the other strain, home life. I am not by nature domestic. While I write books I must keep in touch with my fellow creatures in my family and outside it, and endeavour to be a good member of a family, and a good friend and a pleasant acquaintance.[139]

Despite this continuing tension, she noted that life was easier than it had been for the last three years, and she felt ready to face the future. One thing she would have to face in the next year was another literary scandal, arising from her latest novel.

But in early 1906 it was not the future that had to be faced, so much as the past. In January Mary had just finished reading Hester's papers, the diary alone amounting to 222,000 words. In this diary, since lost or destroyed,[140] Hester had recorded every small event in the life of the family at Hodnet, and now Mary would have read her sister's criticisms of her own first unpublished novel, and presumably her opinion of the young man who came to the rectory to call on her oldest sister. Fourteen years after Hester's death Mary was working steadily on a small volume for private circulation.[141] Her first idea seems to have been to publish some of her sister's work as part of a memoir, in fulfilment of the promise made to Hester on her deathbed. But it would be another twelve years before these reminiscences appeared, and the volume as published bears little resemblance to the original conception.[142]

In February Mary was still making good progress with the work, although she was worried about it appearing disjointed, and she was enjoying the new luxury of having her own maid. She planned to remain in London until Easter, with possibly a run of a few days down to Preshaw, where Florie had recently given birth to another child, Joan.[143] And then once again she was taken ill with asthma. After two years where she had not had to spend a single day in her room, she found herself floored for a solid three weeks. After this she recovered quickly but was still not well enough to attend the private view of Victoria's first exhibition, although she was proud to hear how lovely her sister had looked on the occasion and how Bond Street had positively been blocked with people queuing to see her work.[144] In addition, in the sight of her increasingly feeble father she began to face the eventual prospect of her own decline into old age. He could only creep into a bath chair perhaps once in three weeks, and his children were amazed to hear him confiding to a friend, 'If it were not for my home ties I should travel'.[145] She hoped that she might never grow old, and many years later she would admit that she had once despised bath chairs, until she learned better in what would be her own last years of illness.[146]

That summer she was again visiting friends, including Percy Lubbock, of whom she noted gratefully, that he 'was so kind and considerate of my small powers; such a curious contrast to some of my literary friends'. Already she was feeling nervous about the imminent publication of her new novel, shivering at the thought of its reception.[147] In fact *Prisoners* had already been run in the *Lady's Realm* from November 1905 to October 1906 – Mary had been less than pleased by the illustrations, commenting somewhat acerbically:

> I felt very unwell when I first realized that I was looking on the face of the hero. I had hoped he did not look exactly like a groom. And I did not know my heroine had a 20 inch waist, or that she wore two sausages of hair on her forehead.[148]

As she waited for the release date of the volume – she was relieved that it would at least not be illustrated – and as the first copies were sold, Mary was surrounded by family. There was a rare visit to Tom and Margaret, then to Preshaw to see Regie and Florie, then to Essex and back to Preshaw, where she may well have been staying on the day of publication.[149] A few weeks later she was with friends, being driven by motor to Sussex to meet an ill and suffering Rudyard Kipling:

> I was quite nervous at meeting him. He is not as intellectual looking as his portraits but he gave the impression of being swiftly alive more like some wild animal in his new Jungle Book than a man. His eyes were extraordinarily direct and clear, very human. He insisted on talking about my asthma until I tried to stop him. Then he said people's illnesses were such interesting things, as they moulded character, and he asked if my illness had not thrown me back very much upon myself. I said it had. I was very glad just to have seen him and spoken to him.[150]

She need not have worried about the reception of her own new book. Within three weeks sales had reached 25,000, with seventy reviews, most favourable and few with any insight into her intentions. Few commented on her central theme, 'the very old one, that in life the affections are everything and that egotism – not hate – is the opposite to love'.[151] She confessed to Lord Aberdeen that she was amazed by the book's success, having been warned by her friends that such a sorrowful tale with a 'prig of the most repulsive kind' for a hero would never be popular with readers.[152] But clearly readers were not put off either by the unappealing central characters or by the tragic note struck by the narrator. Anne Thackeray Ritchie told her she was a magician, while Florie said it was a privilege to know the writer of such a book.[153] In fact nearly all her friends claimed that it was an advance on *Red Pottage* – which is patently untrue – and the only shadow on its success was the persistent claim of various bachelors that she had targeted them in her presentation of Wentworth. Again Mary marshals her arguments, claiming that the character is a type, like Gresley before him, and complains in her diary about one man who is foolish enough to write to her rather than simply ignoring what he has taken as a personal attack. Wentworth is certainly a little like him but Wentworth is like so many touchy old-maidy kind of men.[154] Five years later in a note in the margin she is relieved that the man in question has apologized to her, allowing her to confess that she may not have been blameless herself.[155] Blameless she clearly was not. For in the sententious language of this selfish and narrow figure, Mary had repeated, sometimes verbatim, the more pompous pronouncements of her friend Arthur Benson, the most private of men. That Benson was upset and distressed is clear from his own diary, later edited by Percy Lubbock, who presumably considered the oblique reference safe from outside interpretation. In January 1907 Benson writes: 'I reflected sadly today how I tended to squabble with my women-friends ... I have insulted M.C., alienated Mrs. L., shut up Mrs. S. – and so on.'[156] The smart in this case lay in the very public nature of Mary's criticism. As E. F. Benson later recalled, it was an unprovoked and savage attack. Arthur, hurt and angry, presumably wrote to demand an explanation, only to find that the privilege of visiting without an appointment – conferred only on Mary's intimate friends – was peremptorily withdrawn. In his account of the affair, his brother comments that as Arthur had no intention of renewing his visits, he bore this privation well. Nonetheless it was an unpleasant affair, 'a storm in a tea-cup, but the gale was violent and a great deal of hot tea was spilt'.[157]

The Wentworth affair was not the only trouble to cloud Mary's otherwise triumphant progress – it was in 1906 that the Times Book War abruptly divided the literary world. The nineteenth century had seen a determined effort to solve the problem of underselling, i.e. the selling of books at less than their advertised price. In the 1899 the Publisher Association, the Association of Booksellers and the Society of Authors reached an agreement, implemented on 1 January 1900, to the effect that a 'net' book could be bought by a bookseller for a discount but must be sold to the public at the advertised price. This agreement, known as the Net Book Agreement, remained in force until its collapse in 1995.[158] But in 1906 *The Times* newspaper effectively flouted the agreement by obtaining books at a discount with which to set up a circulating library available to anyone taking out a year's subscription, then expanding into a bookshop selling books at up to 50 per cent discount only a few months after publication.[159] The resulting fracas lasted for eighteen months and involved a libel case with Mary's old publisher Murray, which he won.[160] Mary herself was beset by appeals from different quarters – Lady Lugard for one was putting considerable pressure on her to side with *The Times*, she was fending off demands from Mrs Humphry Ward for an expression of opinion, and her position was complicated by the fact that she had already been asked to sell 5,000 copies of *Prisoners* to *The Times* a mere two months after its first publication.[161]

It is from about this time that Mary first shows a disturbing tendency to equate her improving health with some kind of mental degeneracy.[162] During her illness and the resulting battle with morphia in the 1890s, she had persuaded herself that her sufferings might be simply the necessary 'shadow' of her talent, without which she would not be able to write at all.[163] In a sense this idea was the logical corollary of what her doctors had always been telling her. If intellectual effort led to physical collapse, as the mind took vital nerve force from the body, now her body was simply feeding off the nervous energy that was so essential for her work. At this time she was having a course of Swedish massage, which she claimed was helping her body only at the expense of hurting her mind.[164] Clearly she was depressed, and while she felt grateful for the lessening of her sorrow over the last year, nonetheless 'sometimes I feel something in me has become stunted. I am ... so callous, so without feeling or affection. But perhaps this will pass too.'[165] This formulation is suggestive of an acutely introspective mind, as Mary carefully but helplessly observes her own withdrawal from the world, with a detachment that paradoxically forms not the least part of her suffering. George du Maurier attributes just such an affliction to Little Billee in his own *fin de siècle* bestseller *Trilby* (1894), in which the loss of the woman he loves leads to an entire collapse, the most frightening feature of which is the loss of the faculty of loving. In fact, even as she felt herself to be incapable of affection, Mary was regretting her own lost opportunities. A few months before this entry she had told Stella Benson (who likewise worried about her supposed incapacity for emotion) that as she got older she increasingly wished she had a daughter of her own.[166]

One source of consolation was a new friendship, with Mrs Arthur Lyttelton. It is not clear exactly when they met, but in 1906 Mary writes that they have seen a great deal of each other, and that she is beginning to love her.[167] Despite her concerns about her own emotional detachment, Mary's rhapsody about this new friend is uninhibitedly romantic, a reminder that her attitudes were formed in the second half of the nineteenth century, and she retained something of that culture even in her later life.[168] By the early twentieth century emotionalism between members of the same sex was largely discouraged, in the wake of scientific 'discoveries' about sublimated homosexuality. But as her diaries show, Mary combined a sometimes passionate attachment to individuals with a deep reserve, somehow concealing her private misery from her family for years at a time. Now she wrote:

> I seem to have been wanting Mrs Lyttelton all my life. she <u>seems</u> to like me. Yes I am <u>sure</u> she does, tho' I cannot hope that she could ever care for me as I do for her. Oh! I am lucky to have her in my life.[169]

Mary says nothing in her journal about her friend's politics, but in fact Mary Lyttelton, her namesake and near contemporary, was a committed women's activist. Born in 1856 into an aristocratic family, Mary Clive had married a tutor at Keble College, Oxford, the Revd Arthur Lyttelton, in 1880. She became a vice-president of the National Union of Women Workers in 1895, before taking over as president. She also sat on the executive committee of the Central Society for Women's Suffrage, formed in 1888, and wrote the feminist manual *Women and Their Work* in 1901.[170] It was extraordinary that they had not met earlier. In 1894 Mary had been gratified by her sister-in-law Mrs Alfred (Edith) Lyttelton's review of *Diana Tempest* in the *National Review*,[171] and she already knew of this Mrs Lyttelton at that time as someone who moved in the same social circles. It is even possible that she and Mary Lyttelton had attended the same parties without ever being introduced. When they finally became known to each other, Mary seems to have turned to her as an antidote to the misery of the last few years.

But a few days after the entry in Cholmondeley's diary, Mrs Lyttelton died of influenza and weakness of the heart. In her reaction to this event, Mary again reveals a sense of her own public importance, even as she strives to keep her most private feelings from the scrutiny she both acknowledged and rebelled against. She wrote nothing for several months and then in April 1907, 'I could write pages about her and her wonderful dealings with me. But why should I. I shall never forget them, and surely these things are mine, and mine only.'[172] Again the diary becomes a site of contest with an imagined reader, as Mary struggles to keep her deepest feelings private, a reticence enabled by her writing in a private journal. But at the same time she is a public figure, specifically a published *writer*, and in this sense anything she writes becomes part of a dialogue with an unseen public. This threat of being appropriated by her public, and her most intimate secrets being revealed, is something in which Mary was at some level quiescent – it was by her own implied wish that Lubbock wrote a memoir based on these very diaries, and one of the last entries gives as a reason for breaking off the realization that the diary was ceasing to be 'a record' of her life and would therefore by implication not be interesting to a reader.[173] Despite her determination not to reveal more of her relationship with Mrs Lyttelton, the diary immediately continues,

> I never thought she would die, but I acted as if I did. I took every opportunity of seeing her. I took every chance. And she did the same. I am told she cared for me, much. I think I may believe it.[174]

In the spring of 1907 Mary was entertaining as usual, although she now found the constant socializing more tiring than exhilarating. She had paid some pleasant visits with Victoria, including to Flora Lugard. But on her doctor's orders she was not working, and now claimed startlingly that she had been an absolute idler in life. Her health at any rate improved notably under this regimen of absolute idleness – she had put on a stone and was mildly gratified to be constantly told how good her complexion was. But while the doctor reassured her that she would write better than ever if she would only rest now, she noticed that her mind would only fix on the most trivial details, and was not convinced.[175]

Meanwhile another Cholmondeley sister was less idle. In May of this year Diana's first and apparently last play appeared at the Imperial. *A Man's Foes*, of which no known copy now survives, was a melodrama featuring an alcoholic lifeboatman's wife who inadvertently causes her son's death by drinking the brandy that would have been used to restore him after the wreck of his ship on the Cornish coast. Although there was a great stir among the sisters, and an excited Stella Benson recorded that the opening had been a great success, the play ran for only one night.[176] Mary seems not to have attended and she makes no mention of it in her diary or in her surviving correspondence, and *The Times* was making a kindly exaggeration when it later described Diana as being 'known as a writer of plays'.[177]

Mary herself may have been understandably concerned that her mind had apparently lost its elasticity, but she felt ashamed to be doing nothing and inevitably began to worry that she would never write again. In her own words, she 'pulled herself together'[178] and the round of dinner parties went on into the summer. She recalled a long conversation with one Mr Butcher about the male habit of pulling out once the wedding day got too near; on the same night she was complimented by Asquith, who would shortly become Prime Minister, on *Prisoners*, although he was unconvinced by Magdelen's final marriage to Lossiemouth, 'and said she had married him out of magnanimity or something to that effect. I said she had married him because she cared for him.'[179] Another reminder of the past came in a visit from Mark Twain some time in this year: 'He was quite unchanged, his mane of white hair fairly tidy when he first arrived but soon standing straight up as he warmed to his subject and rubbed his hands through it.'[180] He remembered his own fury at the disastrous management of

Condover in her uncle Regie's time, and in her turn Mary was touched by this visit from her uncle's old friend. But if Mary's mind was running largely on her own past and that of her family, she was about to find the refuge she required at times from both.

7 'WINDOWS WIDE OPEN, YET DISCREETLY VEILED': *NOTWITHSTANDING* (1913)

The idea of a country retreat was not a new one – for some years now Mary had depended on the safety valve offered by strategic visits to Preshaw, and she often had the use of Flora Lugard's cottage during her residence abroad. But some time in 1907 she took the significant step of leasing a house of her own in the country.[1]

It is not clear what turned her thoughts to the small Suffolk village of Ufford, not a part of the country she seems to have known particularly well. But perhaps this was the point. She had probably first seen the village while visiting her cousin Margaret Grant (neé Beaumont) at nearby Melton Grange.[2] Mary's sensitive pride had occasionally made her sarcastic about the Beaumonts, but she was on good enough terms with her cousin to take a young Stella Benson to the Grange a year or two later (it was a less than successful visit, and Stella noted acerbically that the Grants were very vain about their garden).[3] Ufford itself was certainly picturesque, as well as continuing the familiar traditions of Hodnet, with its own library, Girls Friendly Society, Women's Institute and mothers' meetings, as well as a parish magazine featuring short stories, local news and advertisements for safety matches and Pear's Soap. In May Mary was writing excitedly to Matthew Nathan, now in Natal, 'I am camping out in a perfect little cottage which I am thinking of taking if it suits my coquettish lungs, which wont inhale every air'.[4]

The house she had alighted on – anyone looking for a cottage is likely to pass it many times in the lane without stopping – was old and attractive, with low ceilings and two front doors, a legacy of its former life as two separate dwellings. Immediately behind one of these doors is a large alcove, now used for bookshelves, but in Mary's day the source of much confusion – to her amusement, visitors would insist on knocking at this door despite the mesh where a panel had been taken out and clearly revealing legs of mutton on the other side. Like other old houses, it came complete with its own ghost – or, in this case, a persistent ghostly smell in the principal bedroom, likened by Mary to the odour of roast hare.[5]

There was a great deal of work to be done to the house itself. There were ants in the pantry, where it turned out there was actually no floor; there were rats in the walls and plaster dropping from the ceilings. Upper floors came dangerously close to collapse and two rooms thrown into one proved to be actually on different levels. But to set against this, there was a bedroom with an oak floor, fastened with the original Tudor pins. The garden, where the soil was good, and 'everything grows like a weed, very like a weed at this moment',[6] backed on to the park of the local landowner, Edward Brooke. As Mary brilliantly expressed it, the cottage was 'in the waistcoat pocket of his park'.[7] This 'kind little bachelor'[8] as Mary described him, owner of Ufford Place (since burned down) and much of the land around, agreed to give her a twenty-five-year lease on the cottage. As it turned out it was just as well he had. But for now the air of Ufford proved congenial in every sense, and in December that year she was clearly still feeling all the invigoration of a new project. She would later have a series of fallings out with her eccentric landlord, but at this stage Mr Brooke, a church warden who took an interest in the doings of the Sunday School, was 'kindness itself'[9] to his new tenant.

The delights of the cottage were to be shared with Victoria and the two of them lay awake at night in London planning refurbishment and laying plans for the garden.[10] A particular source of pride was a pair of brilliant orange curtains put up that autumn, an acquisition that does not actually feature in a poem by their friend Eva Anstruther, written at the time. In fact this poem, later published in the *Westminster Gazette*,[11] seems more descriptive of Mary herself than her curtains – 'Windows wide open, yet discreetly veiled' could almost stand as her epitaph. Clearly the house, the first she had ever been able to call her own, fulfilled a deep emotional need for Mary, but she told Victoria that 'I could not care for it unless she felt it was as much hers as mine. After all it is doing it with Victoria that has made it such a joy.'[12] Her one humorous complaint about her sister was her irrational fear of frogs, which meant that Mary was forced to chase them with a duster. And it was not, she pointed out, easy to carry a frog in a soft duster. But, as she reported happily to Matthew Nathan:

> It really is a rather nice, very little cottage. Victoria and I spent all the summer working on it. We did nearly everything ourselves with my little maid. We laid down the stair carpets, made and put up the curtains, and I nearly broke myself in two polishing the table.[13]

She was also shameless in her scavenging of plants for the garden, with Brooke as her main victim:

> He likes me very much at present, as so many do before they know me well, and I need hardly tell you that I am taking every advantage I can of his friendship. I am working it for all it is worth, and have filled my garden with all his best things. He also is a great gardener, and I tell him it is good for his things not to be planted too close. I have really got so much out of him that I have the comfort of feeling if we do quarrel later on I shall have nothing to reproach myself with. It does not matter being thought grasping

when one has really grasped a lot of things which are <u>rooted</u> in the soil. I little thought this time last year when I began to renovate the cottage what I was in for.[14]

She was planning a low brick wall for the garden, although she complained that as it seemed to cost a sovereign every time you put a spade into the earth, and bricks were about £5 a piece, this would have to wait for a while.[15]

A year later she gleefully told the story of how she had been on the best of terms with her neighbours, who all regarded her as a person of limited means who had the good taste to live in Ufford. But then one day she was working quietly in the garden when she was annoyed to hear the noise of a tractor engine squeezing itself into the stable yard, accompanied by all the village boys. It turned out to be her consignment of bricks, and that evening the father of the small boy who pumped her water called round to suggest that she raise his wages.[16] The low wall, ingeniously arranged, was subsequently buried before being rediscovered by a new owner decades later, and still 'divides the mown grass from the rough broken ground which slopes upwards behind it till it loses itself among the tree trunks'.[17]

Mary's enjoyment is equally apparent in her diary, where she writes 'I had hardly realized how wonderfully healing and resting it is to have an entire change of thought. The country was new to me, the place was new to me, to have a little thing of my own was new to me.'[18] Lubbock remembered it as 'a pretty and simple old house in a leafy village-lane, far from the world', where he enjoyed talking to Mary and Howard Sturgis about their respective works in progress. On Sunday mornings the three of them would sit out in the garden and 'Howard took her to task on the subject of her books', while Mary promised amendment.[19] Mary herself would later recall her first impressions in a preface to her last book, *The Romance of His Life and Other Romances* (1921), much of which was written here and which she dedicated to Sturgis.

Meanwhile back in London Mrs Humphry Ward was inaugurating a Women's Anti-Suffrage Organisation.[20] Of more immediate concern, Mary's father was becoming yet more obviously old and frail,[21] and must have required increasing levels of care, creating an additional weight of anxiety. But, characteristically, Mary's need to escape her domestic responsibilities was counterbalanced by her joy in welcoming her family to the new cottage – Diana (after her less than successful visit to the Abinger cottage a few years earlier), Essex and Regie had all been to stay by the end of 1908 and were unanimous in their approval.[22] This was the period in which Mary had written two stories about a doomed romance revisited in middle age, 'The Understudy' and 'St Luke's Summer' – the latter contains a loving description of an old maid lavishing her taste and energy on her pretty cottage, and it is some relief to see that she planned to spend the proceeds on doing up her own new home. And she was getting stronger every year, although her anxiety about her health now gave way to fear that she would no longer be able to write; even a short story was becoming an effort now, and she was not to know that her most brilliant short story was still some years away.[23] Her plans for the cottage were a merciful distraction, but now that the dark years were finally passing away, she found herself longing again for the comfort of God's presence, a sense of nearness that had comforted her in the worst times of life but which she felt 'so seldom now'.[24]

As Mary's health continued to improve, so her father's declined, and his loyal children could only wait patiently with him for the end, praying that he would be spared any further pain. Mary was not able to spend as much time in her new cottage as she would have liked as a result, but when she did it was to work.[25] She included a satirical self-portrait in 'The Lowest Rung' of a female writer, living alone in a cottage and prone to bronchitis:

> I have no time to be ill in my busy life. Was not Broodings beside the Dieben being finished in hot haste for an eager publisher? And had I not promised to give away the Sunday-school prizes at Forlington a fortnight hence?[26]

The dual imperatives of meeting the publisher's deadline and fulfilling her obligations to the Sunday school are humorously presented, but Mary had clearly not forgotten the constraints of her Shropshire life, or her subsequent troubles. She often gave her own name to the less sympathetic characters in her stories. But if she is Marion, the writer of the story, she is also the nameless morphia addict, whose addiction has lost her everything and whose 'first glimpse of hope came to me in the woods at Abinger in a windless, sunny week at Easter'.[27]

The first-person narrator of the story vaguely resents her family's affectionate teasing, which she knows herself is due in large part to her self-deprecating humour:

> There was a rooted impression in the minds of my own family that I was a flurried sort of person, easily thrown off my balance, making mountains out of molehills (this was especially irritating to me, as I have always taken a broad, sane view of life), who always twisted my ankle if it could be twisted, or lost my luggage, or caught childish ailments for the second time. Where there is but one gifted member in a large and commonplace family an absurd idea of this kind is apt to grow from a joke into an *idée fixée*.[28]

It is hard for a reader to know, as it was perhaps for Mary herself, how to take this joke about the gifted but misunderstood member of a commonplace family. She told Matthew Nathan that the writer narrator *was* a portrait of herself, but that she would forgive him for not thinking it the living image of her.[29] She made no mention of the experience she had drawn on for the agonies of sudden morphia withdrawal, or the insight into the possible fate of an addict, who watches helplessly as she is kicked down the social ladder from one rung to the next.

In the event she was given £75 for the story, which became the title story of a collection that appeared in this year to 'no attention whatsoever', although it was taken up by the American publisher Dodd, Mead as *The Hand on the Latch* and was subsequently translated into French.[30] Her article 'The Skeleton in a Novelist's Cupboard', in which she takes issue with her critics who insisted on seeing real people in her novels, was published in *Pall Mall Magazine*; and in Ufford with Victoria that summer she was finishing the memoir of Hester, that became as she wrote it 'more of a family annual than a memoir'.[31]

Stella Benson was thrilled to be invited for a visit, a prospect she found 'too lovely to believe'.[32] At this stage of her life she felt closer to her aunt Mary than she ever would to her mother, and there was much to bring them together, not least their shared experience of perpetual ill health. In a memorable phrase in her novel *Living Alone* Stella would later comment that pain had the power to put out the sun.[33] Essex by this time was bringing up her children alone, her husband having left them in 1906. And while she was charming and kind in company, her relationship with her daughter seems not to have brought out the best in either of them. Essex was irritably critical of Stella, whom she accused of lacking natural affection; Stella meanwhile admitted that her mother's emotional demands left her ill-tempered and unable to respond as she would have liked.

In 1914, a few months before the outbreak of war, Stella finally contrived to leave home, a feat none of her unmarried aunts had managed to pull off. Mary knew exactly how difficult the relationship between a mother and a daughter could be. But she was close to Essex, thinking her 'a perfect angel',[34] and if she had an inkling of the situation at home, would certainly not have sided against her own sister. However this was not all they had in common. Stella was shy in company[35] and lacked confidence in her personal attractions. She was passionate about the woman question, first against and later for, joining a suffragist organization in 1914.[36] Most importantly, she was an aspiring writer.

Stella fell in love with the house in Ufford just as her aunt had done, describing it as 'all wooden beams and up and down stairs', but the evenings were awkward. She had been warned by her mother that her aunt Mary was not well and would need a certain amount of rest and solitude. What she found particularly difficult was the having to go to bed hours before she was tired because her aunt kept looking 'in an ominous way' from the clock to her.[37] It was perhaps on one of these evenings that they did a word test, writing down the thoughts that occurred to them in relation to various everyday words. Next to 'woman' Stella wrote 'machine in a factory' as well as 'Venus of Milo'. Equally bleak, next to 'home' Mary wrote in her turn simply, 'Strain'.[38]

But it was on one of these evenings, after Victoria had gone, that Stella confided her own self-doubt and social anxiety to Mary, finding her – as well she might – a sympathetic listener. She did not tell her, or anyone else, about the 'thought people' whom she welcomed imaginatively, but who tellingly invaded her at times of particular anxiety or loneliness; as for her aunt, her diary itself was too public a place for her to describe at length the voices she heard in her solitude, and her one entry on that subject was partially destroyed with a sharp pair of scissors. Nor could Stella have realized that Mary was confiding something of her own need for consolation when she told her 'that hardship makes and fosters genius and that everybody who has had a bad time either pain or trouble or poverty has if they meet it bravely generally something more than the others who are brought up and live without any mishaps'.[39]

Mary at this stage of her life may have come across to a caustic and watchful young niece – she sounds something like Hester in fact, as she would later observe herself – as a kindly if occasionally suffocating middle-aged spinster. But still there was the same restlessness and sense of loss as she felt her creative powers ebbing away even as her health was better than ever. Mary had always tended to see in her literary power some consolation, even reason, for her invalid condition, and now, with the failure of any subsequent novel to match the success of *Red Pottage*, she seems to have convinced herself more than ever that one was dependent on the other. Much as she longed to be engaged on another novel, she was reading *Red Pottage* to her father and facing the horrifying thought that she would never write anything so good again. Her power to write was diminishing, in other words, long before she felt ready to give up her writing. 'I am so strong. I have never been so well as I am now. And I have never had so little mental grasp. Will my powers really return. I doubt it.'[40] Just as the 'dark years' came to an end, Mary was having to face an almost greater loss.

Her depression towards the end of that summer was not helped by the absence of Victoria in Sweden, and Diana at the seaside, leaving Mary in sole charge of their aged father, who by now could not stir out of doors and was good 'as a child is "good"'.[41] But once again Mary pulled herself together and by the end of the year she was remarking that this was the happiest time she had ever known, despite her undeniable bouts of depression. Twenty people had visited the cottage, including Tom, Regie and Florie, and Victoria had enjoyed another successful exhibition.[42]

The first few months of 1909 were overshadowed both by her own illness and the near death of her father. In May Mary 'crawled down to Ufford', where at the instigation of the actor Charles Maude she was setting about an entirely new stage version of *Red Pottage* in four acts.[43] With her usual ambivalent response to convalescence, she felt herself getting 'stupider and stronger', and even as she worked on the play she asked herself dubiously, 'Will it ever see the light[?]'[44] Sadly the manuscript of this version has not survived or at least its whereabouts are unknown – what Mary's correspondence with Maude does reveal is her continuing interest in her most important work and something of the modifications she might have made a decade later. After 'looking fixedly at a laurel bush for a week', for instance, she wondered whether if Hester were to attack anyone, it should not be Gresley himself – she had already decided in the original stage version that the dual plots were too separate to be easily accommodated in one play (in fact she questioned their essential unity even in book form, which suggests the extent to which a writer may herself be unaware of what she is doing).[45] The division of the profits was carefully drawn up, with a commission accorded to Kinesey Peile, who had introduced them in the first place.[46]

Maude seems to have told Mary enthusiastically that he was in touch with more than one manager eager to see the script, but in the event his optimism was misplaced.[47] The fault was not necessarily in Mary's powers of dramatic adaptation. A playwright by the name of Barnes, who with Mary's consent was working on his own version of the book, admitted that he had tried three times to get it put on without success, and was quite happy for her to try her chances with her script. But once again the project came to nothing. Or perhaps not nothing. From the extant correspondence it is clear that Cyril Maude, Charles's brother and manager of the Playhouse, was lined up to read the play on its completion in 1910, and a year later *The Hand on the Latch* was put on under his management, with his wife Winifred Emery in the starring role.[48] It seems likely that Maude rejected the four act *Red Pottage* but intimated that he might see his way to producing something in one act at a later date. *The Hand on the Latch* is a one-act play based on the story of the same name, essentially in fact it takes the dialogue from the original and simply leaves out the description.[49]

Aside from the revised script, it had been a fairly successful year. In July the *Cornhill* published 'Vicarious Charities', attacking the parasitic practices of well-bred philanthropists who foist their causes on acquaintances who are too polite to escape; notably the witty Marcella complains of the incessant demands made on a writer for autographed copies of books to be given to charity bazaars. She is particularly scathing about the well-dressed and irresistible eighteen-year-old who shyly extracts money from hapless callers:

> If she really has a charity at heart ... Let her wear a moreen petticoat as I do instead of a silk one. That would be a gain of at least eighteen shillings, the price of four novels, representing four distinct assaults on trembling authors.[50]

Meanwhile 'The Romance of His Life', in which a middle-aged bachelor is redeemed from a life of pompous aridity by falling in love with a correspondent he never meets (and who turns out to be a male prankster), appeared in *Scribner's Magazine* in August.[51] Mary had been able to spend a considerable amount of time at the cottage in Ufford, coming up to London for a few days at a time to take her turn at looking after her father. His increasing frailty meant there were fewer entertainments in the London flat, but there had been the usual visits, to

Tom in Wrexham, and to friends such as the Acton Reynald Corbets, Lord Wantage and Lady Crawford.[52] It is likely that a cousin from New Zealand, the 'other' Mary Cholmondeley, came to London for Christmas this year. In her account in her local newspaper, carefully preserved in the scrapbook where she kept family memorabilia and articles on her famous namesake, she has initialled and dated an article on 'Christmas in London (by a New Zealander)'. In it she describes captivating toy shops and the bustle of Covent Garden on Christmas Eve. On the day itself there is turkey and plum pudding, which she comments appreciatively 'one really could enjoy in this cold weather'. The evening is devoted 'to the children', suggesting that various cousins may have come up to town for her visit.[53]

Despite her indifferent health and the drain of the play, Mary had also inaugurated and drawn up the rules for a weekly ladies' luncheon club (the original idea had come from Evelyn March Philips), meeting at restaurants to 'provide opportunities of informal intercourse between a limited number of genial and convivial spirits'.[54] The Give and Take Club, as it came to be known, provided a forum for discussion as well as conviviality. Something of the atmosphere is captured by another writer, Marie Belloc Lowndes, in her diary of 7 January 1913. She had been lunching at the club with Mary Cholmondeley, Ellen Thornycroft Fowler (Cholmondeley's main rival in the bestseller lists of 1899–1900, who seems to have just outsold her in 1899 because her own novel had been published early in the year, and *Red Pottage* in October) and Mrs Bailey, when the discussion turned to the strictures on contemporary literature. They talked of English prudery and how while unmarried lovers could do what they liked within the pages of a novel, a man could not hold a married woman's hand without causing offence to the average reader.[55] It is a timely reminder that the much recast and misrepresented 'Victorian prudery' did not disappear with the end of the century or even with the queen who gave her name to the era.

Nor should it be forgotten that Mary's own cultural attitudes had been largely formed during that time. But if Cholmondeley appears conservative in her determined allegiance to the country house way of life and also, it has to be said, in her snobbish attitude to outsiders, she was no prude and never had been. Indeed she clearly enjoyed the shock she caused to stuffy moralists with her depiction of sexual temptation in some of her stories. Perhaps she was influenced by her friends Lady Ridley and Lady Lugard, both active in the women's movement, but certain it is that in her stories written in the early years of the new century she quietly drops the satirical references to 'advanced' women and goes beyond the pragmatic call for female employment to write stories that seem to offer at least a qualified support for the female suffrage campaigners.[56] While Mary made no attempt to join an organized movement, she retained and enlarged the concerns that had characterized her as a New Woman novelist ten years earlier. Certainly she would have had no time at all for Mrs Humphry

Ward's anti-suffrage organization, merged with a male group in 1910 to form the National League for Opposing Women's Suffrage.[57]

In July 1909 she published the satirical 'Votes for Men' in the *Cornhill*. Imagining a time 'Two hundred years hence, possibly less',[58] in which women have disenfranchised men, she returns to the periodical debates over the New Woman of the 1890s. A female Prime Minister is reluctant to meet a delegation of male suffragists, and the Woman Question of Cholmondeley's youth is satirically reintroduced, as Eugenia's husband complains that independent women are marrying later and later, leaving single men to the contempt and pity of those around them. Ongoing arguments about the laws of nature are realigned, with Eugenia claiming that while the surplus of men does not justify their being given the vote, the female capacity for reproduction means that she is fundamentally better suited to political rule. Recalling the Victorian England of Cholmondeley's own youth, Eugenia launches a direct attack on the limits artificially imposed on women at that time:

> It seems incredible, looking back, to realise that large families of daughters were kept idle and unhappy at home, after their youth was over, not allowed to take up any profession, only to be turned callously adrift in their middle age at their father's death, with a pittance on which they could barely live. And yet these things were done by educated and kindly men who professed to care for the interests of women, and were personally fond of their daughters.[59]

Mary would later confront her friend Matthew Nathan about his doubts over his own employment of girl messengers, on the grounds that it was a man's department to support his future wife, and the woman's to make a home beautiful. Mary warned:

> There is growing up to a degree that astonishes me a deep bitterness against men in the minds of great numbers of women, and these not only the superfluous women, the unattractive, the incapable, the middle aged. I think this feeling has been growing silently for years. They realize that there are too many of them: consequently a large percentage of them will do anything to get married and are willing to marry any one. The bachelor can be unaware of that fact. But there are also many who would rather support themselves than endure a loveless marriage and there are many more who have no chance of marriage whatever. We get then a large mixed class of women, some of the best and many of the inferior ones who must either support themselves or go on the streets.

Having issued this almost apocalyptic threat, she rather surprisingly denies that she herself is in favour of female suffrage. What women need, she claims, is legislation and greater respect in their desire to be self-supporting:

> Personally I do not think it is a vote, but legislation that she needs. It is hard that women anxious to make an honest livelihood should be stigmatized as hysterical by

men when they agitate for a vote ... As far as I know women, almost no woman wishes to support herself. It exhausts her. The fixed hours, the hopelessness of it all crushes her when her first youth is gone. But she has got to do it[60]

Her proposed solution was typically pragmatic, and at the same time typically conservative. If the indoor and administrative labour market was flooded by women, young men would be all but forced to enter the armed forces, and so supply the current shortage.

Notwithstanding her excoriating attack on traditional roles in 'Votes for Men', in the spring of 1910 Mary took Lady Herbert's house in London in order to take out her nieces Mary and Susan in the approved manner, so that they could 'go to balls and things and get to know people' as Stella Benson wistfully noted in her diary – Mary notes in her own diary that while she herself was responsible for organizing the social side, Victoria took care of the housework.[61] Both sisters went down with influenza immediately afterwards.

In April their father seemed better, and Mary was able to spend a few days with Regie at Preshaw. But it was a short reprieve, and on 10 August, his hand in Victoria's, he died. He was buried at Hodnet Church. 'And then came at us a great deal of business, and the disentangling of all the threads of our lives, and the breaking up of the pretty home at Albert Gate Mansions, and the long search for a new home.'[62] In fact Mary's desolation at this moment almost echoes her expression of misery at leaving Hodnet, 'our pretty house' as she had described it in almost identical language in 1896.[63] For all her resistance to the constraints of domestic life, Mary would always feel a strong emotional attachment to the place she regarded as 'home'.

Why the sisters had to leave their flat in Hyde Park is not clear, but it would be months before Mary found a new home, at 2 Leonard Place, Kensington.[64] Victoria came to live with her here but Diana, perhaps in a belated attempt at freedom, settled in a flat in the Brompton Road. Mary expended a quantity of grim humour on the Uncle Tom style decor of her own new house – walls gravy coloured literally from attic to basement. And, having had one of her letters rescued from between the floorboards of the passage, she had succumbed to a 'letter cage', what she described as 'a horror which acts as a receptacle for correspondence'.[65] It seems likely to have been around this time that Mary came to terms with another horror, the domestic telephone.[66] She had, she felt, added greatly to her experience of the seamy side of life, no detail of crooked flues and scullery sinks remaining unknown. Now 'I have no illusions left, and the poetic side of my nature is for ever dead'.[67]

Within a few weeks of moving in, Victoria fell ill again and Mary sent her to Torquay to recover, before promptly getting influenza herself. Still weak a month later, she reflected sadly that she would miss the opening night of her first play,

The Hand on the Latch, which was going on before George Pleydell's *One of the Dukes* at the Play House.[68] In the event it was probably just as well. The few reviews of her first and last entry into theatre were at best moderately favourable – one critic suggested that it should be replaced with a bassoon solo[69] – and in fact the first night of the play was also to be its last. Mary recorded in her personal notebook that the royalties amounted to a mere £5 and 18s.[70]

By this time her niece Stella, who would herself be publishing her first novel within a few years, was becoming increasingly critical of both Mary and Victoria, who appeared not to have noticed that she was fast growing up and gave her games to play in a corner when visitors arrived. She was 'a dear', but still Stella found all the Cholmondeleys vague and inconsequential in their conversation. Certainly she was 'not so lost in admiration' of her aunt Mary as she had been, becoming increasingly irritated by what she saw as her aunt's intrusive interest in her affairs.[71] She might well have been amazed to realize how alike they seem to anyone reading their diaries in tandem. But Mary was in any case losing interest in keeping a record of her own doings. On the inauspicious opening night of her play she wrote:

> I think it is no use my continuing this diary, or whatever it is ... my interesting years are over. Life has become peaceful and in a way happier than it has ever been. But I have very little to say about it. and I am afraid my own feelings are altogether commonplace: just those of every middle aged woman ... For the things I feel now most deeply, are the things I cannot write; like Father's death which I think of often.[72]

However she retained more of her old energy than such comments would suggest. She took an interest in the employment of boys, suggesting that some at least could be trained as footmen (a comment that says much about her impressions of the world).[73] That April she felt strongly enough to write a letter to *The Times*, complaining that women could not vote on the election of the Academic Committee of the Royal Society of Literature.[74] The nature of Mrs Humphry Ward's dispute with them at this time remains unclear, but this may well have been the reason for her resignation of her Fellowship – for once these two Marys were in agreement.[75]

That October brought another bereavement in the death of Ralph Benson,[76] still estranged from his wife, but in December Mary was the guest of honour at the Authors' Club Annual Banquet at the Hotel Cecil. She admitted that 'It is rather absurd at my age but I liked the applause, and my beautiful bouquet'. But what pleased her most was an old man coming up to her and saying, 'I have come all the way from Wensleydale on purpose to see you. I am one of your "Prisoners".'[77]

That Christmas was spent peacefully alone at her flat, while Victoria went to stay with Diana. And it is here that the diary ends, with Mary's reflection on the lessons she had learned since it began:

> I daresay sorrow and suffering may come again but I feel sure if they do I shall be sustained. Oh! if I had only started life with faith even as a grain of mustard seed. Fifty two long years has it taken me to trust my Friend. And the lesson is not fully learnt yet. but I think I am more ready to be taught, less stubborn, and self willed. And at any rate I know God is my friend.[78]

It was a few weeks after this last entry that her old friend Sir Alfred Lyall died of heart disease.[79] Algernon Heber-Percy was another person whose death she would have regretted in this year.[80] But as she had come close to acknowledging in one of her final diary entries, the things she felt most deeply were the very things that, as she got older, she tended to avoid writing down. And so she did not return to her diary with this last sad news.

In 1912 *Moth and Rust* was reprinted by Hodder and Stoughton, but Mary knew that she was not part of the new generation of writers. D. H. Lawrence mentions in passing that he met Mary Cholmondeley in 1909, but it was not an encounter about which he had much to say.[81] She wrote to Hugh Walpole in April 1912,

> If there is one thing more than another that we elders dislike being told it is that we are dead. That is why we are always pathetically talking about leading a very full life, and keeping in touch with the younger generation.[82]

She was full of admiration for his novel *Mr Perrin and Mr Trail* (1911), in which Perrin the schoolmaster, who feels he has failed in life, is brought to the verge of a full-scale nervous breakdown, convincing himself at moments of particular stress that an ornament in his room is dancing about in front of him. In the course of the term, the stifling routine of the school exacerbates the tensions between him and a new, younger member of staff, Mr Trail, and eventually Perrin decides to kill him. Still highly readable, one of the strengths of the novel is its working out of Perrin's collapse, as he comes to believe that he has a Mephistophelean double, the projection of his own thwarted anger, and rails against a God who fails to save him from himself. The psychological dimension would have greatly appealed to Mary, and she was 'awed' by his courage in presenting Perrin's declared hatred of his God. She told him that she had not been able to put it down.[83] A year later Mary confessed with some embarrassment that she had not thought entirely well of his new novel *Fortitude*, which was set to make his name but which she was convinced lacked the close observation of his previous work. There was, she complained, too little concentration on imaginative facts, which came out helter skelter. As she put it in a letter to Walpole,

> Imagination is the art of drawing the circle from the arc, isn't it: building up the skeleton from the single bone ... If we are gifted with imagination we ought to study it, and be reverently obedient to it, and never expect it to do our bidding. We are there to do its bidding.[84]

But equally she knew – or said she knew – that older writers such as herself should simply enjoy the work of the younger generation and not try to tamper with it.[85] Even as she was writing her own new novel, *Notwithstanding*, she could joke to a correspondent that, 'I am not intended by nature to write novels, but to do crotchet work and arrange flowers'.[86] It is likely that this is precisely what she did in Ufford that summer, between work on her new book, itself based largely in the Suffolk countryside. It details a peaceful rural existence, disrupted by crisis when the heroine can only prove her lover to be the rightful heir to the estate he loves by producing a will she has witnessed, and which will identify her as the supposed mistress of his dissolute cousin. The dilemma is resolved when the hero attempts to burn the will rather than jeopardize her reputation, and succeeds only in eradicating her name without invalidating the document. The real tragedy of the story lies in the monotonous life of his cousin Jane, who watches him fall in love with her friend as she herself stays at home looking after a cantankerous bedridden mother. Old enough now to take a more critical view of the older generation of writers, Stella Benson found this last novel 'very mild and ordinary'.[87] Even the loyal *Bookman* struggled to find something more than the simple plot to relay to its readers, deciding in the end that the life of Riff was 'vividly touched on'.[88]

That October Victoria set off with a friend, Elena Rathbone (another of her aunts' friends whom Stella did not like), for a six-month trip to India – on her return her sister would refer to her jokingly as 'the prodigal'.[89] In the meantime she kept up her long-standing friendship with Matthew Nathan. She had to refuse an invitation to a dance at his country house, for fear of her lungs letting her down at the wrong moment, although she regretted the lost chance of watching her niece Mary, also invited, from the minstrels' gallery – 'she really is lovely at night', remarked the proud aunt. Still she wanted to hear about it all afterwards – clearly she had not forgotten her own enthusiasm for dancing in Hodnet and Cambridge, as a girl. 'I was a great dancer a hundred years ago', she said now.[90] But if she was no longer fit for dances, she could host luncheon parties still, and she asked Nathan as a personal favour to come and make conversation with her nephew Reginald (named after his father), now twenty-three and in the Rifle Brigade, although he was learning to fly planes. He is, Mary admitted, 'the apple of my eye'.[91] She would go further in the next few years and say that he had been almost like her own son.[92]

Increasingly now she was spending her days in the country, where there was time to reflect and time to be alone. In October 1913 the faithful Murray was to publish *Notwithstanding* (which despite the censures of Stella Benson and the indifference of later readers, was still selling well four years later);[93] and this year also saw a new six-penny edition of *Diana Tempest*, one of her most popular works. But in July of that year her old friend Howard Sturgis was unwell, yet another reminder of her own mortality.[94] In a letter to Rhoda Broughton written in the same month, her full narrative powers came into play in a description of a plane crash involving her nephew Regie, now a fully fledged pilot. She was staying with her brother at Dorton, his new house,[95] and the whole party motored up to see his plane land, followed by two more planes. It approached at 'a terrific rate' (sixty miles an hour). In the afternoon Regie went up twice more but the second time there was some slight mishap, putting the plane out of action for a few days. By now a crowd of horses and carriages had arrived in the field to watch. As one of the other airmen went up, a fault with the plane caused it to waver and fall upside down two fields away. And the worst of it was that Mary, with her brother and his son, had to remain with the crowd to prevent them rushing towards the fallen plane. In the event both the pilot and his mechanic were rescued with relatively minor injuries – Mary helped to get her own room, as one of the most comfortable in the house, ready for their reception. But she was deeply shaken by witnessing this event, confessing that 'oh! Rhoda I dont want to see any more aeroplanes. All night afterwards I saw it fall!!' Most of all she thought how hard it must have been for Regie and Florie, thinking 'how easily it might have been their splendid son'.[96] This same son, who had not crashed in his plane and so easily might have done, was killed in action in the second year of the First World War.[97]

But in relaying the details of these incidents, Mary presents them as a noteworthy aberration, disrupting the quite tenor of country life. The agony of suspense re-envisioned and communicated to her reader, her thoughts revert to the past, in a clipped postscript aside that defies enquiry or remark – revealing in its very lack of context, the postscript to this letter remarks briefly and with no explanation that she is going back to Shropshire to visit Condover. At this stage of her life she seems to have felt that nothing important would happen to her again.

And so ended 1913, with the publication of a novel about a simple-minded girl who resists sexual fall and marries into a quietly traditional country family. There is no indication in her letters, still less in her writing, that Mary saw the old traditions as being subject to any particular threat.

8 WAR

While Mary had written what would turn out to be her last long work of fiction,[1] she was still being read and 1914 brought a Nelson's Library edition of *Red Pottage*, some fifteen years after the original debacle with Edward Arnold. But more important, unforeseen events would dominate this year. On 13 June Mary was writing to Rhoda Broughton, one of her staunchest friends of the previous century, with jokes about Percy Lubbock's forthcoming marriage to an unnamed woman (in fact he did not marry during Mary's lifetime), and flippant expressions of jealousy because Victoria was making off with a cool dozen of her friends and inviting them to tea on her own account. Brooke was

> the same as ever only more so: full of endless talk on how it is better to be good than pretty (which it isn't) and how happiness is to be found in thinking of others. He is just like the third leading articles in *The Times*.[2]

This report to her old friend, full of Mary's characteristic irony and humour, is her last extant letter written before the outbreak of the First World War. She had in any case broken off her journal in 1911 and her experience of the next few years is recoverable – in so far as it can be recovered – almost entirely through her correspondence with two old friends, Rhoda Broughton and Sir Matthew Nathan.

The summer of 1914 brought notably hot weather; afterwards people remembered picnics under the trees, and in the first two or three weeks of June Mary was busy arranging motoring parties and issuing luncheon invitations from her house in Ufford.[3] It was on 28 June that the Austrian Archduke Ferdinand and his wife were assassinated, and the question of whether or not war would be necessary, even desirable, began to be debated in the national press – *The Times* alone of the major papers was initially in favour of such extreme measures. Then on 1 August Germany – allied to Austria-Hungary – declared war on Russia, and subsequently on its ally France. Belgium was initially a neutral party in this contretemps, but it was also on the most direct route to Paris. When German troops therefore invaded Belgium, Britain was arguably bound to intervene, both on the grounds of its moral obligation to France and by the more specific terms of a treaty binding her to defend Belgium itself in the event of aggression. The real reasons for Britain's decision to enter this European war are difficult to ascertain. But when war was ultimately announced that August, ostensibly in response to the German invasion of Belgium, the government quickly instituted measures to ensure their control over the way it was perceived. The Defence of the Realm Act, amended six times between 1914 and 1918, arrogated to the government power to intervene in the lives of the English people to an unprecedented extent. Among other powers was censorship of information during the war years.

The German invasion of Belgium, then, provided one argument for going to war. But there is evidence to suggest that many of those who signed up in 1914 were wholly ignorant of the cause they were being encouraged to support. Notoriously, the political obligation was translated by propagandists through-out the war into the more accessible aspiration of dying for one's own country, a sentiment with a long tradition of stirring verse to support it. Before the fiascos of trench warfare, young poets such as Rupert Brooke famously envisaged the English soldier as ennobled by the experience of battle, or even death.[4]

It has in fact been suggested that rather than a feeling of obligation towards an unknown European country, more important factors for the surge in volunteers in these first few weeks included the rousing music played by the military bands outside recruitment offices, pressure from women and friends, and also the unemployment caused by the financial crisis in August, itself a result of the war.[5] Mary would no doubt have been among the more informed English observers of foreign events. She read *The Times*, but more importantly, she was acquainted with members of the Cabinet (including Asquith and Churchill), she knew Kitchener himself, and also had a cousin in the Admiralty.[6] Throughout the next few years she would continue to watch not only the progress of the army in the trenches, but also the political repercussions at home.

The atrocities in Belgium, real or exaggerated, may not have been the most important factor in determining public opinion. But a number of writers, Cholmondeley among them, publicly attested their support for the Belgian people as victims of German aggression. In December 1914 the writer Hall Caine ushered in a host of famous names as contributors to *King Albert's Book: A Tribute to the Belgian People from Representative Men and Women throughout the World*, published by the *Telegraph* and other newspapers with Hodder and Stoughton. Other contributors included Asquith, now Prime Minister, Mary's friend Valentine Chiriol, and popular writers such as Marie Corelli as well as the more heavyweight Kipling and Thomas Hardy. Mary's own article, 'Polydore in England', offers an account of looking after a small group of Belgian soldiers in her country cottage. All five soldiers are described as seriously wounded when they are handed over by a 'jaded Red Cross official' at a roadside station, and their sole luggage is comprised of a packet of English picture postcards and one pipe.[7] Neither the regiment nor the hospital named in the article actually existed, but the affectionate rendering of the foreign soldiers' manner and speech suggest that Mary may well have been fictionalizing a real experience as opposed to simply inventing an engaging story. Certainly by 1915 the eastern counties were not allowed to take in Belgian refugees, possibly due to fears that German forces would attack the coast and necessitate a chaotic evacuation.[8]

But it is conceivable that they passed through Ufford; certainly Mary offered her cottage as a retreat to both soldiers and women in the course of the war, and it is known that at some point she did work for the Red Cross.[9] A further piece of evidence is her use of the name 'West Lowshires' for the regiment in which her Private Dawkins, who befriends Polydore, is based. Lowshire was of course her fictional name for Suffolk, first used in *Notwithstanding*, and certainly both she and more particularly Victoria would become engaged in the war effort over the next few years.[10]

Already in evidence in this article is her characteristic strategy of using humour to allay anxiety – she recalls incidents 'too ghastly to be written here'[11] and how at such moments she would ask to hear again about the contemptible fire of the German infantry, how they fired ineffectually from the hip, so different from the Belgian accuracy. And immediately she moves on to the Belgian soldier who expands his chest, as his comrade demonstrates with a tap on his chest button, momentarily diverting the reader as she has already distracted the soldiers themselves. Nonetheless her reference to events 'too ghastly to be written' effectively persuades the reader, if not the Belgian soldier, to dwell on the brutality of the Germans, even as she ostensibly changes the subject. It has been said that 'At every level of society war propaganda did not have to be produced by governments; it produced itself. Academics, journalists, amateur poets and ordinary people churned it out unprompted.'[12]

Lloyd George, then Chancellor of the Exchequer, was explicit in his praise of Belgian heroism and condemnation of the German invader. 'It was Belgian valour that exposed the sinister character of Prussian militarism ... This unfortunate country is now overwhelmed by the barbarian flood',[13] and so on. No opponent of the war on moral grounds is likely to have written for such a book, particularly bearing in mind that Earl Kitchener likewise contributed a passage of exhortation (although to generations who know him largely from the famous poster in which he points sternly at potential recruits, his words on this occasion seem surprisingly moderate).[14] By the end of the war Mary was clearly horrified both by the devastating effect on its victims and by the mismanagement of military operations at the front.[15] But there is no indication in her extant letters that she thought the war itself had been unnecessary, and she certainly invested in a war loan.[16] She is unlikely to have viewed the conflict at any point with patriotic enthusiasm, but to the end she was suspicious of those who failed to assist it.

The first effect of the war on Ufford was the cancellation of a Sunday school outing to Felixstowe that August, but, as the parish magazine reported, Brooke stepped into the breach with a tea on the terrace for the disappointed children.[17] That September he was in the chair for a recruitment meeting in the school-room, and made a speech to an apparently enthusiastic audience, urging them to respond to the call for 500,000 new soldiers by Christmas.[18] Over the next few years a series of regiments would be billeted on the village, a squadron of the Essex Yeomanry in 1914, a section of the Royal Army Medical Corps under Major Brownrigg from 1915 to 1916, and the 327 Field Ambulance under Colonel Haydon in November 1917.[19] Mary would later recall the impact of war on the community of Ufford, or Riff as she calls it, in her preface to her last published work, *The Romance of His Life and Other Romances*:

> We in Riff learned the meaning of war early in the day. Which of us will forget the first Zeppelin raid, and later on the sight of torn, desolated Woodbridge the day after it was bombed: the terrified blanched faces peeping out from the burst doorways ... It seemed as if it could not, could not be! We had seen photographs of similar havoc in Belgium and France, but Woodbridge! ...
>   Yes, the war reached us early, and it left us late.[20]

Instinctively Mary identifies her own small village with the victims of war in Belgium and France, as the English had been encouraged to do in 1914. On All Saints Day that year the collection was sent to Belgians abroad, and again Brooke stepped in with a top-up, making it up to a total of £10.[21] But equally it seems unreal that the devastation abroad could be repeated at home, among people she knows. Mary's name appears on a list of contributors to Christmas presents for Ufford soldiers that year.[22] At least one of them would later return to work on the land, a victim of shell shock. Twenty-two of the young men from Ufford would not come back at all.[23] But it came closer to her than that. One of the first to be affected by this war was her nephew Reginald, son of the brother to whom she would remain closest for the rest of her life. Reginald had obtained his commission in 1909, shortly after leaving Eton. He joined the Royal Flying Corps in 1913 and was made a captain in the Rifle Brigade shortly after the out-break of war, in December 1914.[24]

In these first months of comparative optimism, Mary and Victoria promptly set themselves to assist in the war effort. Back in London Lord Harrington had lent his house in Kensington Palace Gardens, and Victoria had transformed it, with Lady Lugard, into a home for upper-class Belgian refugees. Despite the exclusion of their own class from the home, local tradespeople rallied round, lending furniture, cleaning the windows for nothing and even donating coal. By December 1914 forty Belgians, including fourteen children, had been installed.[25] Flora Lugard herself was too busy to take an active share in the running of the home, but Victoria worked hard to give the children as happy a Christmas as circumstances allowed, working up to twelve hours a day and ruling the place with a 'kind but firm hand'.[26] Mary herself, in London for at least part of that winter, had some of the children to lunch, 'a chastened joy but they seem to like it', as she reported somewhat dubiously.[27] As the war dragged on, Mary would become increasingly worried about her sister, who was 'virtually living' at the home by the summer of 1915 and growing noticeably thinner.[28] She appears on the Visiting Committee of the Hospital Committee for the Relief of Better Class Belgians for 1914–15.[29] Later she would work equally hard for another hospital, at Lady Ridley's house in Carlton House Terrace.[30] Mary was clearly not robust enough to take on this sort of work, but she appears to have been the Honorary Treasurer for the Camberwell and Peckham branch of the Soldiers' and Sailors' Families Association between 1914 and 1915.[31] It is not clear whether Diana, still living in London, was involved in any of these activities, but she is listed as a volunteer for the Queen Alexandra's Field Force Fund in 1916.[32]

Both Diana and Victoria had long experience of nursing their invalid sister as well as their father, but although amateur nursing was one of the options for women of their class, they may have preferred to direct their energies into less familiar kinds of work. Certainly Diana's deafness by this point would have made nursing a difficult occupation, and she seems to have lapsed into a querulous habit of trivial complaining, at least in her dealings with the younger generation. Stella Benson noticed that even her contemporaries spoke to her with a touch of impatience, and comments like 'I dislike the smell of smoke very much, but as you all want to smoke, what does an aunt matter[?]' do not present her at her best. Stella, in a determinedly tolerant mood, worried that for all her peevishness, Diana was acutely sensitive and must regret the lack of love and enjoyment in her life.[33] War or no war, it comes as something of a relief to read that she could be vivacious, even boisterous, with friends of her own age. From 1914 Stella herself was working for Mary's friend Edwin Konstam (whom she greatly admired and whom she was convinced was in love with her aunt Victoria), organizing relief for poor families in the East End district of Hoxton. By March 1915 she was working five and a half days in Hoxton, four evenings with Southwark factory girls and another evening with a Soldiers' and Sailors' Wives club in Bethnal Green. Never strong, it is hardly surprising that she was now, according to her biographer, heading for collapse.[34]

Meanwhile her uncle Reginald, by now too old for active service, was working as an Assistant Commandant at an alien concentration camp on the Isle of Man. It was not the work he would have chosen, but, Mary said, at fifty-five he was 'thankful to be able to serve his country' even in this capacity. There seems to have been some lack of communication at first, as the War Office began sending 400 prisoners daily, to a camp designed to hold 300. According to Mary, it was not the fault of the War Office – the Isle of Man agreed to take these prisoners and then 'took a gentle nap'. Reginald found himself at the end of 1914 with a total of 1,600 prisoners, three inches deep in mud, and with no facilities for washing. On the last day of the year, Mary was recording her hopes for an honourable peace in 1915.[35]

This hope was quickly dispelled. In February 1915 Mary Braddon died, and there was no end to the war in sight.[36] In May Asquith formed a coalition with Lloyd George's Conservatives.[37] The bishop of London, who had once announced his approval of *Red Pottage* from the pulpit of St Paul's Cathedral, now published a collection of sermons glorifying the war.[38] That year the casualties at Ypres, Neuve Chapelle and Loos, followed by losses on the Somme in 1916, meant that by September 1916 conscription had been introduced as an essential measure.[39]

For Mary personally 1915 brought a new edition of *Nothwithstanding*, her story of stolid integrity in the uneventful Riff, otherwise known as Ufford. On its appearance the year before she had been annoyed by the failure of its various reviewers to grasp her central aim in writing it.[40] In this novel, as in *Moth and Rust* and *Prisoners* before it, she had turned away from her spirited and captivating heroines of the *fin de siècle*. Now middle aged and with a knowledge that had come far too late of how her life might have been different, she was conscious too that the story of her own life was not radically different from that of many other middle-aged women. Her writing from the early years of the twentieth century turns increasingly for inspiration to the more commonplace characters of life, the old maid and her counterpart the inflexible old bachelor, the stolid country squire and the unremarkable woman of the world; all the cast of characters she had so wanted to escape when she feared she would spend the rest of her life among them. But within these banal figures she had now begun to locate integrity, the desire for truth, sometimes even hope. Indeed she seems to be fulfilling the prophecy of her own bishop of Southminster in *Red Pottage*, that Hester will come to appreciate the residents of Warpington as she herself grows older and understands them better. As she wrote, 'What pleasure it would have given me if any one of my many reviewers had commented on my problem and its solution!'[41] By 1915 concerns about whether an unhappy young woman had or had not slept with a dissolute aristocrat, and whether his cousin the country squire should believe and indeed marry her further to this escapade, must have seemed unreal to her younger readers.

But in these fraught months her work was nonetheless being appropriated and redeployed, by propagandists with very different aims. An article in the *Fortnightly Review* that February skilfully brought her into the argument on women's employment, by extending her remark that a man sums up women's friendships as 'Occupy till I come' to include male attitudes towards women's work.[42] In the same month her nephew Reginald was mentioned in dispatches.[43] During the spring she herself was ill, and on 12 March Reginald was killed at Neuve Chapelle. He had been loading bombs in his own plane when one of them exploded, killing Regie and ten other men. As his cousin Stella Benson recorded sadly, 'It is impossible to realise that the world no longer contains that pure and jovial soul'.[44] The Parish of Ufford meanwhile offered condolences in the more public language of its time,

> our sympathy is offered very sincerely to Miss Cholmondeley on the occasion of her painful loss, and yet also our congratulations to her and to her family on the distinction of giving so noble a life for the cause of King and Country.[45]

Mary was in Ufford that spring, where she had both her sister Diana and Stella Benson to stay – Stella records going to see the crater made by a falling Zeppelin bomb.[46] It was here that Mary wrote to Matthew Nathan to tell him of Regie's death, 'I cannot tell you what a grief that was and is. He was almost a son to me. And we were so proud of him. ... We have given our very best to this great war, giving our dear child.'[47] It was still possible in 1915 to maintain the traditional terms of bereavement through war – miserable as she was, there is no trace of irony in Mary's way of expressing her loss; Regie has been 'given' to a cause, not, as a future generation might have said, needlessly lost to a faulty bomb.

Ironically it was only a few weeks later that the YMCA tendentiously quoted her own observation that 'To live much in the past is a want of faith in the Power that gives us the present'.[48] Over the summer Mary took in first a soldier seriously wounded in both hands – quite the most cheerful person she had seen for months – and then a Canadian officer's wife, who had been living in one room in London and simply wanted some fresh air.[49] But she was not well, leading a sardonic Stella Benson to fear that she would 'go dead' suddenly while worrying whether Stella was going dead or not. In any case their relationship was considerably more complicated than it had been a few years earlier. Stella complained that her aunt was always trying to break down her 'golden reserve', even when Mary herself did most of the talking.[50] Percy Lubbock would admit independently that 'it was possible she might be too intent – she might pore too closely, cultivate the young plant of confidence too intensively ... That was always her difficulty'.[51] Increasingly Stella was insisting on her right to her own judgement, remarking that Rhoda Broughton's supposedly witty *Cometh Up as a Flower* (1867) was notable for its utter lack of wit, but that there was no point saying this to her aunt, who could not believe that the young could be right about anything.[52] And she was annoyed that Mary had accused her of copying a half page of her first novel, *I Pose*, from *Prisoners*. It is difficult to imagine which half page she could have meant, as Benson's detached, caustic narrative of a militant suffragette and a gardener who assumes various 'poses' could not be more dissimilar to Cholmondeley's realist style. 'I was too polite to tell her that I had just bounced my eye through *Prisoners*, skipping every moral soliloquy, & did not now remember the outline of her story much less any details', wrote Stella acidly in her diary.[53] In fact the one moment of recognition for an outside reader lies in a passage that could have come from Mary's diary, which Stella could not possibly have seen. In satirizing the novelist whose experiences are all stored away as copy for future books, and who comes out with the classic line, 'I have a passion for air. I sometimes think I should die without it',[54] she becomes momentarily expansive:

> Some of us squeeze our copy into little six-shilling novels, or hack it into so many columns for the benefit of an unfeeling press. Some of us live three-score years and ten, and then wake suddenly to find our copy-coffers full. Upon which we become bores, and our relations hasten to engage a paid companion for us. But some of us carry our lives about with us sealed up in our holy of holies.[55]

Mary clearly did not know what to make of the book, although she was generous with her time, reading the proofs twice over. The second time admittedly her doubts seemed to increase, and Stella complained privately 'She seems to want to squeeze out everything that is peculiarly me and turn it into a sort of pretty Cholmondeley book'.[56]

Despite her irritation, and despite Mary's reported put downs, Stella continued to go to her with proofs of her first novels, suggesting that her dependence on her aunt's approval was more ingrained than she wanted to admit. She was going over the proofs of *This is the End* with her a year later, and acknowledging grudgingly that if her aunt was 'rather damping', at least she liked what she grasped of the book, and had praised the ending.[57] Indeed in her less severe moments, Stella was ready to acknowledge that her aunt Mary could be only too enthusiastic where her beloved nephews and nieces were concerned, giving them credit if anything for being more exceptional than they were. She had for instance sent a copy of Stella's poems to Percy Lubbock, and she alludes directly to Benson's work in her own later work.[58]

It was during this autumn that Victoria broke her leg, narrowly avoiding a permanent limp.[59] Mary continued with her usual entertaining, including a party for Elena Rathbone and Bruce Richmond, who had first met at her house and who were now to return as bride and groom. Mary invited Matthew Nathan to be of the party, as he had been present on the first occasion, and in her letter of invitation she makes a rare allusion to her friendship with the more celebrated Henry James, also on the guest list. But she knew that she herself would never write another novel, 'tho' what I am to do without work I don't know; find another kind I suppose'.[60]

Writing to Rhoda Broughon that winter to condole with her on an accident, Mary reported her sister well but working too hard. She was at least to have ten days' respite at the cottage, before going back to her work in London. To lighten the mood Mary draws on her seemingly endless fund of humorous anecdotes, confiding the incident of a recent dinner guest who had been scathing about Lady Balfour turning up at a house on the wrong evening. Mary simply remarked that it was infectious, only reminding him at the end of the evening that she had not invited him to this particular dinner at all. As ever she was ready to laugh at the world and her place in it. Victoria looked very nice in her new gown with pockets on the hips, a vogue which clearly Mary had no intention of taking up. 'It seems right now to look as if you had a bag of potatoes on each hip. I, in my tight old skirts look so old fashioned that I hardly dare go any where except down Earls Court Road.'[61]

By 1916 enthusiasm for the war had abated and the losses of the previous year had made conscription necessary. In January the Military Service Act conscripted all serviceable single men (by now the total number of Ufford men serving in either the Army or the Navy stood at an estimated 13 per cent),[62] and married men were called up that April. It was at this time that the Battle of the Somme, a name so familiar to future generations, brought on the first major wave of desertions. Mary would later recall this as the worst period of the war, an insight that the combined efforts of the press had been anxious to prevent at the time (Stella Benson writes in her diary of victories, albeit marred in her own mind by heavy losses, at the Front that July).[63] It is not clear whether Mary had brought her own clear-sighted attention to bear on this deliberate obfuscation, or whether she gained her information from friends involved in foreign policy. But her interest in governmental politics, so notable in her as a child, is no less obvious in her brief comments on the progress of the war.[64]

In the summer of 1916 the harvest failed.[65] That August the parishioners of Ufford were reminded that it was as patriotic to pay for a shell as to make one, and invited to buy War Certificates.[66] In September the Sunday scholars were busy selling postcards and managed to raise 30s. for the Belgians.[67] Mary kept one letter from this year:

> My home is a little cellar deep down & covered with sand-bags just a few hundred yards from some German machine guns. I live alone here with my terrier who keeps away the rats – rats that for numbers and size would scare the Pied Piper of Hamelin ... When I came here last week I found among a heap of old stuff – papers, food, old clothes, ammunition, & dirt of every description – I found 'Diana Tempest' ... It has helped me much in this depressing work & I am truly grateful to the author.[68]

In December Asquith resigned from office, leaving Lloyd George to take his place as wartime Prime Minister. Meanwhile Mary was taking on a different problem, publishing an article on a new handloom industry operating in small premises in London, partly with the aim of giving disillusioned prostitutes an alternative means of earning a living, without turning them over to the drudgery of mindless, purely mechanical labour. In an echo of Stella Benson, she went so far as to make the point that women should unite to campaign for higher wages. In evidence here too is her refusal to subscribe entirely to the sexual double standard of her time – shifting the focus somewhat from the traditional view of the prostitute as morally lost through rash trust in a man, she redeploys conventional platitudes about the nurturing role of women to configure the male client as himself lost:

> Every woman is potentially a mother ...
> And these women have ruthlessly destroyed that which some other woman has built up in years of devotion. That is one of the principal reasons why some of them have fled with loathing from the predatory life of the prostitute, not only because its poisoned wine is destroying their own souls, but because there is death in the cup for the young ignorant lips to which they proffer it.[69]

In certain respects she even seems to identify with the women whose experience, apparently so different from her own, she is describing. Rejecting the argument that prostitutes fall through a love of luxury, she retaliates by pointing out that for some of them luxury simply means a bath every day and time to go out into the open air during the hours of daylight. What is necessary for them is work, and it is here that she seems, if not literally to conflate her feeling with theirs, at least to move so rapidly between the two subjects as to break down the boundaries between them in the mind of the reader. It is only by an apparent effort that she recalls herself to the question of the specific girls she is supposed to be talking about, moving from a transparently personal use of the third person to the ostensible subject of her article, 'these girls':

> To create something is to feel that you are of use in the world: it gives self-respect. It gives more: creative work leads to peace of mind. The ugly pictures in memory are gradually replaced by harmonious designs. Only those know who have laboured and loved their labour, the healing and serenity that such work brings to the smarting soul which has fallen on the thorns of life. It comes like starlight into the darkened mind. In the case of these girls it sets a gulf between the past and the present.[70]

Despite her determined focus in these lines on an individual past and present, the war itself was a rupture between that past and present, experienced by the whole nation. And it continued to drag on. February 1917 saw the beginning of the German U-boat campaign along the British coast.[71] By the summer Mary was telling Rhoda Broughton that nothing ever happened in Ufford, bar the one terrifying incident of the Zeppelin raid on 17 June[72] – although she could not know it, this attack would be the last of the war to affect the residents of the village. In the introduction to her last volume of stories, she recalls the attack in detail. She had woken up to hear bombs at around 3 a.m. and the walls of the cottage shook as if they had been made of paper. She could not see the plane in the dark but she could hear anti-aircraft fire. What follows is presented as a kind of apocalypse. Mary and her visitors watched through the dawn as the Zeppelin caught fire and flamed from end to end. Then from every throat in the village rose 'a shout of triumph, the shrill cries of the children joining with the voices of the elders'. And then the smoke rose:

> like some solemn upraised finger pointing from earth to heaven.
> No one stirred. No one spoke. The light grew. And, in the silence of our awed hearts, a cuckoo near at hand began calling gently to the new day, coming up in peace out of the shining east.[73]

The symbolism is nothing if not heavy. But the triumph of the children is a darker moment than Mary intends, as is the image of the villagers spectating as the plane falls. In her letter to Rhoda Broughton, Mary treats the incident altogether less poetically, although the voyeuristic triumph is in evidence here too. She describes it as 'an hour of deafening bombardment and bomb dropping in the dark' before they could finally see the plane outlined against the dawn, and watched it slowly sinking in flames. Mary alone did not go to look at the wreck, and she was only glad it had happened before her sister Essex arrived to recover after an illness. Essex is not mentioned often in Mary's last diary, but in this letter written a few years later the affection between the sisters is obvious, as Mary praises her cheerfulness and willingness to be pleased, stating almost as a matter of course that Victoria had taken the difficult part of the nursing into her own hands. But serious topics are not allowed to predominate, and Mary follows up these accounts in the letter to Broughton with a remark on the humourless local rector, who has been admonishing his congregation with the story of the parents of John the Baptist, who led holy lives although nothing seemed to come of it. But something did come of it, the holy child was born to them. So Mary has not been to church quite so often lately for fear she too like a second Elizabeth might have a holy child. Only in that case, she goes on, Brooke ought to have a dozen at least. The little she has seen of him has led her to fear he is 'less normal year by year'. Apparently he had told Diana that he thought he was jolly mad, and told Mary herself that the whole world had gone mad. And to her fury he was still, in this third year of the war, deliberating whether or not to give his large and empty house as a convalescent home.[74]

Typically in her letters from these years, Mary resolutely tenders anecdotes and sprigs of gossip, interspersed with matter of fact allusions to the backdrop of ongoing war. She says now that she is writing in a tremendous thunderstorm, and cannot believe with every clap that the village is not undergoing a Zeppelin raid. But of course the clap of thunder has not after it the sickening quiver of the falling bomb. She goes on to tell Rhoda that she stayed in the garden for an hour in the last raid, as her cottage shook so that she was not sure it would stand even if it was not hit. And all the time she was comfortably unaware that a neighbouring garden was being plastered with shrapnel.

Rhoda herself seems to have been more struck by the signs of Brooke's growing eccentricity than by the account of Zeppelins and flying shrapnel. In her next letter Mary is grieved that she has 'taken this foolish comedy so much to heart'. She admits that her brothers warned her against coming to Ufford as his tenant, although neither of them has been unkind enough to say 'I told you so'. By this stage it seems that Brooke had threatened her with a court summons on some grounds or other, and as she and the other principal residents of the village had all taken the side of the poor in another dispute, he was now pouring forth abuse by letter, and, she could not resist adding with delight, 'Even the morals of my books have not escaped'. For some weeks previous even to this she had been denied her daily walk, the habit of ten years, across his garden and into the park to a certain pretty lawn. Brooke had told her that for reasons connected with religion and the war, he would from now on be locking the gate. Mary herself agreed that regrettably they ought to leave. But she was unwilling to cross Victoria, who had put so much work into the garden. And besides, the cottage was to be let to a couple over the summer. These reassurances duly administered, Mary then passes to the latest war news. Her cousin in the admiralty had told her that German submarines were instructed to practice sinking the unmanned English fishing trawlers before taking on more important targets; but in two recent instances the trawler had unmasked a gun and sunk its antagonist. The result was that the submarines had almost ceased attacking trawlers along the coast. Her cousin had given her leave to repeat this heartening tale. Returning to the most immediate source of concern to her correspondent, the postscript of the letter is an assurance that Brooke hardly knows what he is saying or doing.[75]

Mary herself was in London now, helping Victoria, who was working 'with a kind of enthusiastic doggedness'[76] at Lady Ridley's London house at Carlton House Terrace (now the British Academy), which had been adapted for use as a military hospital in collaboration with the Red Cross Society. While an assembly of doctors and nurses looked after the inmates, volunteers involved themselves in the administrative work that continued to pile up. No detailed records of Mary's work here survive, and it is unclear precisely what she was doing in the spring and summer of that year, but what is known is that she began her work for the Wounded and Missing Detachment in April 1917.[77] Stella Benson had briefly worked here as well, finding it far less congenial than her usual work among the poor of Shoreditch. With characteristic asperity, she recalled the incongruity of the splendid house and '"beautifully gowned" workers flitting about', and was infuriated by the condescension of 'gabbling Mayfair females who don't know what work is'.[78] Meanwhile news of the war at the Front continued to arrive through Sir Matthew Nathan, who would report back after breakfasts with Lloyd George and Sir Edward Carson; and Mary herself would pass on details 'direct at fifth-hand from the Admiralty'.[79]

On 17 September 1917 there was a mutiny at the military base at Étaples. That autumn Mary had spent a week at Dorton with Regie and Florie,[80] who had taken in a houseful of wounded Belgian soldiers and had the gramophone and piano playing all day long. Many of these soldiers, Mary told Rhoda, came back each year for their holidays from the trenches, having nowhere else to go. Then back to Ufford, where she had the chairman of the parish council to dine, in order to discuss the question of Brooke and the right of way. The mere mention of her landlord was usually enough to bring on a fit of combined amusement and exasperation – had she ever told Rhoda about his lament that England would never be the same again after the war? 'No more room maids! No more house-keeper's rooms!'[81] Of more immediate concern to Mary, who suffered badly from the cold, was the fear that coal would soon be compulsorily rationed.

While these conferences were taking place in Ufford, Victoria was actually planning to rest for a weekend, and visit Essex at the seaside. So Mary was to go up to London and take her place at the office. She had, she confided to Rhoda, strict injunctions only to deal with the correspondence she understood, and not to meddle in matters too high for her. It is interesting to remember here that while her diary may talk about 'ugliness and incompetence' as the obstacles she had early had to face and overcome, she had once described herself to Bentley as 'an orderly, methodical person'. Now she is almost ostentatiously playing the disorganized one – the one who need no longer take responsibility for managing large num-bers of people. She recalled with some amusement that she had made one or two bad mistakes, but if only Percy and Miss Howard would listen to her for about two hours she could explain how it happened. Here she is led away by an anecdote about the Custom House fining her for supposedly importing sugar, which had arrived as a present from Dick in Australia. When the next parcel arrived she was threatened with legal proceedings. Between the Custom House on the one hand and Brooke on the other, she thought she should hardly emerge alive.

Thinking it better to set her house in order while she is still 'at large', here at the very end of the letter, as a sort of afterthought, is a reference to her literary work, the 'flame' which had kept her alive for so many years now.[82] She had been to see Murray about bringing out a 'little book' after Christmas. She was clearly nervous about discussing this 'little book'; writing another letter the next day to say that she has called on Murray, she apparently forgets that she has broached the subject at all, and admits that she trembles in her shoes wondering what her brothers (strangely she talks about her 'two brothers', presumably being less con-cerned about a written reproof from Australia) will have to say. What she sees as character drawing, she fears they will interpret as disloyalty. Though Mary does not name it, the book in question was *Under One Roof*, the result of her work begun more than ten years earlier, when she first set herself to fulfil her promise, and start arranging the papers of her dead sister Hester.

This second letter is equally remarkable in other respects. It begins on an apparently light-hearted note, with, 'We live in stirring times', as Rhoda had apparently accused her of having said when she bought a new coat. But just one day after her entertaining account of her own maladministration at Carlton House Terrace, Mary goes on to suppose that Victoria only tells Rhoda the humorous side of her work there, and the delightful things the soldiers say to her. For it is, she now admits, heartbreaking, and she has no idea how Victoria keeps up her power of sustained work there. Now that the winter has set in, Mary herself no longer works on site. Her new work, she tells Rhoda, is to bring home quantities of reports and work out from them what a given regiment was doing on a particular day; she then writes a letter to be reproduced for the families of soldiers missing in action. She has written nineteen so far, all but three relating to disasters – tragedies in which whole companies were destroyed; attacks that were hopeless from the first, our own artillery killing our men; failures owing to lack of support when trenches had been gallantly won, etc. She cannot of course allude to these events as they happened, but makes suitably guarded references to the movements of the regiment on the day in question.[83] This deliberate obfuscation was characteristic of the way people at the time were encouraged to write and speak about the war – after 1916 the parents of soldiers shot for desertion or insubordination were told that they had 'died of wounds'. As one literary historian puts it, 'The war began for the British in a context of jargon and verbal delicacy, and it proceeded in an atmosphere of euphemism as rigorous and impenetrable as language and literature skilfully used could make it'.[84]

Mary's youth in the Shropshire rectory must have seemed a world away. But fifty years later her letters to Rhoda show much of the same personality that comes through in her first journal written while she was still in the schoolroom; the ready irony and the political urgency – she is glad Lloyd George has pulled through, 'He is the best we have got, tho' he is an impulsive ignorant creature' – only partially screening the controlled despair, 'Week follows week and our lives are exactly the same'.[85] Mary was following the events of the war closely. She feared for the Tommies so delighted to go to Italy from Flanders, stood amazed at the efficiency and enthusiasm of the American allies, found time in the middle of it all to ask Rhoda what she thought of Edith Wharton's *Summer*, and, of course, to fear for the reception of her own new work.

In this instance Mary quite possibly had reason to feel apprehensive. While *Under One Roof*, dedicated to her brother Tom, contains loving and sometimes poignant recollections of family life in late Victorian Shropshire, it also presents a stark picture of her own position in that household, and there is little doubt allowed as to where she places the blame. While the book began as a memoir of Hester, Mary decided, as she says in her introduction, that the short life of a woman who never became known beyond her own circle would attract little attention so many years after her death. She admits to the temptation she as a writer would feel not to present her sister as she was but to turn her into a fictional creation. Somehow she convinces herself that by placing Hester in the context of the family in general, she will be able to obviate this dilemma. And so what she does is to offer sketches of Hester, her parents and the family nurse Frances Coupland (Ninny). In so doing she contrives, consciously or not, to present a version of her own difficult place in that family, without damaging her sense of her own privacy or deflecting the focus of attention too completely from Hester herself. As one critic of women's writing has suggested, some write memoirs as opposed to personal autobiographies 'because it allows them ... to tell their stories between the lines, to narrate their histories as part of a larger story'.[86]

In this 'family record' (the subtitle of the book) her father is a largely unproblematic figure, disorganized in his affairs but large hearted and benevolent, not particularly intellectual but gifted in the arrangement of the china and pictures in which Mary and her siblings delighted. The constant wear and frustration of the parochial duties he imposed on her are seemingly forgotten, and that aspect of her life in Hodnet merits only the passing comment that as they grew older he involved all the children in his work. Their old nurse is lovingly pictured, and Mary makes the rather startling claim that her love was greater than that of the parents themselves, bestowed as it was on children who were not even her own.[87]

Her presentation of her mother is more ambiguous by far, and she seems wholly unaware even that she contradicts herself from one page to the next. Admitting that her mother both wrote the plays for her children's theatre and sang in accompaniment, she describes the scripts as 'vivid, dramatic, and in a flowing verse which children could understand'. It comes as a shock then to be told a few pages later that 'the artistic side of life did not appeal to her. It repelled her.'[88] Mary is adamant that her mother had no aesthetic sense, took no pleasure in beautiful things and would have enjoyed life as a don because it would have rescued her from all contact with the complex world of other people. She evidently forgets her own letter to Richard Bentley at the time of Emily's death, saying that her mother had died 'a poet's death', finally killed by her intense enjoyment of a piece of music.[89] But she recollects in *Under One Roof* how her mother, whose beautiful hands were not dextrous, was unstinting in the creation of paper boats which her children then ruthlessly destroyed. She might also have recalled that it was her mother who usually left Christmas bonbons under the younger children's pillows, and wrote the accompanying cards from the fairies. Instead she claims that her mother should have been 'a bachelor professor in a white-washed laboratory, instead of the invalided mother of many children'.[90] And the proud parent who once 'went into ecstasies'[91] over her daughter's new wardrobe is now remembered only for resolutely putting her children into plain undergarments, such as the poor were obliged to wear. Mary comments that one of the reasons for her father's almost intrusive interest in his children's appearance was probably that their mother showed so little interest.

Clearly these accusations, with their constant implication of maternal unfitness, are not met by the facts that Mary herself also musters. In the four character sketches given in *Under One Roof*, this is the only one to show signs of vindictiveness. One of the reasons lies in the account she gives of her own assumption of the housekeeping responsibilities at such a young age. From her diary written at the time it seems that her mother's abandonment of this role came abruptly in the wake of a serious illness, and at a time when, to complicate matters, Dick had scarlatina.[92] The scathing account offered in retrospect is misleading here to say the least:

> Even before her health failed, her mind could not grapple with the practical side of life. Her housekeeping was non-existent ... At sixteen it became necessary that I should leave the schoolroom and undertake the management of our household of eighteen people. I never received from her any hint as to how to perform that duty. I feel sure she did not withhold knowledge. She had it not.[93]

Very similar reflections would one day be made on Mary herself, who in later life would be only too happy to leave the housekeeping to Victoria. This suggests one of the reasons for her deep-seated and abiding resentment of her mother. Not only was she still blaming her, over forty years later, for thrusting her young and ill equipped into adult life. In many respects she was also very like her.

It is quite possible that she blamed her mother for her own ongoing invalidism, forgetting that there was asthma on her father's side as well – in the 1890s she had written to Bentley of the 'hereditary taint'[94] responsible for her condition, a cruel enough expression more generally used to suggest hereditary insanity or even venereal disease. And now she wrote, 'The Spartan element in her succeeded better in the rearing of her strong children than her delicate ones'.[95] But her accounts of her mother's heroic response to her own debilitating depression and constant illness read uncannily as if she were writing about periods of her own life. As Emily grew older she became increasingly incapacitated by creeping paralysis and, her daughter recalled, 'She had never, even in youth, possessed buoyancy of temperament' but 'She was sometimes helped by her sense of humour. I have seen her laugh till she cried over parts of Dickens ... I have seen her smile grimly at her own expense. But these were only momentary gleams across long stretches of gloom.' She even uses the very term applied to her own mental afflictions in her journal, referring to Emily's 'anxious, over-apprehensive mind'. And in her mother's increasing alienation from the rest of her family, she is finally able to feel pity, even perhaps empathy. 'How often she must have felt lonely, thwarted, misunderstood!'[96]

It is impossible to say how far Mary saw her mother in herself. To her own mind, the rendering of her mother's portrait apparently seems straightforward enough, and it is rather the account of Hester that she admits to be problematic. For in writing this part she comes up against her sister's minute recollections of the years in Hodnet, in which Mary's own sad story of the young man who visited the house regularly for seven years, and then went away, must have figured. Well might she say, 'It is a grave moment when one looks back into the same past through the eyes of another'.[97] But if the reading of her sister's journals was painful in connection with her own life Mary gives no indication of it. She admits to being confused, confronted with her sister's narrative, as she tries to order her own memories. Still she must 'do the best I can. For there is no one else to take up the task if I relinquish it.'[98]

Hester's tragedy, Mary never forgot, was that she had died too young to take up the fight herself. In her account of her sister, she uses terms she had applied to her own life. Possessed of great gifts, Hester had also had 'an indomitable determination and energy, which often go further in the long run than talent'. For a woman to make a literary career for herself when Hester was young was not easy, as Mary well knew. And her sister had had 'no time'. No wonder that the image she turns to is of a war, a battle to be fought. 'But she had no time. Before she could sharpen her blade, before she could even disentangle it from the scabbard, it fell from her eager childish hand.'[99] It could so easily have been the fate of Mary herself. Once more before her own death, in one of the last stories she ever wrote, 'The Goldfish', she would revisit this theme of the young and creative woman, whose sole desire for work is routinely thwarted.

But if Mary herself thought that she had written the tragic story of a woman who lived and died before her time, one member of the new generation was largely unimpressed. Stella Benson had herself undergone a battle to leave home, to pursue a writing career and to work long hours among people whom she could hardly have introduced to her mother. Fully cognizant of the internalized pressures that prevented women even of her own generation from seeking independence, she had little time for the constraints of class consciousness that she saw as largely responsible. From her closer position, her excoriating attack on the older generation is both penetrating and merciless:

> I think [*Under One Roof*] misses a lot of chances of explaining a misunderstood generation to the present lot. Aunt Hester seems to have followed much the same lines as me to a certain point, but of course never got the chance of freedom & the feeling for work, as I have. If she had lived I think she would only have collected like the other aunts a lot of amateur interests. It was apparently the only thing to do in their generation, nobody could so far forget they were ladies as to break away at all.[100]

To later generations, the tragedy of all the Cholmondeley girls lies in precisely this adherence to social expectation, their undoubted talents for writing and painting trammelled by their acceptance that the only way of leaving home was through marriage. From here it takes only a leap of imagination to establish the classic narrative of female ambition thwarted by a purblind society – it takes someone much closer to that world to insist so directly on the complicity of the women themselves. A successful rebel herself, what Stella cannot see or will not acknowledge is the anger in Mary's presentation of the ways of her youth.

But if her mind was running largely on the past in these days, Mary was also contending with what would prove the final stages of the war later generations would see as the turning point between her time and theirs. In February she was in London, arranging dinner parties and accepting pragmatically that no one would have time to change into evening dress when they attended them. Despite earlier disagreements, she was still in touch with Hugh Walpole, inviting him to dine with Sir Valentine Chiriol and praising his book *The Dark Tourist*.[101]

That summer her nephew Hugh, Reginald's only surviving son, left Eton for the trenches with the Coldstream Guards, from whence he would send home reports of having to pass under fire to get his meals, but also of his flower arrangements in the mess, using empty shells to put the flowers in; and of the kitten with the 'angelic face' who lived with him in his dugout.[102] Meanwhile Mary, quite possibly at his request, published a humorous article, 'How to be Happy on Railway Journeys', in his old school magazine, published in aid of the Red Cross. Quite simply the title referred to a game supposedly played during the Boer War. The aim was to induce a fellow traveller to open a conversation, and points were awarded according to the perceived inaccessibility of the passenger selected. 'Young ladies of open-work stockings and a haughty manner, immersed in a novel and a box of caramels, score *six*. Archbishops and newly-married couples score *ten*. We have no instance on record when *ten* has ever been scored.'[103] In her private journal at the time, Mary had been far from finding amusement in the Boer War, and her letters of the next few months show that she was no less anxious during the last year of this 'war to end all wars'.[104]

Apart from her constant anxiety about Hugh, and her equal solicitude for her favourite brother, whose suspense was so much worse, she was clearly worried about Victoria. Insisting to Rhoda that she had not the influence over Victoria that her friend thought she possessed, she was able to reassure her that for the first time in her life she was free from indigestion and the small ailments that attacked her every winter. Furthermore, she had reached a state of mental calm and power which took friction and anxiety from her: those two causes of fatigue and brain weariness (as Mary herself had good reason to know). But despite her apparent health, Victoria was determined to 'spend herself' for her country – 'with us all I think it is the anxiety about the war that is beginning to tell on us. It never lifts its weight, and it is easier to bear when one is fully occupied. I think V feels it at times a relief to throw herself into her work.' Nineteen Ufford lads were dead and, Mary told Rhoda, she could not help hoping for peace that autumn. Meanwhile sales of *Under One Roof* continued to be modest but steady. Mary herself saw almost no one, which she said made her mind less about the spots wearing through into 'ugly hooks' with which she and others of her friends were now afflicted. But she was free of asthma and, after a further access of rage, Brooke had apparently offered her his cordial forgiveness, saying that he never remembered injuries done to himself. Again Mary moves on, with no obvious rush, from the anguish she feels for her brother Regie, whose only remaining son was in the trenches, through Brooke's latest escapades, to the amusing comment of an unmarried mother – her older child had told his mother she 'should not have had Emily', and that Arthur always knew what was right, being a clergyman's son.[105]

July brought promising news, in the shape of a French victory in the Marne. In Ufford Mary took in a couple of her country neighbours for three days while they moved house – a long enough time, as they never picked up a book, but, she hastened to add, somewhat guiltily, he was involved with food control, as well as the Defence of the Realm and the getting up of volunteers. Here Mary's ambivalent attitude, even at the end of the war, is at its most visible. While she had come to dread the thought of further conflict, she is supporting as a matter of course the authorities whose 'valuable work' includes press censorship and propaganda. She was eager for his opinion on the current state of the war. Was it true, as her brother Reginald believed, that the Germans were planning an invasion? To which the reply was that they had tried, and their submarines had been sunk. Less hopefully, he was also disparaging about the High Command of the volunteers, who had apparently ordered men of sixty to march through the rain for twenty miles without their overcoats. She was expecting Regie, still deeply anxious about his son, for the August bank holiday; and looking forward too to the arrival of Victoria and Essex, whose daughter Stella they now heard had reached America safely.[106] It was during this visit that a Zeppelin raid sounded overhead, and she with her 'vast experience' of raids, was able to assure Regie that it was not practice, although in the event it did not come near them. She was also just finishing a story, 'The Stars in Their Courses', 'about an asthmatic old maid who hid in a cottage. Is not that an alluring subject!'[107] The story centres round a woman in later middle age, who lives on excellent terms with her landlord, a rejected suitor from her youth, until his new wife takes a dislike to her because her niece appears set to marry the man she wants for her own daughter. The 'old maid' from the cottage is then exiled on the orders of this wife, who claims that she sees her destiny 'in the stars' and it is not in the village. In the same self-deprecating vein, she hopes Rhoda will like to hear that a course of bacon has now cleared her of spots.

Then too she was to let the cottage while she returned to London to keep an eye on Victoria. She was busy getting things ready as if her tenants were 'entirely paralysed', and noted with evident amusement that her landlord was choosing this period – for the first time in eleven years – to pay his respects to the cottage in the evenings. He was in trouble with the water authorities now for failing to clear out his dykes in twenty-five years, a serious matter in the marshy country round Ufford. Mary could not resist quoting his exact words as he looked round at the assembled company, that he had written back saying, 'they were very ignorant about my estate as there is not a single water course in it'.[108] It was a few weeks later, on his own very different property in Australia, that her brother Dick died suddenly, sitting on the verandah with a copy of *Red Pottage* in his hand.[109]

But the war, as Mary had hoped, was coming to an end. In October she reported that Victoria had banned her from going in to the office – by this time they had been relegated to makeshift huts on the terrace, which must have been freezing during the premature cold spell. Victoria herself was now hoarding beads, as methodical in wresting them from her, remarked Mary, as the Germans in deporting young females from Belgium. There was a man in the hospital known as the Bead King, who made them into chains which he then sold back to them at extortionate rates. Mary, although banned from going to the office, was sedulously working at home, making her way through forty-six cases all requiring a special letter which no one else had time to write. Mothers whose sons were officially dead and buried 'have a feeling' they might be 'suffering from loss of memory' and enclosed photographs, or a last letter, to help her to identify them. She should not, she told Rhoda grimly, like to be one of those who brought about this war when the Day of Judgement arrived.[110]

Mary's next letter is dated 18 November, one week after the news that the Great War had finally come to an end. In the immediate aftermath of the news, Londoners had been terrified by all the noise, thinking they were the victims of another air raid. Regie's daughter Mary, 'that stately calm personage', had run hatless down the street calling that it was peace.[111] Overwhelmed by the magnitude of it, Mary let fly at Rhoda with the thoughts that now came crowding in on her. Hugh never to go back to the front. Oranges for Christmas. The Swiss would have to take home rule. A serge all-in-one gown from Bradley, braided in broad lace from the neck to the foot. She supposed it was her duty to resist the urge to get drunk.

Her response to the ending of hostilities is telling, in that she takes as read the moral victory of the English Parliament who had declared war in the first place, regarding the nation as heroic even as she admits to her own nervous exhaustion. Certainly she has no time for neutral Switzerland, a country she insists on presenting as having been in cahoots with Germany:

> My dear Rhoda I am tired to death, are you? I suppose emotion is fatiguing at all ages, but it is <u>prostrating</u> when one's hair is white. I am afraid England has a bad time coming, but I hope and pray ignorant hands wont pull her down, for we are at this moment the greatest nation in the world.[112]

But despite her prostration the note of exultation – even jingoism – is obvious. And she reports to Rhoda that even the pessimistic Valentine Chiriol had telephoned to say that he was entirely satisfied with the armistice.

The 'stately calm personage' Regie's daughter was staying with her aunt Mary, but out all day with her husband-to-be Roger Plowden. Both his brothers had been killed in the war, his mother had died before it began and his father in the course of it. He himself had been over the top five times. Now he was waiting to be married, the wedding having had to be put off when Florie fell victim to the influenza epidemic now sweeping Europe. Regie himself was not entirely well. As Mary confided to Rhoda,

> My brother Reginald and I who have always a great deal in common have at last confided to each other – we have both become very thin – that life for both of us has become one long stomach ache! I cured myself by fat bacon, but he is still suffering intermittently.[113]

Not only was Mary thin, but she was forced to invest in a bottle of Harle's hair restorer, having found the war 'a great depilatory'. But again she came back to the old refrain, what a relief it was. She wished her brother Dick had lived to see it.

9 'I DONT THINK I WAS EVER BRAVE':
THE ROMANCE OF HIS LIFE (1921)
AND THE LONGING FOR REST

Mary was still keeping abreast of the peace negotiations, expressing concerns about the American President Wilson,[1] who would in fact disagree with both Britain and France over the terms of the settlement. She would remain convinced that Kitchener had been right in warning against plans for a German invasion of England itself, which helps to explain something very like hatred in her response to Germany and its allies.[2] But these last months of the year were not given over entirely to reflection. A week after the armistice, Victoria was in Ufford with Essex, working on her new initiative to help disabled soldiers by teaching them to paint on old furniture. The new work and the armistice combined to restore Victoria's health, and she now began to busy herself once again in the garden of the cottage. Even before the coming of peace it had become clear that, despite Percy Lubbock's tenacity, the hospital would have to do without her as she began her new furniture project.[3] In January 1919 Mary reported to Rhoda that she was writing because Victoria was too busy with her work. The dining room and morning room had been turned into workshops, and a subtle aroma of stove oil was blending with paint and cheap tobacco all over the house. Two disabled soldiers were comfortably installed and making great progress – with the war safely over, Mary risks a joke about one of them being so stout that she would have thought the bullet to his stomach would have got lost as in a maze. But Victoria worked with them all day, showing them how to paint trays with regimental badges, stools, tables, chests and mirrors. The house was crammed with wet furniture and a resigned Mary relays the story of a van stopping at the door and solemnly expectorating no fewer than thirty tables – they had been expecting six.[4]

That of course was the moment when a wounded Hugh arrived asking them to take him in, which they duly did. He was growing strong and handsome now, 'but oh! such a child to have been through all he has been through'. And just as she was writing this, the arrival of a telegram to say that he had been awarded a Military Cross for gallantry during the crossing of the Canal du Nord, first rushing his platoon to aid an advanced post and later remaining on his feet to command his troops hours after half his heel had been cut through by flying shrapnel. He was not, Mary went on, 'the least a soldier by nature, a rather dreamy, artistic youth. When Victoria was with his family a week ago Hugh and another comrade in arms played games on the floor with toy trains!'[5]

Now Mary, as many others must have done, could start to rework the significance of the war in her own mind. Her impressions of course were not of battles or trench warfare, but of the impact on those who had remained at home. She was drawn to Barrie's *Echoes of the War* (1918), with its humour and its sympathy for the marginalized and the lonely: the father who feels displaced by a young fighting generation, the woman who pretends to have a son at the Front because without one it is everyone's war but hers. Notwithstanding Victoria's determined efforts at Carlton House Terrace, they were both entertained by E. M. Delafield's *The War Workers* (1919), in which an upper-class woman devotes herself to hospital administration not least because it makes her feel she is being 'splendid'. She is satirized with only a little more mercy than her mother's friend Mrs Willoughby, who declares rapturously at one point, 'I adore Belgians – positively adore them!'[6]

Meanwhile the work for Victoria's new project went on. She was planning to take furniture up to Liverpool in March, for an exhibition of work by disabled soldiers. One cold and dry Friday in February the house in Leonard Place emptied a vast confusion of chests, tables, mirrors, frames and chairs into a lorry, which then set off with Victoria in it (the soldiers knew better than to risk their wounds and took the tube) for new premises in the Caledonian Road. There she now went every morning in all weathers, despite many anxieties and what Mary circumspectly referred to as 'a little labour trouble'. Loyal as she was, Mary could not help admitting that it was pleasant to have the use of the dining room again and promptly asked some friends to dinner. But she was clearly not in good health herself, and more than that, she was generally unsettled. The end of the war had not diminished her anxieties, although she could now remark on how odd it seemed to feel safe. 'I have never forgotten the bored anger I used to feel as soon as the first distant bomb reached my ear.' On her doctor's orders she was immersing herself in a Turkish bath every fortnight, and she was worried about the perpetual threat of strikes, which she convinced herself were instigated by political radicals in order to bring about anarchy.[7]

But in these days after the war Mary was writing to Rhoda not just about the changes affecting them and their friends. Mrs Humphry Ward had just published her autobiography, and her failure to mention either Mary or Rhoda among her illustrious acquaintance did not go unnoticed. But what a useful happy life she must have had, and what perfect health and prosperity and wealth: 'I do envy her the health especially, and a sort of satisfaction she seems to have'.[8] Evidently

Mary Ward was as adept at concealing her ill health as Mary Cholmondeley herself – she had in fact suffered a series of illnesses over many years, including periodic bouts of neuralgia.[9]

It was many years now since Mary Cholmondeley had kept a diary, but she was still, to use Lubbock's expression, 'beating in solitary hours against the barriers that were round her life'.[10] Still she was working, and 'swelled with pride' at Rhoda's praise of 'Stars'. She had, she told her in confidence, received £100 for it between England and America, and never was money more urgently needed. Victoria was now 'most unkindly' pressing her to write another to meet that year's deficit. As a cook of theirs had always said, 'You can't make somethink out of nothink'. But this was precisely what writers, now 'our unhappy profession', had to do. With her masterpiece now twenty years behind her, and the new generation of post-war modernist writers poised to take the place of this once celebrated Victorian, she told Rhoda, 'My imagination has dropped dead into the giant crevasse of the war'.[11]

That spring brought further anxieties, as Mary and Victoria both fell ill. Worse, their sister Essex, although unwell herself, was nursing their old Shropshire friend Rowland Corbet through his final illness. They could only hope that the old man, whose hopes were now fixed on death, would not linger for too long (in fact he died a few days after this comment, on 4 April).[12] It seemed to her that everyone she knew was either just falling ill, or dead, or trying to get better. Among other friends she must have had in mind Anne Thackeray Ritchie, who had encouraged her as a girl and who had now died on the Isle of Wight.[13] She tried to rally herself from the yellow fog that she decided had got into her pen, and managed to express a hope that she would before long 'be strolling hand in hand with Brooke through buttercupped meadows'. And there was cheering news after all. Her brother Regie had been honourably mentioned in *The Times* for his war work; and Percy Lubbock, who was deserving of any happiness, was setting off to Italy, where he would take up permanent residence in the year after Mary's death.[14] But still, while the Carlton House Terrace hospital had officially closed, her work for it went on – there remained 60,000 soldiers missing and unaccounted for. Mary was, as she put it, 'drooping' with regard to the Peace Conference, and all were in need of 'spring and peace, and Cooper's Oxford Marmalade, and half a pound of butter apiece a week'.[15] To make matters worse, she found that she would not be able to renew the lease on her house in Leonard Place. As she approached her sixtieth birthday, yet another home was to be lost to her and she would have to begin again the arduous business of house hunting. To add to the stress, she was desperately worried about money.

In this first year after the war Stella Benson's third novel, *Living Alone*, appeared. Set in the London of falling bombs and charitable committees, it features an impecunious witch who runs a boarding house for which the residents pay no rent and agree among other things not to burden each other with too much conversation. The novel stands as a fine example of what we would now call 'magical realism', but it could in no respect be termed what Stella had once dismissively called a 'pretty Cholmondeley book'.[16]

In Ufford that spring, Mary was exuberant about the luxury in which she now found herself after the deprivations of London; there was a leg of mutton in the larder, and a pound of butter; in the cellar a ton of coal. 'A ton do you realise, I, who have seen nothing but hundredweight for months past.'[17] She felt, she told Rhoda Broughton, that she ought to throw a ring into the sea. But this unwonted luxury by no means signalled the end of her financial problems, and she sympathized entirely when Rhoda had to refuse an invitation to Ufford on the grounds that she could not afford it (Rhoda herself would continue to publish novels until her death the following year, but she would never again be a celebrated writer).[18] *Under One Roof*, which Mary had hoped would tide her over for the time being, had brought in only £27 (slightly less after commission), although it would continue to bring in small sums until 1920, and she was forced to write a story for *Pear's Annual* to bring in some extra cash.[19] The theme of the collection was to be events taking place in fifty years' time, and Mary's contribution was a story about a man who lies in a coma after being shot in the trenches, only to wake up in the 1960s. The story treats the war only briefly, charting the military career of John Damer, who enlists 'all patriotism and good cheer' for what he thinks will be a short conflict. Coming to feel profoundly unhappy when, a year later, there is no sign of a quick end to the war, he is still prepared to fight not for European allies, but because this was 'England in peril calling to him her son who dumbly loved her, to come to her aid'.[20] Among monotony, mud and lack of sleep against the roar of guns, he is shot and falls forward senseless, and comes round fifty years later after a groundbreaking operation. The story is remarkable not so much for its ingrained sense of patriotism as for the continuing concern with women's rights that it evinces. To Mary's disbelief the story was returned by the editor with a request to make it 'six inches shorter'.[21] She was not amused, but, as she grimly put it, cupidity gained the day and she complied with his request.

However other anxieties were at last beginning to lift. In May 1919 Victoria had a successful exhibition for the YMCA but she was finally closing down her workshops and winding up her work with the soldiers, while Mary was remarking that she herself deserved an Order of the British Empire for having kept up her Thursday dinners all through the war. But she had had enough of London for the time, and leaving the house in Leonard Place with her sister as a tenant, she decamped to Ufford, where 'Instead of struggling to get into a no 9 I wander in a little wood of dancing green, and pick a bunch of cowslips and bluebells'.[22]

As ever she was able to regale Rhoda with Brooke's latest escapades. He was putting up a memorial in the church, with a soldier and a sailor holding a cross

– above it was to be not an angel, nor a deity, but his own coat of arms. 'Priceless', was Mary's comment on this act of self-glorification. There was further trouble when Mary, thinking that she was getting on with him much better of late, spoke to him about his obligations to her roof, which was not in a good way. Brooke flatly refused to contribute to the cost on the grounds that she spent so little time in the cottage, winding up with the words, 'From what I hear the short time you are here makes in no way towards the calming of the world's unrest, and makes several more besides myself wish you never came here at all. However it is a burden we must bear.'[23] So that was the end of that. But roof or no roof, guests continued to arrive every Friday to Monday until Mary moved out again in August, leaving the cottage to tenants who, to her relief, would be bringing in five guineas a week for the next two months.

That autumn she paid a visit to Rhoda, as Rhoda could not come to visit her.[24] It was then back to Leonard Place, where her furnishing was now in a deplorable state, and she mended holes in the carpet while the sofa collapsed completely, its bowels rusting on the carpet. Mary was left wearing her own hair and seeing no visitors. She could not resist joking, 'I attribute the fact that I have lost nearly all my hair this summer to pining at Brooke's coldness'. But pointedly she goes on, 'I dont think even if he were to relent I should ever grow a fresh crop'. As the cold weather came on she set herself to endure it with her usual stoicism, and at least this year there was no war to worry about:

> I feel in a minute we shall be in for it again: the continual struggle against cold; the chilblains; the red nose; the anxiety as to feet: the endlessness of winter: and the departure of my temper early in the autumn with the swallows. However the war is won. Even if our ex soldiers join in a revolution and burn down our houses and take our food and throw us out of the windows they can't alter the fact that the war is won.[25]

As she prepared for winter, she was also planning, not a novel – she would never write another book now – but what would be her final collection of short stories, *The Romance of His Life and Other Stories*. These stories, written after the war and just at the time that women over thirty gained the vote, contain few references to the women's movement, but those that approach the subject at all evince a more settled and conclusive view than she had been willing to put forward in *Red Pottage*, her famously 'New Woman' novel. One character wryly comments that:

> My sisters became workers, and they also became ardent Suffragists, which would have shocked my father dreadfully if he had been alive, for he was of opinion that woman's proper sphere is the home, though of course if you have not got a home or any money it seems rather difficult for women to remain in their sphere.
>
> I, being provided for, remained perfectly womanly, of the type that the Anti-Suffrage League, and the sterner sex especially, admire.[26]

The collection contains not only this passage from the darkly comic 'Her Murderer', but also the inflammatory 'Votes for Men'. The theme is continued In 'The Dark Cottage', her story set fifty years in the future, as Mary – who had once denied that she was in favour of female suffrage – imagines a time when the women left bereft by war will enter parliament and educate for the vote not only the working class, but also other women like themselves. While her soldier husband lies in a coma, Catherine Damer does not devote herself to the children and the poor, as he assumes her to have done when he miraculously wakes up – instead she has taken advantage of her new vote and forged a political career. Their grandson later demands, 'why instead of opposing female suffrage you did not combine to place the franchise on an educational basis, irrespective of sex; the grant of the vote to be dependent on passing certain examinations, mainly in history and geography'?[27] But this future of female emancipation and unrestricted energy is not one that can be easily achieved, and *The Romance of His Life* also contains a tragedy of unfulfilled female promise in perhaps the most compelling story she ever wrote, 'The Goldfish'.

In the midst of these plans and speculations, and just as all the business of packing up the house, and the sale of pictures and china began, Mary became ill again. She was writing to Rhoda in November to explain that she would come and see her when she could, but all she could do for the moment was to toddle in the sun for a hundred yards and then collapse. She was delighted to receive the grapes, direct descendants of the ones in their picture Bible brought by the patriarchs whose names now escaped her. And as Percy was coming to see her and there was to be a party, she was going to exchange her mummifying shawl for an under vest in order to present 'a less repulsive appearance'.[28] Victoria, she complained, was not allowing her to touch the grapes, which she insisted must be saved for the party. On a more serious note, she would look to Rhoda for news of Howard Sturgis, now in his last illness.

By early December Mary and Victoria were preparing to leave Leonard Place. Regie, who had himself moved house, bought their sixteen-seat mahogany dining table for his new home; they had held their final dinner party in the old house, and the rugs and curtains were being collected for the cleaner. Now Victoria was off to some outlandish place to look after a group of unmarried Women's Auxiliary Army Corps members who were approaching what a few decades earlier Mary would have called their 'confinement'. She commented wryly, 'I suppose their young men were "backward in the <u>Church</u> part of matrimony", as Hardy so admirably puts it.'[29] She herself was still unable to leave the house, and so instead she wrote a last letter to Rhoda before the chaos began on 14 December. This time she had good news to impart about one of the stories from her new collection. The ever efficient Curtis Brown, despite her demurral, had managed to sell the serial rights of 'The Goldfish' to the American market for over £200, the most she had ever received for a short story.

By the New Year of 1920 the sisters were in their new house at 4 Argyll Street and busy putting up pictures. But then, with what must have been a sense of inevitability, not only Mary and Victoria, but most of the workmen involved in renovating the new house succumbed to the second of the influenza epidemics that would kill more of the English population than the war itself.[30] In February Mary wrote to Hester Ritchie, daughter of her old friend Anne Thackeray Ritchie, to say that she was still too unwell for more than one visitor a day. The ever faithful Essex was 'a perfect angel' in this emergency, coming twice a day to check on Mary and Victoria, and also tending to Diana, who was lying ill in a hotel. Later Victoria would go to Bognor with Essex to recuperate, leaving Mary in London, from where she wrote cheerfully enough to Rhoda Broughton, who had been out to see her and was clearly concerned, 'I fear your remedy for me of a ceaseless flood of port wine would land me in an inebriates home. I think on the whole I should prefer 4 Argyll Road for the present.'[31]

Then came a series of deaths. First Howard Sturgis in February, as Mary herself was convalescing from the influenza. She saw him continually, she said, with his head bent over his work, sitting in a greatcoat in the large room at Carlton House Terrace. 'Dear dear Howard, so warm hearted and generous, and unselfish, such a real friend. I never met any one in the least like him.'[32] Then in March she wrote from Ufford to Tom's son Richard, admitting that Alice Heber-Percy's recent death had left her full of memories of the past; Mary herself was clearly still feeling frail (her handwriting around this time is wobbly and uncertain, very different from the 'small and businesslike' hand described by a journalist in 1900).[33] She was still in Ufford that May. And before she could have had time to rally herself, on 5 June her old friend and confidante Rhoda Broughton died of cancer at her home in Oxford.[34] Of all Mary's friends, perhaps Rhoda had been the most significant to her literary career. It was she who first introduced the younger writer, then in her twenties, to the firm of Bentley; she had been unstinting in her praise of *Red Pottage* at a time when her own status was becoming less assured; throughout the war years she had acted as confidante and sounding board. For the already frail Mary this rapid succession of deaths must have been horrifying, and such a series of disasters may certainly explain why *The Romance of His Life and Other Romances* did not finally appear until 1921.

She returned to London that October, but her last published work received little attention now. Already in these years the first modernist writers were challenging the older realist mode, which they perceived as portentous and cluttered. Mary had never been in sympathy with their apparent preoccupation with style, once commenting that she had never forgiven Tennyson for saying of the public, 'The fools don't see that it is not what I say that matters, but the form in which

I say it'. For her own part, she said, 'I don't believe that for a moment'.[35] The new century brought with it new fashions in style, and she was not always able to perceive the seriousness of its intent, insisting that

> Thought and as far as I know thought alone is able to take into its crucible the trivial, the raw material of our lives, our lopsided love affairs – can anything be rawer – our absurd mistakes, our crude garish experiments, our commonplace misfortunes and to transmute them by slow unperceived processes not into one book or picture but into worthy material for the hand of the artist, into that which gives dignity and value to our book or picture.[36]

Viriginia Woolf, now publishing her early work, would later regret the passing not of the Victorian Mary Cholmondeley, but of her greatly admired niece, the suffragist novelist Stella Benson.[37] Mary's style had been formed in another time altogether, and she shows no signs in these last stories of taking on the concerns of the post-war generation. But if her writing remains determinedly pre-modernist, she can nonetheless claim to have anticipated one of Virginia Woolf's most famous comments, by a cool seven years.

In 'The Goldfish', one of the most powerful stories she would ever write, Mary returns to the theme that had haunted her for much of her adult life – how can a woman find a room of her own? Woolf would later say that a man sees himself reflected and enlarged in the mirror of a woman's admiration. In Mary's last, incisive treatment of the woman artist, the talented and visionary Blanche Robinson is married off at seventeen to a man she believes will share her passion for art and encourage her career. Instead he becomes jealous when an artist of renown wants to take his wife as a pupil but not him. While himself dying of a consumptive complaint, he puts her to reproducing and enlarging his own dull canvases, when he becomes too ill to paint on a large scale. Ironically it is the wife herself who is confined by her husband's fatal illness; not only is he unwilling to let her leave the house alone, he appropriates her talent very much as the Victorian Gresley had taken up Hester's time in improving his own weak compositions.

The reader is forced to witness Blanche's betrayal by a series of male characters, to each of whom she has turned for help. In the course of the story she is offered or forced into a series of different roles: her uncle and guardian has initially wanted her to enter a convent where he argues she could laminate books and embroider sacred texts if she is interested in art; her husband tries to relegate her to the role of muse before realizing that his sole chance of success lies in her representation of his work; even the doctor who tries to help her views her at first only as an object of psychological interest. The one character who would save her, a famous but dissolute artist, accuses her of having sold her talent for silk dresses and urges her to take to the streets before abandoning her art. But he is himself dying and has no time to destroy her reputation and force her husband to divorce her, by taking her to live with him as she requests.

The ambivalent portrayal of Blanche herself is achieved through the supposedly detached observations of the doctor who attends her husband. She is first seen as lethargic, wandering and unable to fix her mind on what is said to her. Mrs Robinson, whose inane kindness masks a cruelty never fully acknowledged by the narrator, describes Blanche as her pet, linking her to an obese goldfish which she fatuously claims is trying to get to her in his repeated attempts to jump out of his tank. She has placed a mesh over the top to keep him in, and Blanche will repeatedly identify herself with this goldfish. She herself goes into her husband's splendidly equipped studio only to rework his pictures, and must do her own work surreptitiously in a garret. She explains her inability to leave the house that is destroying her health and even her sanity, to the dying artist, 'I don't want to be married ... No pretty clothes, no amusements, no expense. I don't want anything except a little time to myself, to paint.'[38] But this time to herself is the one luxury she is systematically denied.

In her garret room in secret she paints the goldfish, bringing out the misery of his well-fed existence in a compelling picture which will later be exhibited at the Royal Academy. But by this time both will be dead. After the death of the great artist who alone has sympathized with her condition, Blanche deliberately removes the mesh from the aquarium, allowing the goldfish to jump out to his death. Completing the parallel between them, she herself will jump into the water of the Serpentine, the traditional death of the despairing prostitute. Over two decades and a world war lie between *Red Pottage* and 'The Goldfish'. But, as far as Mary was concerned, clearly little had changed since the Victorian age for a woman whose whole consolation lay in her art. As in the case of Hester Gresley, the final irony is that the insuperable obstacle is not the opposition of others, but the fears of the woman artist herself. It is possible that the choice of a painter rather than a writer for this story is a tribute to the sacrifices made by her sister Victoria, whose own career might have been more successful had she not spent much of her adult life looking after Mary and their father. Whatever the intention in writing it, 'The Goldfish' stands as a horrifying indictment of the resistance faced by creative women; and it came just as a new generation of female writers was emerging, determined to distance itself from everything they thought Victorian writers had represented. But if she did not adopt the style of the modernists, she was as troubled as they could wish by Victorian assumptions that she was perceptive enough to see had not been laid to rest by the war. Women would be accorded the vote on the same terms as men in 1928, although the perceived conflict between a woman's vocation and her domestic life would continue to polarize opinion into the 21st century. But Mary herself had only four years left to live.

Percy Lubbock remembered that after the war 'she began to look older, to seem frailer',[39] a perception that is borne out by the uncertain hand of her last extant letters. But she retained enough energy to make jokes at his expense. In 1920 she was recommending the controversial *Diary of Opal Whitely*, published earlier in the year, to Matthew Nathan. Purportedly the authentic diary of a seven-year-old American girl who befriends animals, the book was acclaimed on its first publication, before scepticism about its origins caused it to be vilified as a fraud. In one scene the unfortunate Opal is forced to assist in the killing of her friend the pig, for sausages, and Mary could not resist commenting, imagine having to do that to Percy Lubbock![40]

In the spring of 1921 her brother Dick's widow returned to England with her six children and Mary responded with both delight and understandable bewilderment to their exuberant presence in her home, 'Such splendid children, tho' I felt as if they would take the roof off my quiet London house! All dowered with health and strength and high spirits, and some of them with great good looks.' It is likely that in these children she saw something of her lost brother, that 'splendid vivid handsome creature, overflowing with affection and high spirits'.[41] It was around the same time that the unexpected death of her uncongenial landlord removed one major source of stress. She made no pretence of mourning – as she wrote candidly from Ufford, 'a sense of relief envelops the place'.[42] She must have appreciated the production of *Moth and Rust* in this year by the Progress Film Company. But a sudden illness – most likely linked to a stroke – now left her more fragile than before, and she spent most of her few remaining years in London, where Lubbock remembered 'her smiling welcome as she looked up from her sofa, the firm pressure of her hand' the same as ever.[43] In fact she would not be the same again. Her death certificate records that from around this time she was the victim of cerebral thrombosis which left her paralysed down the left side, and she would from now on have to be nursed almost perpetually by Victoria, 'the great blessing of my life' as Mary was the first to acknowledge.[44]

In February 1922 their brother Tom died, 'a great loss to us',[45] but was it perhaps enviable to die before old age set in? That summer would be her last in Ufford and, after her return to London in October, she was never again to set foot outside her own door. A further series of illnesses left her in pain and virtually helpless, and by 1923 she made no secret of the fact that she was simply waiting to die. In what she expected to be her last winter she wrote, 'Dear Victoria is beyond anything words can tell you, a measureless selfless love – I am greatly blessed – and I have no anxieties, no cares, and my brothers and sisters are full of sympathetic affection'.[46]

By the summer of 1924 she was describing herself as 'very tenacious of life, in spite of my great wish to go'. Her life now was 'just a thin thread of existence spent between two rooms, and an armchair on the balcony in summer time', and she may have been too ill even to be pleased by the appointment of her old friend W.

B. Maxwell as the Chairman of the Society of Authors that year.[47] In her final letter to Matthew Nathan in November, she tells him of the pain she has undergone in her last illness – there is no euphemistic 'weakness' in these last years – and,

> I am ashamed to say I have lost any courage I may have had in bearing it. I dont think I was ever brave, but now that I am weak, I am alas! a coward, and how to endure patiently sharp pain I know not. I can only pray that the worst attacks of it are over.[48]

While she was still able to indulge her love of books, she could no longer remember what she read, and it was now two years since she had been outside. No wonder that she assures him yet again of her readiness to die, and he must 'then thank God for me that after my long trial I am at rest. For I do long for rest.' Reading this from his new post in Australia, Nathan may have caught something of his friend's old zest in her next words, 'We have been deeply interested in the elections'. But he must have known that it was, at least in part, a characteristic distraction technique intended to help them both. She manages to work herself up on a favourite topic, the previous Labour government's refusal to support emigration. She hopes he will publish his lecture on Charlotte Brontë, 'a wonderful creature'. And then, with an assurance that he will hear from Victoria if she becomes too weak to write again, she is gone.[49]

The last recorded memory of her comes from Curtis Brown, who went to see her a few weeks before her death. He found her 'very frail and pale', but interested to hear any news about his family and himself, and able to talk a little about books and authors. Then Victoria took him to the door to explain why she had written asking him to visit her sister, 'She wished to say good-bye to you'.[50] She died on 15 July 1925.

The obituary in *The Times* begins with a sketch of her lineage before moving on to her books, not necessarily an instinct she would have resented. She is described as having 'the temperament of the true artist, patient, conscientious, never satisfied with anything but the best possible realization of the idea in her mind'. Inevitably it is *Red Pottage* that is recalled as her most important work, but the writer admires as much as her satirical humour, her 'simple and unaffected' style, with its 'admirably concealed art'.[51] An unnamed correspondent adds,

> her seriousness, her fine courtesy, her deep sense of duty, were full of traditions of an honourable past. But she had added to these something entirely of her own, in quite another vein – her observant and ironic humour ... Mary Cholmondeley will be badly missed by everyone who knew her; she was one whose friendship was peculiarly needed, sought and securely counted on by all her friends, men and women – a very wide gathering of both.

Astutely this correspondent notes that 'Ill-health, it was possible to guess, had taught her many sharp lessons: but it seemed chiefly to have determined her to keep it out of sight, as a matter that concerned nobody but herself, in her relations with the world'.[52] It is likely that Percy Lubbock, and Mary's other close friends, suspected something of her troubles and knew not to ask too many questions.

Now after her death Lubbock found that she had left him the three volumes of her journal, along with carefully labelled packets of correspondence. It may have been with this in mind that she cut out a number of pages from the last volume, most radically the sixteen pages following on from the entry where she records having learned that her lover had not rejected her in her youth, but thought that she had rejected him. Nowhere is her old conflict more apparent than in this gesture, leaving the most personal record of her life to an old friend who was also known as a biographer, but leaving it with some of the most important passages cut out.

Three years later, in 1928, Percy Lubbock published his memoir *Mary Chol-mondeley: A Sketch from Memory*. It is every bit as guarded as Mary herself, as she appears in her extant letters. He hails her courage in the face of illness, but gone are the harrowing allusions to morphia addiction and the subsequent pain of withdrawal; her 'unhappy love affair' seems to have slipped in almost as an oversight, or at least a titillating secret that he has no intention of explaining; the loss of Condover is barely registered.

Some years later Sir Matthew Nathan would lend Cholmondeley's letters to their mutual friend Lady Jane Lindsay, who returned them with the comment:

> Before such a character revealed as this: Mr Percy Lubbock's laboured pages become more and more firmly glued to the shelf. The fact is no pen but her own – no wit but her own – could reveal Mary Cholmondeley – any other pen would be heavily shod beside hers which danced so readily to her quick brain's piping.[53]

Since this was written the increasing number of scholars interested in her work have been less interested in the witty, satirical side of Cholmondeley's mind than in the fury and frustration so tantalizingly and incompletely proffered by Lubbock, and so powerfully relayed in her most famous heroine, Hester Gresley. It would be another seventy years before the other aspect of Mary Cholmondeley's writing, her private pen, would come to light.

NOTES

The following abbreviations are used throughout the notes:

ATRP Anne Thackeray Ritchie Papers, Eton College Library.
BA Bentley Archive, Mic.B.53/177, British Library.
BL British Library.
DBC Box M, Delves Broughton Collection, Cheshire Records Office.
Diary the original manuscript of Cholmondeley's diary, held in a private archive, unless otherwise stated.
HRHRC Harry Ransom Humanities Research Center, University of Texas at Austin.
MA Murray Archive, Acc. 12604/1217, National Library of Scotland.
MSN MS Nathan 132, Bodleian Library, University of Oxford.
NPC Nancy Price Correspondence (C0642), Box 1, Folder 86, Manuscripts Division, Department of Rare Books and Special Collections, Princeton University Library.
ODNB *Oxford Dictionary of National Biography*.
Red Pottage MS the original manuscript of *Red Pottage*, held in a private archive.
SA Shropshire Archives, Shrewsbury. All manuscripts quoted are from SA 1536: Condover Hall and its successive owners.
SU *Ufford Monthly Magazine* (1908–17), S Ufford 283, Suffolk Record Office.

All birth, marriage and death references are to the index held by the Southport General Records Office.

Prologue

1. S. Jordison, 'Bestseller versus Groundbreaker', *Guardian*, 21 April 2007, Supplement: 'Time Lines: 50 Books that Defined their Era', p. 3.
2. *Guardian*, 11 April 1900, p. 528.
3. P. Lubbock, *Mary Cholmondeley: A Sketch from Memory* (London: Jonathan Cape, 1928), p. 24.
4. M. Cholmondeley, preface to *The Hand on the Latch* (New York: Dodd Mead & Co., 1909), p. xi.
5. The basic facts of Cholmondeley's upbringing in Hodnet Rectory were often used as a preface to discussion of her work, while her residence in London was glossed over. See, for instance, the romantic account in E. Hodder Williams, 'The Reader: Mary Cholmondeley', *Bookman*, 18 (May 1900), pp. 40–7. This article discusses Cholmondeley's

lineage and early life, but in noting her departure from Shropshire, the writer does not specifically mention her move to London.

6. M. Cholmondeley, 'Scrapbook, relating to Family 1864–1920, 1936, 1940', 98/46, Canterbury Museum, New Zealand, p. 16, newspaper cuttings, undated. Not traced. See also Hodder Williams, 'The Reader'.
7. Mary Cholmondeley to James Payn, 3 January 1895, Wolff 1212b, HRHRC.

1 'Water Tinted with Gold'

1. First in Hodder Williams, 'The Reader'. Details were repeated in *Book Buyer*, 11 September 1903 (untraced) and 'An Authoress's Childhood', *Woman's Weekly* (16 June 1900), p. 2.
2. Sources for the Cholmondeley and Beaumont family histories include *Burke's Genealogical and Heraldic History of the Landed Gentry*, ed. P. Townend, 18th edn, 3 vols (London: Burke's Peerage, 1965–72) as well as Mary Cholmondeley's own account as given to Ernest Hodder Williams, in Hodder Williams, 'The Reader'.
3. For details of Reginald Heber's time in Hodnet, see M. Watt, *The History of the Parson's Wife* (London: Faber, 1943), pp. 71–3.
4. Mary Heber to Richard Heber, 3 August 1820, in *The Heber Letters 1783–1832*, ed. R. H. Cholmondeley (London: Batchworth Press, 1950), p. 286.
5. For details of Mary Heber's marriage to Charles Cholmondeley and his subsequent appointment as rector, see ibid., pp. 292–3.
6. Mrs Charles Cholmondeley to Richard Heber, 10 June 1829, in ibid., p. 335.
7. See M. Cholmondeley, *Under One Roof: A Family Record* (London: John Murray, 1918), p. 4.
8. G. Mothershaw, *St Luke's Church, Hodnet: A Brief History* (n.p., 2005), p. 5, gives details of the Heber-Percy family and their connection with Hodnet, including memorials to family members in the church.
9. Marriage index, Market Drayton, vol. 18, p. 205.
10. Letters from Thomas Cholmondeley in New Zealand to his brothers Richard and Reginald, in the early 1850s, include affectionate messages to the rector, making this supposition likely. See, for instance, Thomas Cholmondeley to Charles Cholmondeley, undated, 1536/5/3/1a, and Thomas Cholmondeley to Reginald Cholmondeley, 29 July [1852], 1536/5/4/1b, SA.
11. There is no account of it, for instance, in *Under One Roof*.
12. For details of the Beaumont family history, see *Burke's Genealogical and Heraldic History*, vol. 1, pp. 126–7.
13. Marriage index, Marylebone, vol. 1, p. 204. Both brothers are listed in the 1851 Census, HO107, Piece 2129, f. 37, p. 30, GSU roll 87759, National Archives, Kew.
14. See *Under One Roof*, pp. 3–52, for Mary's account of her parents' early lives.
15. *Bagshaw's Gazeteer of Shropshire* (n.p., 1851), p. 282.
16. Rugby School Registers 1675–1842 (1901) and 1842–74 (1903), Revd A. T. Mitchell. With thanks to Jo Outhwaite, and records held at Rugby School. With thanks to the Rugby archivist.
17. Obituary in *Newport and Market Drayton Advertiser*, 30 January 1897, 1536/5/3/2, SA.
18. *Crockford's Clerical Directory* (London: Horace Cox, 1876).

19. See note 10 above.
20. Their daughter Mary claims inaccurately in *Under One Roof*, p. 6, that they married in 1854. In fact they married in 1855. See Marriage index, Pickering, vol. 9d, p. 585.
21. *Under One Roof*, p. 15.
22. Ibid., p. 11.
23. With thanks to Gerard Boylan, archivist of Oscott College.
24. Obituary in *Newport and Market Drayton Advertiser*, 30 January 1897, 1536/5/3/2, SA.
25. M. Abbott, *Preserve their Memory – Shrewsbury Diocesan Priests (Deceased) 1850–2001*, unpaginated in-house publication of the Diocese of Shrewsbury.
26. Thomas Cholmondeley to Reginald Cholmondeley, 29 July [1852], 1536/5/4/16, SA.
27. C. Godley, 'Cholmondeley, Thomas', in 'G. R. Macdonald Dictionary of Canterbury Biographies', c294, Canterbury Museum, New Zealand.
28. Mary Cholmondeley, 'Scrapbook', 98/46, Canterbury Museum, New Zealand.
29. T. Cholmondeley, *Ultima Thule; or Thoughts Suggested by a Residence in New Zealand* (London: Chapman, 1854), p. 52.
30. See *Under One Roof*, pp. 46–7.
31. Ibid., pp. 41–2.
32. Ibid., p. 43.
33. See J. Grant, *Stella Benson: A Biography* (London: Macmillan, 1987), p. 15.
34. She notes in *Under One Roof*, p. xi, that 'some of us' were born there, an allusion which can only logically be to herself, Tom and Regie.
35. Death index, Market Drayton, October–December 1886, vol. 6a, p. 518.
36. *Under One Roof*, p. 49.
37. Census 1861, Banbury, Class RG9, Piece 917, f. 85, p. 2, GSU roll 542721, National Archives, Kew.
38. *The Times* recorded on 1 July 1863, p. 14, that Thomas had been granted licence to change his name by the Queen.
39. Thomas Cholmondeley to Reginald Cholmondeley, 12 June [no year], 1536/5/4/1a, SA.
40. Untitled newspaper cutting, 1536/5/1/14–15 (1864), SA.
41. For details of the various mortgages on the Condover estate, see D3651/B/3/3/128, SA.
42. Diary, 19 July 1896.
43. Twain was a loyal friend to Reginald, and was deeply distressed by the mismanagement of the Condover estate, for which he blamed the agent. A later conversation on the subject is recorded in Mary Cholmondeley's Diary, in an undated entry from 1907.
44. V. Colby, '"Devoted Amateur": Mary Cholmondeley and *Red Pottage*', *Essays in Criticism*, 20:2 (1970), pp. 213–28, on p. 221.
45. For the origin of this story, see the preface to *Diana Tempest* (1893; New York: Appleton, 1900), p. vi.
46. M. Cholmondeley, 'The Cottager at Home', *Murray's Magazine* 6 (July–December 1889), pp. 238–50.
47. 'Jet's Story' (February 1872), unpaginated MS, private archive.
48. Mary Cholmondeley to George Bentley, 14 December 1894, L51, BA.
49. See Thomas Cholmondeley to Reginald Cholmondeley, 12 June [1851], 1536/5/4/1B, SA.
50. See *Under One Roof*, p. 101.

51. A modern reader would share Mary's ironic view of cigarettes as a cure for her condition, as suggested to her in this year. However Salter recommends tobacco as a palliative second only to chloroform in its efficacy. See H. H. Salter, *On Asthma: Its Pathology and Treatment*, 2nd edition (London: John Churchill and Sons, 1868), p. 215.
52. Diary, 22 June 1872.
53. For the first definite reference to Dr Radcliffe, see Diary, 1 May 1876.
54. Cholmondeley's note on an envelope containing a letter from John James proposing marriage to Frances Coupland, 3 February 1889, private archive.
55. Diary, 14 April 1872.
56. Diary, 15 November 1872.
57. Diary, 18 January 1872. Uncle Charles visited on 20 March and 5 May 1872, Cholmondeley's grandmother was a visitor between 28 May and 16 September 1872.
58. Diary, 24 July 1872.
59. Diary, 8 January 1872.
60. Diary, 2 October 1872.
61. Diary, 24 May 1872, 10 February 1872, 30 March 1872.
62. Diary, 27 January 1872.
63. *Under One Roof*, p. 44.
64. See Diary, 22 August 1875; and, for instance, 'Water-colour sketches of Rome, Bruges, Scotland, Hertfordshire, etc: by Miss Victoria Cholmondeley and Sir William Baillie-Hamilton', Catalogue, Modern Gallery, National Art Library, London.
65. *Under One Roof*, pp. 32–3.

2 'One Great Hope'

1. Lubbock, *Mary Cholmondeley*, p. 9.
2. Diary, 22 August 1875.
3. Diary, 26 December 1872.
4. *Under One Roof*, pp. 41–55.
5. Diary, 26 December 1872.
6. Diary, 1 January 1873.
7. Diary, 8 January 1873.
8. 'Jet's Story' (February 1872), unpaginated MS, private archive.
9. On 24 July 1877. Undated Diary entry.
10. Diary, 6 June 1873.
11. Diary, 3 July 1873.
12. Diary, 11 August 1873.
13. Ibid.
14. See Hodder Williams, 'The Reader', p. 41, where Cholmondeley says that she was about fourteen at the time.
15. This admission, included in several newspaper articles, including 'An Authoress's Childhood', was first made in Hodder Williams, 'The Reader', p. 41.
16. Diary, 1 November 1873.
17. Ibid.
18. *Crockford's Clerical Directory*, 1879–96.
19. The Diary entry of 3 October 1874 describes moving into the rectory as if to a new house. There is no indication that she is returning to a house she has previously lived in.

20. Diary, 3 October 1874.
21. Diary, 1 November 1873.
22. Ibid.
23. Diary, 25 December 1873.
24. Diary, 2 February 1874.
25. Diary, 3 February 1874.
26. For an account of this election see T. H. Hoppen, *The Mid-Victorian Generation* (Oxford: Clarendon Press, 1998), p. 612.
27. Diary, 8 March 1874.
28. Diary, 23 May 1874.
29. Diary, 11 April 1896.
30. Diary, 3 October 1874.
31. Diary, 19 October 1874.
32. Diary, 16 November 1874.
33. Diary, 11 December 1874.
34. Diary, 15 July 1876.
35. Due to ill health Cholmondeley was not always able to accept these invitations. She notes in her Diary on New Year's Day 1875, for instance, that her uncle Regie had made a point of inviting her but that she had been unable to go.
36. For a detailed picture of Reginald's increasingly involved affairs, see all D365, SA.
37. D. Cannadine, *Aspects of Aristocracy: Grandeur and Decline in Modern Britain* (New Haven, CT, and London: Yale University Press, 1994), p. 45.
38. See, for instance, 'MS book [by Reginald Cholmondeley] relating to a natural history trip to the West Indies [no title]', 1876, 1536/5/4/52, SA.
39. For details of the auction on 27 May 1874, see 665/3/1135, SA.
40. See J. Harris, *Private Lives, Public Spirit: Britain 1870–1914* (London: Penguin, 1993), p. 69.
41. See *Under One Roof*, p. 98.
42. For Mary's account of her circumscribed social life in Hodnet, see 'The Motive-Hunting Reader and the Theory of Malicious Origins', *Bookman*, 28:4 (1908), pp. 313–17, on p. 316.
43. *Sir Charles Danvers* begins with just such a visit. See *The Danvers Jewels and Sir Charles Danvers* (London and New York: Harper Bros, [1900]), pp. 93–6.
44. Diary, 27 December 1874.
45. Diary, 1 January 1875.
46. Ibid.
47. Diary, 13 February 1875.
48. Ibid.
49. Ibid.
50. Ibid.
51. Diary, 9 April 1875.
52. Cholmondeley's Diary for Christmas Day 1875, for instance, indicates that her mother was literally made ill by any emotional disruption.
53. Diary, 9 April 1875.
54. See Diary, 1 August 1875. Even at this stage of her life, Cholmondeley was deeply conscious of class difference, commenting in the same entry on the social gulf between actors and her own class.
55. Ibid.

56. Diary, 5 September 1875.
57. Diary entry begins on 24 December 1875 and then continues undated 'as I find time'.
58. Ibid.
59. Diary, 4 May 1876.
60. *Under One Roof*, p. 47.
61. Ibid., p. 52.
62. Diary, 1 May 1876.
63. Diary, 4 May 1876.
64. Ibid.
65. Diary, 3 June 1876.
66. Ibid.
67. Diary, 1 July 1876.
68. Annotated pictures, private archive.
69. Note in Cholmondeley's writing dated October 1906, private archive.
70. Diary, 1 July 1876.
71. Diary, 15 July 1876.
72. Diary, 17 July 1876.
73. Diary, 17 September 1876.
74. Diary, 25 September 1876.
75. Ibid.
76. Diary, 27 September 1876.
77. Diary, 18 January 1877.
78. Diary, 16 May 1877.
79. Ibid.
80. Mary mentions this in her Diary on 17 June 1877, but I have been unable to trace an account in the local press.
81. Ibid.
82. Diary, date assumed to be on missing pages.
83. Diary, 20 August 1877.
84. Note added Christmas Day 1882.
85. Diary, 20 August 1877.
86. Diary, date assumed to be on missing pages.
87. Diary, 16 May 1877.
88. Diary, 6 September 1877.
89. After her mother became incapable of running the household, Cholmondeley took over for an indefinite period, and given the involvement of all the children in adult duties in the parish, it seems most likely that she was assisted on the domestic front by Diana at least.
90. Diary, 13 January 1878.
91. Diary, 21 January 1878.
92. Diary, 6 April 1878.
93. Diary, 29 April 1878.
94. *Diana Tempest* (1900), p. vii.
95. Diary, 2 April 1899.
96. Diary, 28 May 1878.
97. Ibid., and Diary, 29 May 1878.
98. Diary, 28 May 1878.
99. Diary, 29 May 1878.

3 'If I Found I had no Power at all'

1. Cited in *Under One Roof*, p. 94; and see Hodder Williams, 'The Reader', p. 44.
2. In addition to Mary's achievements, Victoria was a talented artist, Hester wanted to be a writer, while Diana would later publish a play (discussed in Chapter 6). See *Under One Roof*, p. 79.
3. Ibid., p. 77.
4. Ibid., p. 103.
5. *Diana Tempest* (1900), p. vii.
6. Lubbock, *Mary Cholmondeley*, p. 79.
7. See *Under One Roof*, p. 103. Date of entry not given.
8. Lubbock, *Mary Cholmondeley*, p. 87.
9. 'The Lowest Rung', in *The Hand on the Latch*, pp. 42–74, on p. 50.
10. Linda Peterson speculates plausibly that this was 'All is Fair in Love and War', published under the name of Lee Russ. Cholmondeley later used the initials L.R. as a pseudonym. See 'The Role of Periodicals in the (Re)Making of Mary Cholmondeley as New Woman Writer', *Media History* 7 (2001), pp. 37–44.
11. Lubbock, *Mary Cholmondeley*, p. 80.
12. Reginald Cholmondeley to Emily Cholmondeley, 27 December 1882, private archive.
13. Diary, Christmas Day 1882, quoted in Lubbock, *Mary Cholmondeley*, p. 79. The ellipsis is almost certainly Lubbock's rather than Cholmondeley's.
14. Lubbock, *Mary Cholmondeley*, p. 80.
15. Mary Cholmondeley to James Payn, 3 January 1895, Wolff 1212b, HRHRC, which also gives evidence that Cholmondeley was sending work to journals.
16. 'Lisle's Courtship', *Household Words*, 36 (May 1884), pp. 501–7. Mary identified herself as the author on her personal copy.
17. Hodder Williams, 'The Reader', p. 42.
18. M. Cholmondeley, *Red Pottage* (1899; London: Virago, 1986), p. 200.
19. A key source for Cholmondeley's activity in the parish is Victoria's 1885 cartoon, 'Too Many Irons in the Fire, Mary' (original in private archive). See also Mary Cholmondeley to George Bentley, 3 February 1894, L41, BA; Diary, 10 June 1895.
20. 'Too Many Irons in the Fire, Mary'.
21. Untraced but presumed to be a local Friendly Society.
22. *Red Pottage*, p. 87.
23. Ibid., p. 119.
24. Reginald Cholmondeley to Emily Cholmondeley, 27 December 1882, private archive.
25. Letter to the Editor of the *British Weekly*, 11 April 1918, p. 25.
26. *Under One Roof*, pp. 14–15.
27. Diary, 4 June 1895.
28. Ibid.
29. *Under One Roof*, p. 16.
30. M. Cholmondeley, *A Devotee: An Episode in the Life of a Butterfly* (London: Edward Arnold, 1897), p. 90; *Red Pottage* (play), unpaginated MS, Department of Manuscripts, LCP 1900/16, BL.
31. MS of 'The Silent Member', private archive. No published version traced, but from the positioning of the manuscript, written some time before 'A Latter-Day Prophet', Cholmondeley's article on Hamilton Thom published in 1894.

32. Tellingly, Emily was reading one of Cholmondeley's books when she died. See Mary Cholmondeley to Richard Bentley, 20 April 1895, 140, Add. MSS 59634–5, BL.

33. Lubbock, *Mary Cholmondeley*, p. 79.

34. *Diana Tempest* (1893; London: Macmillan, 1909), p. 3. This edition of the text was based on the 1894 edition.

35. Diary, 23 March, 1898.

36. Diary, Christmas Day 1882, quoted in Lubbock, *Mary Cholmondeley*, p. 79.

37. Diary, 3 October 1901.

38. Ibid.

39. Ibid.

40. M. Cholmondeley, 'Geoffrey's Wife', *Graphic* (Summer 1885), pp. 28–32, reprinted in *Moth and Rust together with 'Geoffrey's Wife' and 'The Pitfall'* (London: Murray, 1902), pp. 243–66, on pp. 245–6.

41. Ibid., p. 259.

42. The controversial Contagious Diseases Acts, designed to protect the armed forces from venereal disease transmitted by prostitutes, were passed in 1864, 1866 and 1869 and repealed in 1886 after over two decades of campaigning by opponents of the legislation.

43. Grant, *Stella Benson*, p. 6.

44. Charles Cholmondeley to Mary Cholmondeley, 17 November 1885, private archive.

45. Cited in Lubbock, *Mary Cholmondeley*, p. 83.

46. Programme, 28–9 January 1886, private archive.

47. Thomas Cholmondeley to Richard Hugh Cholmondeley, 27 August 1897, D3651/3/3/1/55, SA.

48. Mary Cholmondeley to Hester Cholmondeley, 4 February [1886?], private archive. The same letter to Hester discusses her proposed submission of work to the *Sunflower* magazine. Later comment in *Under One Roof* suggests that Hester was probably not contributing to the magazine until late 1885 or 1886, but by her birthday in November of that year there had been time for her to become a regular contributor and to write a letter claiming that she had not sent in work for some time. It is also significant that Emily told an acquaintance her daughter *wrote*, not that she had published a novel, suggesting that the letter could not have been written as late as 1887.

49. Mary Cholmondeley to Hester Cholmondeley, 4 February [1886?], private archive.

50. Most obviously in the preface to *Diana Tempest* (1900), p. vii.

51. Diary, 2 April 1899.

52. For instance she wrote in her Diary for 7 June 1895 that *A Devotee* would be published unless Diana and Victoria considered it to be 'very bad'.

53. *Diana Tempest* (1900), p. viii.

54. *Under One Roof*, p. 88.

55. *Little Folks* (Summer 1883). With thanks to John Rylands Library, Manchester.

56. Mary Cholmondeley to Hester Cholmondeley, [May/June 1886], private archive.

57. *Under One Roof*, p. 94.

58. Ibid., p. 102.

59. Ibid., pp. 102–3.

60. Mary Cholmondeley to Hester Cholmondeley, [March 1886], private archive.

61. E. C. Cholmondeley to Mary Cholmondeley, 3 March [1888], private archive.

62. Diary, 18 August 1886, cited in Lubbock, *Mary Cholmondeley*, p. 83. The plot of Collins's 1868 sensation novel hinges on the theft of a fabulous jewel, taken from an Indian

temple during the mutiny. As in Cholmondeley's novel, the scapegrace hero immediately becomes the prime suspect.

63. See note 32 above.
64. For instance *Red Pottage* was finished at Tolmers on 13 August 1899; see Diary, 9 October 1899. See also Reginald Cholmondeley to Mary Cholmondeley, 30 October 1899, private archive.
65. *Under One Roof*, p. xiii.
66. Lubbock, *Mary Cholmondeley*, pp. 54, 51–2.
67. Notably Dick and Regie feature in *Red Pottage*, while Condover, to which Tom was the heir, appears in both *The Danvers Jewels* and *Sir Charles Danvers*. *Under One Roof* is dedicated to Tom.
68. Mary Cholmondeley to Richmond Ritchie, 3 June [1886], ATRP.
69. Lubbock, *Mary Cholmondeley*, p. 34.
70. M. Cholmondeley, 'Personalities and Powers: The Late Miss Rhoda Broughton', *Time and Tide* (27 August 1920), pp. 323–5, on p. 323.
71. E. Arnold, 'Rhoda Broughton as I Knew Her', *Fortnightly Review*, 108:644 (August 1920), pp. 262–78, on p. 268.
72. Mary Cholmondeley to Richmond Ritchie, 3 June [1886], ATRP.
73. Mary Cholmondeley to Richmond Ritchie, 30 June 1886, ATRP.
74. Lubbock prints this letter, copied in its entirety from Mary's missing Diary, in *Mary Cholmondeley*, p. 83. See also Mary Cholmondeley to George Bentley, 30 August [1886], L71, BA.
75. Diary, 17 August 1886, cited in Lubbock, *Mary Cholmondeley*, p. 84.
76. Diary, 25 September 1886, quoted in Lubbock, *Mary Cholmondeley*, p. 85.
77. Lubbock, *Mary Cholmondeley*, p. 85.
78. Diary, 25 September 1886, quoted in ibid., pp. 84–5.
79. Lubbock, *Mary Cholmondeley*, p. 87.
80. Charles Dickens to Thomas Beard, 17 December 1839, in *The Letters of Charles Dickens: The Pilgrim Edition, 1820–1839*, ed. M. House, G. Storey, K. M. Tillotson and W. J. Carlton (Oxford: Oxford University Press, 1982), p. 619.
81. Mary Cholmondeley to Richard Bentley, 11 July 1895, 148–9, Add. MSS 56934–5, BL.
82. James Legard to Mary Cholmondeley, 27 September 1886, private archive.
83. Charles Cholmondeley to Mary Cholmondeley, 14 January 1887, private archive.
84. Mary Cholmondeley to George Bentley, 1 March 1887, L74, BA.
85. Charles Cholmondeley to Mary Cholmondeley, 20 March 1887, private archive.
86. Preface to *The Hand on the Latch*, p. xi. The review appeared in 'Our Booking Office', *Punch* (22 October 1887), p. 192a.
87. See for instance Diary, 4 November 1899, in which Cholmondeley notes that the Heber-Percys have not congratulated her on *Red Pottage*.
88. See preface to *The Hand on the Latch*, p. vii.
89. Diary, entry 25 September 1886, cited in Lubbock, *Mary Cholmondeley*, p. 85.
90. One such letter is invoked in Cholmondeley's response, Cholmondeley to George Bentley, 10 July 1891, L10, BA.
91. Diary, 2 April 1899.
92. *Sir Charles Danvers*, in *The Danvers Jewels and Sir Charles Danvers*, p. 120.
93. For this continuing interest, see, for instance, Cholmondeley to Richmond Ritchie, 9 June [1886], ATRP.

94.   *Under One Roof,* pp. 90–1.
95.   Ibid., p. 98.
96.   Ibid., p. 9.
97.   Quoted in ibid., p. 100.

4 'The Only Life I Know'

1.   Cholmondeley later remembered 'being hampered [at the start of her career] at every turn I feebly made by constant constant illness', Diary, 1 March 1901.
2.   E. Cholmondeley, 'A Day of my Life in Chambers. By a Briefless Barrister', *Cornhill Magazine,* 58:11, (July 1888), pp. 1–12, on p. 12.
3.   Edward Cholmondeley to Mary Cholmondeley, 3 March [1888], private archive.
4.   Cholmondeley to Richmond Ritchie, 5 March [1888], ATRP.
5.   Ibid.
6.   Ibid.
7.   Mary Cholmondeley to Richmond Ritchie, 3 June [1886], ATRP; Mary Cholmondeley to Richmond Ritchie, 5 March [1888], ATRP.
8.   Mary Cholmondeley to Hester Cholmondeley, [spring 1890], private archive.
9.   Mary Cholmondeley to George Bentley, 5 September 1892, L14, BA.
10.   Mary Cholmondeley to Richard Bentley, 11 July 1895, 148–9, Add. MSS 56934–5, BL.
11.   Richard Bentley to Mary Cholmondeley, 28 May [1888], ATRP.
12.   Mary Cholmondeley to Richmond Ritchie, 5 June [1888], ATRP.
13.   Mary Cholmondeley to [Richard Bentley], 12 June 1888, L1, BA.
14.   Cholmondeley's changing attitude towards publishers after the publication of *Red Pottage* will be discussed in detail in Chapter 6.
15.   Information on the Mills family from Ruth Plowden.
16.   This is implied in Hamilton Thom to Mary Cholmondeley, 4 January 1889, private archive.
17.   M. Cholmondeley, 'A Latter-Day Prophet, *Temple Bar,* 103 (1894) pp. 479–91, on p. 480.
18.   Thom replied on 4 January 1889, saying that her letter had only reached him the night before. The obvious supposition is that it had therefore been written more than a few days earlier, but not at a sufficient distance of time to render a full explanation necessary.
19.   J. H. Thom, *Laws After the Mind of Christ* (London: Kegan Paul, Trench & Co., 1883), pp. 155–6.
20.   Ibid., p. 165.
21.   Hamilton Thom to Mary Cholmondeley, 4 January 1889, private archive.
22.   Florence Cholmondeley to Mary Cholmondeley, 30 October 1899, private archive.
23.   Mary Cholmondeley to Richmond Richie, 28 February [1889], ATRP.
24.   Marriage certificate of Robert Grant and Victoria Alexandria Owen, widow (née Cotes), 24 November 1875, Pitchford MSS, Personal Papers, box XXI/4 – PC/3, National Library of Wales, Aberystwyth.
25.   Mary Cholmondeley to Anne Thackeray Ritchie, 27 March [1889], ATRP.
26.   Ibid.
27.   Mary Cholmondeley to John Murray, 26 October 1901, MA.

28. Mary Cholmondeley to Richard Bentley, 28 December 1896, L63, BA. Allusion untraced.
29. *Diana Tempest* (1909), p. 255.
30. Birth index, Hatfield, December 1889, vol. 3a, p. 527.
31. Undated note of Hester Cholmondeley, private archive.
32. James Legard to Mary Cholmondeley, 14 February 1890, private archive.
33. Charles Cholmondeley to Mary Cholmondeley, 25 November [1889], private archive.
34. Cited in Mary Cholmondeley to Hester Cholmondeley, 29 December [1889], private archive.
35. Mary Cholmondeley to Hester Cholmondeley, 29 December [1889], private archive.
36. Mary Cholmondeley to George Bentley, [1890], [no number], BA.
37. Mary Cholmondeley to Hester Cholmondeley, [spring 1890], private archive.
38. Ibid.
39. Ibid.
40. Mary Cholmondeley to George Bentley, [spring 1890], [no number], BA.
41. Mary Cholmondeley to George Bentley, 28 March 1890, L3, BA.
42. Mary Cholmondeley to George Bentley, 13 April 1890, L11, BA.
43. Mary Cholmondeley to George Bentley, 19 April [1890], L85, BA.
44. Mary Cholmondeley to Richmond Richie, 17 August 1890, ATRP.
45. Figures taken from Cholmondeley's personal record book, private archive.
46. Mary Cholmondeley to George Bentley, 19 April [1890], Bentley Archive, L85, BA.
47. *Under One Roof*, p. 108.
48. Mary Cholmondeley to George Bentley, 15 May [1890], L86, BA.
49. Mary Cholmondeley to George Bentley, 29 July [1890], L84, BA.
50. Ibid.
51. Mary Cholmondeley to Richmond Richie, 17 August 1890, ATRP.
52. Ibid.
53. Mary Cholmondeley to George Bentley, 18 October 1890, L4, BA.
54. Mary Cholmondeley to George Bentley, 4 December 1890, BA.
55. *Torquay: Queen of the Watering Places*, Local Studies Education Series (Torbay: Torbay Library Services, n.d.), unpaginated.
56. *Bradshaw's General Railway and Steam Navigation Guide for Great Britain and Ireland* (November 1890). With thanks to the National Railway Museum, York.
57. Mary Cholmondeley to George Bentley, 18 October 1890, L4, BA; Mary Cholmondeley to George Bentley, 31 October 1890, L5, BA.
58. *Under One Roof*, p. 109.
59. Mary Cholmondeley to George Bentley, 4 December 1890, L6, BA.
60. Diary, 7 November 1897.
61. *Under One Roof*, p. 110.
62. Mary Cholmondeley to George Bentley, 4 December 1890, L6, BA.
63. Ibid.; Mary Cholmondeley to George Bentley, 20 December 1893, L36, BA.
64. *Under One Roof*, p. 110.
65. Reproduced in ibid., p. 111.
66. Reproduced in ibid., p. 112.
67. See *Diana Tempest* (1900), p. viii.
68. Hodder Williams, 'The Reader', p. 47.
69. Mary Cholmondeley to Hester Cholmondeley, [spring 1890], private archive.
70. *Under One Roof*, p. 112.

71. Ibid., p. 113.
72. Mary Cholmondeley to George Bentley, 21 April 1891, L7, BA.
73. Mary Cholmondeley to George Bentley, 12 June 1891, L8, BA.
74. Untitled newspaper cutting, 1536/5/5/16–17, SA.
75. M. Kent, 'A Novelist of Yesterday', *Cornhill*, 151 (February 1935), pp. 194–200, on pp. 195, 196.
76. *Under One Roof*, p. 116.
77. Ibid., pp. 117–18.
78. Ibid., p. 118. Cholmondeley writes that she returned home with Hester, but she at least spent some time in London on the way back. See Mary Cholmondeley to George Bentley, 21 April 1891, L7, BA.
79. Mary Cholmondeley to George Bentley, 12 June 1891, L8, BA.
80. *Under One Roof*, p. 119.
81. Mary Cholmondeley to George Bentley, 9 July 1891, L9, BA.
82. Mary Cholmondeley to George Bentley, 10 July 1891, L10, BA.
83. Mary Cholmondeley to George Bentley, 5 September 1892, L79, BA; Mary Cholmondeley to George Bentley, 9 July 1891, L9, BA.
84. Cholmondeley described her mistake with Edward Arnold in her Diary, 24 October 1900.
85. Mary Cholmondeley to George Bentley, 5 September 1892, L79, BA.
86. *Under One Roof*, p. 119.
87. Diary, 10 January 1909.
88. This information was passed on by a modern-day asthma sufferer, who had experienced similar difficulty in breathing while suffering from asthma and bronchitis simultaneously.
89. *Under One Roof*, p. 120.
90. Ibid. Even in her final illness, Cholmondeley tells a friend that her ailments leave her 'weak' rather than focusing on the pain. See Mary Cholmondeley to Matthew Nathan, 9 April 1923, MSN.
91. *Under One Roof*, p. 121.
92. Ibid., p. 122.
93. Ibid., p. 124.
94. Lubbock, *Mary Cholmondeley*, p. 87.
95. Diary, 31 December 1906.
96. Mary Cholmondeley to George Bentley, 11 July 1892, L12, BA.
97. See Cannadine, *Aspects of Aristocracy*, ch. 2.
98. Mary Cholmondeley to George Bentley, 30 August 1892, L13, BA.
99. Mary Cholmondeley to George Bentley, 3 February 1894, L41, BA.
100. Ibid.
101. Mary Cholmondeley to George Bentley, 25 November 1892, L18, BA.
102. Mary Cholmondeley to George Bentley, 5 December 1892, L22, BA; Mary Cholmondeley to George Bentley, 15 December 1892, L23, BA.
103. Margaret Oliphant's *John: A Love Story* had appeared in 1870.
104. Mary Cholmondeley to George Bentley, 1 January 1893, L24, BA.
105. Mary Cholmondeley to George Bentley, 23 September 1892, L15, BA.
106. See, for instance, R. Park, 'Some Cases in which Morphia has been Administered in Large Doses Hypodermically; with Remarks', *Practitioner*, 24 (1880), pp. 424–33, on p. 426.

107. J. K. Anderson, 'On the Treatment of Spasmodic Asthma by the Subcutaneous Injection of Morphia', *Practitioner*, 15:89 (November 1875), pp. 321–2, on p. 322.

108. S. Ziegler, '"How Far am I Responsible?" Women and Morphimania in Late-Nineteenth-Century Britain', *Victorian Studies*, 8:1 (Autumn 2005), pp. 59–81, on p. 70.

109. Ibid.

110. Mary Cholmondeley to George Bentley, 14 December 1894, L51, BA.

111. Mary Cholmondeley to George Bentley, 1 January 1893, L24, BA.

112. Mary Cholmondeley to George Bentley, 25 February [1893], Add. MSS 46623–45, 322–3, BL.

113. Mary Cholmondeley to George Bentley, 27 March 1893, L25, BA.

114. Mary Cholmondeley to Richard Hugh Cholmondeley, 22 March 1893, private archive.

115. Ibid.

116. Victor Horseley to Richard Hugh Cholmondeley, postmarked 22 March 1893, private archive.

117. For a detailed discussion of the rest cure, see E. L. Bassuk, 'The Rest Cure: Repetition or Resolution of Victorian Women's Conflicts?', *Poetics Today*, 6:1/2 (1985), pp. 245–57.

118. Described in S. W. Mitchell, *Fat and Blood* (Philadelphia, PA: J. B. Lippincott and Co., 1885). The confinement to bed might last for six weeks or more in extreme cases. For a discussion of the opposition to this prolonged prescription of rest, see J. Oppenheim, *Shattered Nerves: Doctors, Patients, and Depression in Victorian England* (New York and Oxford: Oxford University Press, 1991), p. 121.

119. See Winifred Mayo to Mrs Billinghurst, 26 January 1913, Autograph Letter Collection: Letters of Rosa May Billinghurst and Dr Alice Ker, 9/29/42, Women's Library, London Metropolitan University.

120. Oppenheim, *Shattered Nerves*, p. 121.

121. W. S. Playfair, *An Introduction to a Discussion on the Systematic Treatment of Aggravated Hysteria and Certain Allied Forms of Neurasthenic Disease* (London: Smith Elder & Co., 1883), p. 69.

122. Ibid., p. 81.

123. Oppenheim, *Shattered Nerves*, p. 81.

124. Mary Cholmondeley to Richard Hugh Cholmondeley, 4 June 1893, private archive. See also Mary Cholmondeley to George Bentley, 27 April 1893, L26, BA. For a discussion of the perceived relationship between intellectual work and reproductive capacity, see E. Showalter, *Sexual Anarchy: Gender and Culture at the Fin de Siècle* (London: Virago, 1992).

125. Mary Cholmondeley to George Bentley, 27 April 1893, L26, BA.

126. Mary Cholmondeley to Richard Hugh Cholmondeley, 4 June 1893, private archive.

127. Note of Dennis Embleton to Richard Hugh Cholmondeley, 8 June 1893, private archive.

128. Ibid.

129. C. P. Gilman, 'Why I Wrote the Yellow Wallpaper', in A. Richardson (ed.), *Women Who Did: Stories by Men and Women, 1890–1914* (London: Penguin, 2002), pp. 398–9.

130. Oppenheim, *Shattered Nerves*, p. 16.

131. K. Prior, 'Lyall, Sir Alfred Comyn (1835–1911)', *ODNB*.

132. Mary Cholmondeley to George Bentley, 24 October 1893, L27, BA.

133. Ibid.

134. A. Tennyson, *In Memoriam*, 80, in *The Poetical Works of Alfred Tennyson, Poet Laureate, Etc: Complete in One Volume* (Boston, MA: Ticknor and Fields, 1857).

135. Mary Cholmondeley to George Bentley, 27 October 1893, L28, BA.

136. Mary Cholmondeley to George Bentley, 1 January 1894, L37, BA.

137. A. Lang, 'At the Sign of the Ship', *Longmans*, 23 (January 1894), pp. 322–30, on p. 328.

138. Mary Cholmondeley to George Bentley, 9 January 1894, L38, BA.

139. See, for instance, 'Novels', *Saturday Review*, 76 (9 December 1893), pp. 653–4, on p. 653. Others untraced, but see Mary Cholmondeley to George Bentley, 1 April 1894, L43, BA.

140. See Mary Cholmondeley to George Bentley, 16 December 1893, L35, BA.

141. Mary Cholmondeley to George Bentley, 11 December 1893, L34, BA.

142. Unlike today, the Victorian children of unmarried parents were not entitled to use their father's name.

143. M. Cholmondeley, *Diana Tempest*, 3 vols (London: Richard Bentley & Son, 1893), vol. 3, p. 167.

144. See 'Novels', *Saturday Review*.

145. Mary Cholmondeley to George Bentley, 1 April 1894, L43, BA.

146. Mary Cholmondeley to George Bentley, 16 December 1893, L35, BA. The term seems to have been implied but not necessarily used in Harrison's letter.

147. *The Times*, 12 January 1894, p. 15a.

148. Mary Cholmondeley to George Bentley, 3 February 1894, L41, BA.

149. 'News Notes', *Bookman*, 32:6 (May 1894), pp. 37–8.

150. Review of *Diana Tempest*, in 'New Novels', *Academy*, 44 (July–December 1893), pp. 563–4, on p. 563.

151. Review of *Diana Tempest*, *Dial* (1 January 1894), p. 19.

152. Mary Cholmondeley to George Bentley, 17 January 1894, L39, BA.

153. Mary Cholmondeley to James Payn, 3 January 1895, Wolff 1212b, HRHRC.

154. Mary Cholmondeley to George Bentley, 14 November 1893, L32, BA.

155. *Red Pottage*, p. 334.

156. Mary Cholmondeley to George Bentley, 3 February 1894, L41, BA.

157. Ibid.

158. Mary Cholmondeley to George Bentley, 1 April 1894, L43, BA.

159. Mary Cholmondeley to Richard Hugh Cholmondeley, [April 1894], private archive.

160. Mary Cholmondeley to George Bentley, 3 February 1894, L41, BA.

161. Mary Cholmondeley to George Bentley, 9 July 1891, L9, BA.

162. Ibid.

163. Diary, 4 June 1895.

164. Mary Cholmondeley to George Bentley, 14 December 1894, L51, BA.

165. Ibid.

166. Lubbock, *Mary Cholmondeley*, p. 87.

167. Diary, 7 November 1897, describes leaving off morphia as being 'like a second illness', while 26 February 1899 describes the unsuccessful attempt to do without it during an illness.

168. M. Cholmondeley, 'The Lowest Rung', *Windsor Magazine*, 28 (August 1908), pp. 264–74.

169. This seems to have been the effect of medicinal drugs on another New Woman writer, Oliver Schreiner. See Y. Draznin, 'Did Victorian Medicine Crush Olive Schreiner's Creativity?', *Historian*, 47:2 (February 1985), pp. 195–207.

170. *Moth and Rust* (London, New York and Toronto: Hodder and Stoughton, 1912), p. 178.

171. Mary Cholmondeley to George Bentley, 22 January 1895, L53, BA.
172. Mary Cholmondeley to George Bentley, 4 February 1895, L55, BA.
173. Mary Cholmondeley to George Bentley, 9 February 1895, L56, BA.
174. Mary Cholmondeley to George Bentley, 15 March 1895, L57, BA.
175. M. Cholmondeley, 'An Art in its Infancy', *Monthly Review*, 3 (June 1901), pp. 79–90.
176. DYB 622811, National Archives, Kew.
177. Mary Cholmondeley to Richard Bentley, 20 April 1895, 140, Add. MSS 46623–45, BL.
178. Mary Cholmondeley to George Bentley, 20 April 1895, 140–1, Add. MSS 59634–5, BL.
179. *Under One Roof*, p. 46.
180. Mary Cholmondeley to Richard Hugh Cholmondeley, 2 May [1895], private archive.
181. Ibid.
182. R. L. Patten, 'Bentley, George (1828–1895)', *ODNB*.
183. For an analysis of Bentley's influence on Cholmondeley's career, and the impact of the sale of the firm, see Peterson, 'The Role of Periodicals in the (Re)Making of Mary Cholmondeley'.
184. Diary, Whitsunday 1895.
185. *A Devotee*, pp. 40, 11, 195, quoting 'Pilot's Wife's Dream', from Lyall's *Verses Written in India* (1889).
186. *A Devotee*, pp. 103, 38.
187. Ibid., pp. 185–6.
188. Information from Ruth Plowden.
189. Diary, 7 June 1895.
190. Diary, 10 June 1895.
191. From E. Barrett Browning, *Last Poems* (London: Chapman and Hall, 1862).
192. Diary, 11 June 1895.
193. Diary, preceding page cut out, but follows on from 12 October 1902. Notably Cholmondeley refers to her old lover in this way, making his identity impossible to ascertain, Diary, 25 June 1900.
194. Diary, 5 August 1895.
195. Ibid.
196. M. Cholmondeley, 'Waste', *Monthly Packet*, 527 (1 January 1895), pp. 81–90, on p. 81.
197. Diary, 19 September 1895.
198. D3651/B/3/1/49, SA.
199. Mary Cholmondeley to Richard Hugh Cholmondeley, 14 November 1895, private archive.
200. Mary Cholmondeley to Richard Hugh Cholmondeley, 21 November 1895, private archive.
201. Diary, 14 December 1895.
202. Mary Cholmondeley to Richard Hugh Cholmondeley, 11 December 1895, private archive.
203. Victoria Cholmondeley to Richard Hugh Cholmondeley, 16 December [1895], private archive.
204. Diary, 17 February 1896.
205. On board the *Rome*, departing from London, bound for Sydney. See http://www.ancestorsonboard.com/. With thanks to the National Archives.
206. Diary, 17 February 1896.

207. Ibid.
208. Mary Cholmondeley to Richard Hugh Cholmondeley, 13 January 1896, private archive.
209. Ibid.
210. Mary Cholmondeley to Richard Hugh Cholmondeley, 24 January 1896, private archive.
211. Ibid.
212. Ibid.
213. Salter, *On Asthma*, p. 273.
214. Mary Cholmondeley to Richard Hugh Cholmondeley, 24 January 1896, private archive.
215. Mary Cholmondeley to Richard Hugh Cholmondeley, 10 March 1896, private archive.
216. Ibid.
217. M. Cholmondeley, 'A Day in Teneriffe', *Chatauquan*, 33 (April–September 1901), pp. 591–7, on p. 591.
218. Mary Cholmondeley to Richard Hugh Cholmondeley, 10 March 1896, private archive.
219. Mary Cholmondeley to Richard Hugh Cholmondeley, 2 May [1895], private archive.
220. Mary Cholmondeley to Richard Hugh Cholmondeley, 10 March 1896, private archive.
221. Mary Cholmondeley to Richard Bentley, 23 March 1896, Add. MSS 59634–5, BL
222. No review of it in the English press has been traced and, despite its position immediately between *Diana Tempest* and *Red Pottage*, it has not received critical attention since.
223. Diary, 21 February 1896.
224. Diary, 11 April 1896.
225. 'A Day in Teneriffe', *Monthly Packet*, 92 (November 1896), pp. 492–501. See also 'A Second Day in Teneriffe', *Monthly Packet*, 92 (December 1896), pp. 615–23.
226. Mary Cholmondeley to Richard Hugh Cholmondeley, 9 April 1896, private archive.
227. Diary, 11 April 1896.
228. Diary, 19 July 1896.
229. Diary, 19 July 1896. The Appeal against Female Suffrage was first published in *Nineteenth Century*, 25 (June 1889), pp. 781–8, reprinted in C. C. Nelson (ed.), *A New Woman Reader: Fiction, Articles and Drama of the 1890s* (Plymouth: Broadview Press, 2001), pp. 120–3.
230. Diary, 19 July 1896.
231. This reasoning is suggested in Mary Cholmondeley to Richard Hugh Cholmondeley, 24 January 1896, private archive.
232. Obituary in *Newport and Market Drayton Advertiser*, 30 January 1897, 1536/5/3/2, SA.
233. 'Printed letter of Richard Hugh Cholmondeley', 1536/5/5/13, SA.
234. Diary, 19 July 1896.
235. Ibid.
236. *The Times*, 2 April 1897, p. 10.
237. Mary Cholmondeley to George Bentley, 24 July 1894, BA.
238. Described in Diary, 21 November 1909, list of rules enclosed.
239. Lubbock, *Mary Cholmondeley*, p. 19.
240. Diary, 28 August 1896.
241. Diary, 2 October 1896.

242. *Women, Writing and Travel: Diaries of Stella Benson, 1902–1933 from Cambridge University Library*, 10 microfilm reels (Marlborough: Adam Matthew Publications, 2005), 2 August 1912, Reel 3.

243. Diary, 2 October 1896.

244. Ibid.

245. Mary Cholmondeley to Richard Bentley, 5 October 1896, 222, Add. MSS 46623–45, BL. Mary's Diary of 29 August states that the family burned a number of papers, including two of her unpublished novels, her father's sermons and 'endless letters and manuscripts' as part of their preparations for leaving Hodnet.

246. Diary, 22 November 1896.

247. Diary, 23 November 1896.

248. Diary, 1 December 1896.

249. Ibid.

5 'Strumming on Two Pianos at Once'

1. Mary Cholmondeley to George Bentley, 1 November 1893, L30, BA.

2. Diary, 9 October 1899.

3. Hodder Williams, 'The Reader', p. 41.

4. *Newport and Market Drayton Advertiser*, 30 January 1897, 1563/5/3/2, SA.

5. Obituary of Charles Cholmondeley, *The Times*, 26 January 1897, p. 5.

6. See 'The Motive-Hunting Reader'.

7. Mary Cholmondeley to Stephen Gwynn, 5 February 1901, MS 8600(3), National Library of Ireland.

8. B. Bennett, 'Arnold, Edward Augustus (1857–1942)', *ODNB*.

9. J. Sutherland, *Mrs Humphry Ward: Eminent Victorian, Pre-Eminent Edwardian* (Oxford: Oxford University Press, 1990), p. 27. See P. Wachter, *Introduction to Platonics* (Bristol: Thoemmes Press, 1995), p. xi.

10. Mary Cholmondeley to Rhoda Broughton, 27 January 1919, DDM/M/C/2/18, DBC.

11. Ibid.; Diary, 19 July 1896, 10 July 1898. See also Mary Cholmondeley to Henry Newbolt, 4 April 1911, Wolff uncat., HRHRC.

12. She complains that Mary Ward does not mention either her, Rhoda Broughton or Edith Wharton in her memoirs. Mary Cholmondeley to Rhoda Broughton, 27 January 1919, DDM/M/C/2/18, DBC. If Cholmondeley knew that Ward and Wharton were acquainted, this was presumably because she had met them together.

13. Lubbock, *Mary Cholmondeley*, pp. 65, 62.

14. E. Wharton, *A Backward Glance: An Autobiography* (1934; London: Everyman, 1993), pp. 152, 154.

15. Lubbock, *Mary Cholmondeley*, pp. 66, 68.

16. Wharton, *A Backward Glance*, p. 55.

17. Ibid.

18. Diary, undated entry [1907], 1 March 1901.

19. Mary Cholmondeley to Matthew Nathan, 20 November 1897, MSN; C. Newbury, 'Nathan, Sir Matthew (1862–1939)', *ODNB*. For Cholmondeley's discussions on the Woman Question, see her letters to Matthew Nathan, 14 March [1911] and 6 July 1924, MSN. For her criticism of the Labour government see her letter to Matthew Nathan, 6 July 1924, MSN.

20. See Mary Cholmondeley to Richmond Richie, 17 August 1890, ATRP.
21. 'A Day in Teneriffe', *Chatauquan*, p. 591.
22. *Red Pottage* (play), unpaginated MS, Department of Manuscripts, LCP 1900/16, BL.
23. For a range of Victorian responses to the 'New Woman', see Nelson (ed.), *A New Woman Reader*.
24. See, for instance, S. Grand, 'The New Aspect of the Woman Question', *North American Review*, 158 (March 1894), pp. 270–6.
25. The most famous of these articles was E. L. Linton, 'The Girl of the Period', originally published in the *Saturday Review* (14 March 1868), pp. 339–40.
26. A *Punch* cartoon from 1904 features four women playing cards, with the caption: "'Is Florrie's engagement really off, then?" "Oh, yes. Jack wanted her to give up gambling and smoking, and goodness knows what else." (Chorus.) "How absurd!!"', H. Somerville, 'Primum Vivere, Deine Philosophari', *Punch* (25 January 1904), p. 69; Mrs F. Miller, 'How I Made my First Speech', *Woman's Signal* (4 January 1894), p. 5. Talia Schaffer convincingly argues that the New Woman was a fictional construct in '"Nothing but Foolscap and Ink": Inventing the New Woman', in A. Richardson and C. Willis (eds), *The New Woman in Fiction and Fact, Fin-de-Siècle Feminisms* (Basingstoke: Palgrave 2001), pp. 39–52.
27. See Grand, 'The New Aspect of the Woman Question', p. 270. Cholmondeley alludes to the idea of the 'brawling brotherhood' in 'Votes for Men', *Cornhill*, 100 (July 1909), pp. 34–43, reprinted in *The Romance of his Life and Other Romances* (London: John Murray, 1921), pp. 200–15, on p. 203. See Mary Cholmondeley to Matthew Nathan, 14 March [1911], MSN for 'superfluous women'.
28. In *No Name* (1862) Magdalen Vanstone proposes to her future husband.
29. *Red Pottage*, p. 83.
30. Ibid., p. 31.
31. Ibid., pp. 34, 35.
32. Ibid., p. 130.
33. Showalter, Introduction to *Red Pottage*, p. xi.
34. *Red Pottage*, pp. 120, 151.
35. In 'Votes for Men'.
36. *Red Pottage*, p. 84.
37. Ibid., p. 154.
38. Her Diary of 27 December 1900 shows a feeling of gratification that *Red Pottage* can console the troops in the Boer War. Both Lubbock (*Mary Cholmondeley*, p. 11) and E. F. Benson (*Final Edition: An Informal Autobiography* (London: Longman's, 1940), p. 75) note her evident sense of responsibility when speaking of her work.
39. See, for instance, Mary Cholmondeley to George Bentley, 5 September 1892, L14, BA.
40. *Red Pottage*, p. 52.
41. *Red Pottage* MS.
42. *Red Pottage*, p. 56.
43. Hester demands of her brother why he has killed her 'child' when she did not let his die, a confrontation that is immediately followed by her attack on Regie. See ibid., pp. 276–7.
44. Ibid., p. 78.
45. *Red Pottage* MS.
46. Ibid.
47. *Red Pottage*, p. 76.
48. *Under One Roof*, pp. 127, 97.

49. *Red Pottage*, p. 79.
50. Diary, 25 September 1886, quoted in Lubbock, *Mary Cholmondeley*, p. 84.
51. Peterson, 'The Role of Periodicals in the (Re)Making of Mary Cholmondeley', pp. 34–5.
52. Diary, 22 November 1896, 29 April 1897. For a general description of Bournemouth at this time, see E. Edwards, *A History of Bournemouth: Growth of a Victorian Town* (Sussex: Phillimore, 1981).
53. Diary, 29 April 1897.
54. *Red Pottage* MS.
55. *Red Pottage*, p. 29.
56. Ibid.
57. Diary, 29 April, 1897.
58. Diary, 8 June 1897.
59. Peterson, 'The Role of Periodicals in the (Re)Making of Mary Cholmondeley', p. 38.
60. Mary Cholmondeley to Stephen Gwynne, 5 February 1901, MS 8600(3), National Library of Ireland.
61. Diary, 19 June 1897.
62. Mary Cholmondeley to Algernon [Percy], 11 April, 1536/5/9/2, SA. The year is not given but the family left Hodnet in July of the year before, making 1897 the most likely date.
63. *Red Pottage*, pp. 63–4.
64. Mary Cholmondeley to Miss Pack, 27 June 1897, Wolff uncat., HRHRC.
65. Diary, 19 July 1897.
66. Diary, 21 August 1897.
67. The Diary entry for 30 September 1897 notes that she will return to London the following day.
68. Diary, 7 November 1897.
69. Ibid.
70. Diary, 26 February 1899.
71. Diary, 7 November 1897.
72. *Red Pottage*, p. 15.
73. Diary, 7 November 1897.
74. *Red Pottage*, pp. 155–6.
75. Diary, 2 December 1897.
76. *Red Pottage*, p. 85.
77. Diary, 2 December 1897.
78. *Red Pottage*, p. 85.
79. Ibid., p. 87.
80. Diary, 31 December 1897.
81. Diary, 6 March 1898.
82. Ibid.
83. Diary, 23 March 1898, 13 January 1878.
84. Diary, 29 May 1878.
85. *Red Pottage*, p. 258.
86. Mary Cholmondeley to George Bentley, 24 July 1894, L46, BA.
87. *Red Pottage*, pp. 276, 278.
88. *Red Pottage* MS.
89. See, for instance, Lubbock, *Mary Cholmondeley*, p. 24.

90. Ibid., p. 88.
91. Diary, 30 March 1898.
92. Her Diary, of 20 July 1898 shows that she was particularly struck by her meeting with Aubrey de Vere.
93. Lubbock, *Mary Cholmondeley*, p. 30.
94. *Red Pottage*, p. 44.
95. Diary, 2 April 1899. This visit was postponed when the servants became ill.
96. Diary, 15 June 1898.
97. Ibid.
98. *Red Pottage*, pp. 80–1.
99. Ibid., p. 87.
100. Diary, 15 June 1898.
101. This is strongly implied in Lubbock, *Mary Cholmondeley*, p. 24. On p. 87 he claims that he met her one evening 'in the new century'. But see Diary, 15 June 1898.
102. Diary, 15 June 1898.
103. Diary, 21 June 1898.
104. Diary, 10 July 1898.
105. Plot outline, *Red Pottage* MS.
106. *Red Pottage*, p. 335.
107. Mary Cholmondeley to Rhoda Broughton, 30 October 1899, DDB/M/C/2/1, DBC.
108. Diary, 13 September 1898.
109. Diary, 20 July 1898.
110. Diary, 13 September 1898.
111. For Cholmondeley's continuing engagement with this controversy, see the preface to *The Hand on the* Latch, pp. xi–xiv.
112. *Red Pottage*, p. 65.
113. Hodder Williams, 'The Reader', p. 44.
114. Mary's unacknowledged precursor Wilkie Collins, for one, repeatedly backs up his fictional scenarios with details of the real events on which they are based. See for instance the appendix to *Armadale* (1866).
115. Diary, 13 September 1898.
116. Diary, 11 January 1899.
117. Diary, 1 January 1899.
118. Ibid.
119. Diary, 26 February 1899.
120. M. Cholmondeley, 'Dick's Ordeal', in L. B. Walford et al., *Life's Possibilities* (London: Mowbray, 1899), pp. 61–81.
121. Diary, 26 February 1899.
122. Contract between Mary Cholmondeley and Edward Arnold, 29 January 1899, private archive.
123. C. Brown, *Contacts: Autobiographical Reminiscences* (London: Cassell and Co., 1935), p. 111.
124. C. Brown, 'Bargaining with Writers', *Harper's Magazine*, 171 (June–November 1935), pp. 26–35, on p. 27.
125. For Brown's recollections of Cholmondeley, see Brown, *Contacts*, pp. 110–12.
126. See, for instance, '*Red Pottage* and Other Stories', *Saturday Review*, 88 (11 November 1899), pp. 622–3.
127. Diary, 2 April 1899.

128. Diary, 5 June 1899.

129. *Red Pottage*, p. 64.

130. Diary, 9 October 1899.

131. Ibid.

132. Mary Cholmondeley to Rhoda Broughton, 30 October 1899, DDB/M/C/2/1, DBC.

133. Diary, 9 October 1899.

134. Reginald Cholmondeley to Mary Cholmondeley, 30 October 1899, private archive.

135. Florence Cholmondeley to Mary Cholmondeley, [30 October 1899], private archive.

136. Lubbock, *Mary Cholmondeley*.

137. Diary, 4 November 1899.

138. Cholmondeley, 'Scrapbook', 98/46, Canterbury Museum, New Zealand, p. 16, newspaper cuttings, undated. Not traced. See also Hodder Williams, 'The Reader'.

139. Diary, 4 November 1899.

140. Mary Cholmondeley to Rhoda Broughton, 30 October 1899, DDB/M/C/2/1, DBC.

141. Mary Cholmondeley to M. Ward Cook, 28 November [1899], MS Autogr.b.11, no. 1012, Bodleian Library, University of Oxford.

142. Diary, 4 November 1899.

143. Cholmondeley, 'Scrapbook', 98/46, Canterbury Museum, New Zealand.

144. See J. Crisp (ed.), *Mary Cholmondeley 1859–1925: A Bibliography*, Victorian Fiction Research Guides, 6 (St Lucia, Queensland: Department of English, University of Queensland, 1981).

145. 'Recent Novels', *The Times*, 25 December 1899, p. 13.

146. 'Some Notes on "Red Pottage"', *Critic*, 37 (July 1900), pp. 30–1, on pp. 30, 31.

147. 'New Novels', *Nation* (New York), 70 (March 1900), p. 245.

148. For Lang's discussion of Cholmondeley's career, see A. Lang, 'At the Sign of the Ship', *Longman's Magazine*, 35:208 (February 1900), pp. 371–84.

149. 'Some Younger Reputations', *Academy*, 57 (July–December 1899), p. 689.

150. Review of *Red Pottage*, in 'New Novels', *Athenaeum*, 114 (18 November 1899), p. 683; '*Red Pottage* and Other Stories', p. 623.

151. 'Fiction', *Literature*, 5 (1899), p. 495.

152. Review of *Red Pottage*, *Dial* (Chicago, IL), 27, (16 December 1899), pp. 492–3, on p. 493.

153. '*Red Pottage*', *Literary World* (Boston, MA), 30:26 (23 December 1899), p. 450.

154. Cutting from *Sydney Daily Telegraph*, 10 December 1900, private archive. Untraced.

155. 'Some Recent Novels of Manners', *Edinburgh Review*, 192:393 (July 1900), pp. 208–28, on pp. 222–3.

156. *Spectator* (28 October 1899), pp. 612–13.

157. 'The English Clergy in Fiction', *Edinburgh Review*, 212:434 (October 1910), pp. 477–500, on p. 492.

158. Quoted in the preface to *The Hand on the Latch*, pp. xiii, xii.

159. For Cholmondeley's discussion of the controversy surrounding James Gresley, see M. Cholmondeley, 'The Skeleton in a Novelist's Cupboard', *Pall Mall Magazine*, 42 (July–December 1908), pp. 413–17.

160. Hodder Williams, 'The Reader', p. 41.

161. 'The Motive-Hunting Reader', p. 314.

162. Kent, 'A Novelist of Yesterday', p. 197.

163. Diary, 4 November 1899.

164. Mary Cholmondeley to Ernest Hodder Williams, 15 March 1900, MS 16368, Guildhall Library, London.

165. Hodder Williams, 'The Reader', p. 41.
166. Diary, 4 November 1899.

6 'Not Mine to Keep'

1. *Diana Tempest* (1909), p. 126.
2. Diary, 1 December 1896.
3. Diary, 16 May 1877.
4. Mary Cholmondeley to William Frederic Tillotson, 8 December 1899, ZBEN/4/1/33, Bolton Archives and Local Studies; Mary Cholmondeley to John Murray, 5 December 1899, MA.
5. Diary, 17 June 1877.
6. J. M. Barrie to Mary Cholmondeley, 23 January 1918, private archive.
7. Hodder Williams, 'The Reader', p. 40, describes her as being 'literally besieged' by publishers around this time.
8. Mary Cholmondeley to John Murray, 5 March 1900, MA.
9. Diary, 25 June 1900.
10. D. Barry, *The St James's Theatre: Its Strange and Complete History 1835–1957* (London: Barrie and Rockliff, 1964), pp. 224, 79. See also A. E. W. Mason, *Sir George Alexander and the St James' Theatre* (London: Macmillan, 1935).
11. Diary, 25 August 1900.
12. Mary Cholmondeley to Matthew Nathan, 13 April 1900, MSN.
13. Agreement between Mary Cholmondeley, George Alexander and Kinsey Peile, 16 April 1900, private archive.
14. Mary Cholmondeley to John Murray, 5 March 1900, MA.
15. Mary Cholmondeley to Caroline Bridgeman, 29 May [1900], 4629/1/1897/32, SA.
16. Diary, 17 August 1886, cited in Lubbock, *Mary Cholmondeley*, p. 83.
17. Diary, 25 August 1900.
18. 16 April 1900 agreement between Cholmondeley, George Alexander and Kinsey Peile with regard to the play of *Red Pottage*, private archive.
19. Edward Arnold to Mary Cholmondeley, 22 March 1900, private archive; Diary, 24 October 1900.
20. Diary, 24 October 1900.
21. Correspondence in Macmillan Archive, 364 F, BL.
22. Diary, 24 October 1900.
23. See W. E. Henley, 'Some Novels of 1899', *North American Review* 170:2 (February 1900), p. 253; article in *Sydney Daily Telegraph*, 10 December 1900. Cutting from private archive, page untraced.
24. Harper Brothers records, private archive.
25. Brown, 'Bargaining with Writers', p. 27.
26. Brown, *Contacts*, p. 111.
27. Edward Arnold to Mary Cholmondeley, 22 March 1900, private archive.
28. Brown, 'Bargaining with Writers', p. 27.
29. Diary, 24 October 1900.
30. For a recent account of the war, see D. Judd, K. T. Surridge and K. Surridge, *The Boer War* (Basingstoke: Palgrave Macmillan, 2003).
31. Diary, 27 December 1900.

32. Diary, date cut out.

33. Diary, 25 August 1900.

34. Ibid.

35. *Red Pottage*, p. 137.

36. Diary, 25 June 1900.

37. M. Cholmondeley, *Prisoners: Fast Bound in Misery and Iron* (London: Hutchinson, 1908), p. 226.

38. Diary, 25 August 1900.

39. Marriage index, Chelsea, vol. 1a, p. 766.

40. 'One sustains a first love for a long time when one does not take up with a second.' F. de La Rochefoucauld, *Réflexions ou Sentences et Maximes morales* (Paris: Garnier Frères, 1961), p. 104. My translation.

41. Diary, 25 June 1900.

42. Ibid.

43. Diary, 3 October 1901.

44. Diary, 25 August 1900.

45. Diary, 24 October 1900.

46. Ibid.

47. Mary Cholmondeley to Matthew Nathan, 13 April 1900, MSN; Diary, 25 August 1900.

48. This scene might suggest a passing nod to Wilkie Collins's play *The Frozen Deep* (1857), which was available to read as a prose narrative from 1874. Equally, the resemblance is slight enough to be coincidental.

49. *Red Pottage* (play), Department of Manuscripts, LCP 1900/16, BL, p. 115.

50. Barry, *The St James's Theatre*, p. 259.

51. Mary Cholmondeley to Matthew Nathan, 24 July 1901, MSN.

52. Mary Cholmondeley to Charles Maude, 13 April [1910], NPC.

53. A. Klauber, 'Plays and Players', *New York Times*, 13 July 1902, p. 11.

54. Arnold owned half the UK film rights. Contract between Edward Arnold and Mary Cholmondeley, 29 January 1899, private archive.

55. Mary Cholmondeley to Henry Newbolt, 15 October 1901, Wolff 1251, HRHRC; not traced; Mary Cholmondeley to Henry Newbolt, 12 February 1901, Wolff 1219, HRHRC.

56. Diary, 24 July 1901.

57. Diary, 1 March 1901.

58. Ibid. Cholmondeley noted 'I was quite delighted and I suppose if the truth must be said somewhat elated by my evening'.

59. Ibid.

60. Lubbock, *Mary Cholmondeley*, p. 91.

61. Diary, 24 July 1901.

62. Benson, *Final Edition*, p. 75.

63. Letters of E. F. Benson to Mary Cholmondeley, undated, private archive.

64. Benson, *Final Edition*, p. 75.

65. Ibid., p. 77.

66. A. Ritchie, 'Notes of Happy Things', in *Letters of Anne Thackeray Ritchie with Forty-Two Additional Letters from her Father William Makepeace Thackeray*, ed. H. Ritchie (London: John Murray, 1924), p. 264.

67. Mary Cholmondeley to unknown recipient, quoted in Benson, *Final Edition*, p. 76.

68. M. Culley, 'Introduction to *A Day at a Time: The Diary Literature of American Women, From 1764 to 1985*', in S. Smith and J. Watson (eds), *Women, Autobiography, Theory: A Reader* (Madison, WI: University of Wisconsin Press, 1998), pp. 217–21, on pp. 218–19. Benson's first novel, published by Macmillan in 1915, was called *I Pose*.

69. Diary, 3 October 1901.

70. Diary, 25 August 1900, 3 October 1901.

71. In the Diary entry for 3 October 1901, Cholmondeley remarks that he came to the house despite their estrangement.

72. Culley, 'Introduction to *A Day at a Time*', p. 220.

73. Diary, 2 December 1897. The entry says that she had read her old Diary, 'the other day'.

74. *Prisoners*, pp. 89–90.

75. Ibid., p. 156.

76. 'The Understudy', in *The Hand on the Latch*, pp. 75–93, on p. 85.

77. Mary Cholmondeley to Matthew Nathan, [spring/summer] 1922, MSN. See M. Cholmondeley, 'St Luke's Summer', *Cassell's Magazine* (1908), pp. 447–61, reprinted in *The Hand on the Latch*, pp. 94–127. In fact it became a standing joke that Uncle Tom was based on a connection of Matthew Nathan's in the Post Office. See, for instance, Mary Cholmondeley to Matthew Nathan, 14 September 1909, MSN.

78. Diary, 27 July 1901.

79. Diary, 20 August 1901.

80. Mary Cholmondeley to Henry Newbolt, 15 October 1901, Wolff 1219, HRHRC.

81. M. Cholmondeley, 'Notes on Recent Books by their Writers', *Dublin Review*, 4th series, 154:308 (January 1914), pp. 71–3.

82. Described in a retrospective entry in the Diary, 25 March 1901.

83. Undated MS entry, but from the context it can be placed in the summer of 1902.

84. Diary, previous page cut out, but between October 1902 and December 1903.

85. *Prisoners*, p. 91.

86. Undated Diary entry (preceding page cut out), between 12 October 1902 and 31 December 1903.

87. *Red Pottage*, p. 323.

88. Diary, previous page cut out, but between October 1902 and December 1903.

89. Diary, 31 December 1903, 31 December 1906.

90. Diary, 31 December 1906.

91. Diary, 31 October 1905.

92. Diary, 31 December 1906.

93. Mary Cholmondeley to John Murray, 17 October 1904, MA.

94. Brown, *Contacts*, p. 111.

95. Mary Cholmondeley to John Murray, 26 October 1901, MA.

96. Mary Cholmondeley to John Murray, 5 November 1901, MA.

97. Mary Cholmondeley to John Murray, 18 December 1902, MA.

98. Mary Cholmondeley to John Murray, 5 January 1904, MA.

99. Mary Cholmondeley to Henry Newbolt, 15 January 1902, Wolff 1213d, HRHRC; Mary Cholmondeley to John Murray, 22 November 1901, MA.

100. Mary Cholmondeley to John Murray, 27 August–1 September [1902], MA; Mary Cholmondeley to John Murray, 31 July 1902, MA.

101. *Monthly Review* (New York; 10 January 1903), pp. 15–16.

102. Review of *Moth and Rust*, in 'New Novels', *Athenaeum*, 2 (6 December 1902), p. 753.

103. Diary, 25 March 1901.

104. M. Cholmondeley, 'We Twain', in Mrs F. H. Williamson (comp.), *The Book of Beauty – Era King Edward VII* (London: Hutchinson 1902); reprinted in *Pearsons Magazine*, 15 (January–June 1903), p. 236.

105. Diary, 25 March 1901.

106. Undated Diary entry (preceding page cut out), between 12 October 1902 and 31 December 1903. Cholmondeley's letter of 24 April 1903 to John Murray (MA) was written from Preshaw, making it most likely that she was writing her novel there during this period.

107. Undated Diary entry (preceding page cut out), between 12 October 1902 and 31 December 1903.

108. Mary Cholmondeley to Edmund Gosse, 6 June 1902, Gosse Corrrespondence, Brotherton Library, University of Leeds.

109. Diary, [summer 1902].

110. Mary Cholmondeley to John Murray, 17 October 1902, MA; Mary Cholmondeley to John Murray, 20 November 1902, MA.

111. Undated copy of paper read to the Friday Club, private archive. On the Friday Club, see R. Shone, 'The Friday Club', *Burlington Magazine*, 117:866 (May 1975), pp. 278–84.

112. Philip Burne-Jones to Mary Cholmondeley, 12 April 1905, private archive; Letters of W. B. Maxwell to Mary Cholmondeley, 15 September 1903 and 14 October 1903, private archive.

113. Diary, 31 December 1903, 'The experience was not too hard. I thought it was through most of the days of this darkest year, but it was not.'

114. Undated Diary entry (preceding page cut out), between 12 October 1902 and 31 December 1903.

115. Mary Cholmondeley to Henry Newbolt, 26 December 1903, Wolff uncat., HRHRC.

116. Diary, 31 December 1903.

117. S. Gardner, 'To Her Own Hurt', *Sunday Stories*, 413 (19 March 1904), pp. 1–14.

118. Mary Cholmondeley to John Murray, 18 August 1904, MA; S. Gardner, in *Sunday Stories*, 434 (13 August 1904), p. 16.

119. Diary, 8 September 1905.

120. Mary Cholmondeley to Matthew Nathan, 12 August 1904, MSN.

121. Diary, 31 December 1904.

122. Mary Cholmondeley to Matthew Nathan 12 August 1904, MSN.

123. *Diaries of Stella Benson*, 2 September 1908, 16 September 1911, Reel 2.

124. Mary Cholmondeley to Matthew Nathan, 12 August 1904, MSN.

125. Mary Cholmondeley to Henry Newbolt, 3 September 1904, Wolff 1220a, HRHRC.

126. Mary Cholmondeley to Matthew Nathan, 12 August 1904, MSN.

127. Ibid.

128. Review of *Prisoners, Bookman*, 31 (October 1906), pp. 41–2.

129. Mary Cholmondeley to John Murray, 17 October 1904, MA.

130. Mary Cholmondeley to Matthew Nathan, 31 December 1904, MSN.

131. Diary, 31 December 1904.

132. Diary, 31 December 1906.

133. Diary, [spring 1905].

134. Diary, 8 September 1905.

135. Ibid.

136. See Crisp, *Mary Cholmondeley*.

137. Diary, 20 December 1905. See *Diaries of Stella Benson*, 6 April 1917, Reel 5.

138. Diary, 20 December 1905.
139. Ibid.
140. In another context, a note from Mary dated 1920 points out that the more bulky family papers are, the more likely they are to be destroyed, 1536/6/1, SA.
141. Diary, 10 January 1906.
142. *Under One Roof* was finally published in the New Year of 1919, and presents Hester as part of a family memoir.
143. Diary, 17 February 1906.
144. Diary, 15 July 1906.
145. Mary Cholmondeley to Matthew Nathan, 1 June 1906, MSN.
146. Mary Cholmondeley to Matthew Nathan, 27 December 1921, MSN.
147. Diary, 15 July 1906.
148. Mary Cholmondeley to Matthew Nathan, 19 October 1905, MSN.
149. Diary, 8 October 1906.
150. Diary, 17 December, 1906.
151. 'Notes on Recent Books by Their Writers', p. 71.
152. Mary Cholmondeley to Lord Aberdeen, 21 October 1906, Wolff 1213e, HRHRC.
153. Anne Thackeray Ritchie to Mary Cholmondeley, 8 July [year unknown], private archive; Florence Cholmondeley to Mary Cholmondeley, 19 September 1906, private archive.
154. Diary, 8 October 1906.
155. Diary, December 1911, no day given.
156. *The Diary of Arthur Christopher Benson*, ed. P. Lubbock (London: Hutchinson & Co., 1926), 31 January 1907, pp. 156–7.
157. Benson discusses the quarrel in detail in *Final Edition*, pp. 78–9, see p. 79.
158. For an analysis of the Net Book Agreement and its significance for the publishing world, see N. N. Feltes, *Modes of Production of Victorian Novels* (Chicago, IL: University of Chicago Press, 1989), p. 77.
159. Ibid., p. 81.
160. C. Davis, 'The Net Book Agreement', at http://apm.brookes.ac.uk/publishing/contexts/20thcent/nba.htm.
161. Mary Cholmondeley to Henry Newbolt, 23 November [1906], Wolff 1215b, HRHRC; Mary Cholmondeley to Mrs Humphry Ward, 1 November 1906, Wolff uncat., HRHRC.
162. The Diary entry for 22 December 1907 makes a specific link between bodily vigour and mental torpor. The Diary entry for 17 November 1906 makes a similar point.
163. Diary, 7 November 1897.
164. Diary, 17 December 1906.
165. Diary, 31 December 1906.
166. Mary Cholmondeley to Stella Benson, 14 September 1906, Add. 8367/5, Cambridge University Library.
167. Diary, 17 December 1906.
168. For my discussion of romantic friendship in the late nineteenth century, including its portrayal in *Red Pottage*, see C. W. de la L. Oulton, *Romantic Friendship in Victorian Literature* (Aldershot: Ashgate, 2007), pp. 139–44.
169. Diary, 31 December 1906.
170. S. Kelly, 'Lyttelton, Mary Kathleen (1856–1907)', *ODNB*.
171. Mary Cholmondeley to George Bentley, 9 January 1894, L38, BA; *National Review*, 23 (January 1894), pp. 703–5.

172. Diary, 14 April 1907.

173. Diary, 15 March 1911.

174. Diary, 14 April 1907.

175. Diary, 17 April 1907.

176. *Diaries of Stella Benson*, 25 July 1907, Reel 2; J. P. Wearing, *The London Stage 1900–1909: A Calendar of Plays and Players*, 2 vols (Meuchen, NJ: Scarecrow Press, 1981), vol. 1, p. 563.

177. *Stage* (30 May 1907), p. 9, notes simply that Diana was accompanied by Miss Irene Vanburgh. See the obituary of Richard Hugh Cholmondeley in *The Times*, 12 August 1910, p. 9e.

178. Diary, 11 June 1907.

179. Undated Diary entry (part of preceding page missing), [11 June 1907?].

180. Undated Diary entry. For Twain's friendship with Cholmondeley's uncle Reginald, see note 43 to Chapter 1.

7 'Windows Wide Open, yet Discreetly Veiled'

1. I have not been able to locate a written agreement, but see Mary Cholmondeley to Matthew Nathan, 18 May 1907, MSN.

2. Marriage index, Huddersfield, vol. 9a, p. 578.

3. *Diaries of Stella Benson*, 5 July 1908, Reel 2. For the failure to congratulate her on *Red Pottage*, see Diary, 4 November 1899.

4. Mary Cholmondeley to Matthew Nathan, 18 May 1907, MSN.

5. Preface to *The Romance of His Life*, p. 17. Two subsequent owners of the house have confirmed, independently of each other, that there is something uncanny about this bedroom (details withheld).

6. Mary Cholmondeley to Matthew Nathan, 30 December 1907, MSN.

7. Mary Cholmondeley to Hugh Walpole, 10 April 1912, Wolff uncat., HRHRC.

8. Mary Cholmondeley to Matthew Nathan, 14 June 1908, MSN.

9. Diary, 22 December 1907.

10. Ibid.

11. Untraced.

12. Diary, 22 December 1907.

13. Mary Cholmondeley to Matthew Nathan, 30 December 1907, MSN.

14. Mary Cholmondeley to Matthew Nathan, 14 June 1908, MSN.

15. Mary Cholmondeley to Matthew Nathan, 30 December 1907, MSN.

16. Mary Cholmondeley to Matthew Nathan, 9 December 1908, MSN.

17. *The Romance of His Life*, p. 19.

18. Diary, 22 December 1907.

19. Lubbock, *Mary Cholmondeley*, pp. 63, 65.

20. Sutherland, *Mrs Humphry Ward*, p. 65.

21. Diary, 22 December 1907.

22. Diary, 30 December 1908.

23. Diary, 22 December 1907. 'The Goldfish' was first published in the *Pictorial Review* (October 1920), pp. 18–19, cont. pp. 32–133, 160, 162 as 'The Refuge'.

24. Diary, 22 December 1907.

25. Diary, 31 August 1908.

26. 'The Lowest Rung', in *The Hand on the Latch*, pp. 42–74, on p. 48.

27. Ibid., p. 65.

28. Ibid., p. 50.

29. Mary Cholmondeley to Matthew Nathan' 14 June 1908, MSN.

30. Diary, 30 December 1908. The work was translated as *Les Vers et la Rouille*, trans. L. Pezet (Paris: Librairie Universelle, 1906).

31. Diary, 31 August 1908.

32. *Diaries of Stella Benson*, 20 June 1908, Reel 2.

33. S. Benson, *Living Alone* (1919; London: Macmillan, 1920), p. 176.

34. Mary Cholmondeley to Rhoda Broughton, 1 February [no year], DDB/M/C/2/24, DBC.

35. Mary Cholmondeley to Marie Belloc Lowndes, 27 February [1915 or later], Wolff uncat., HRHRC.

36. *Diaries of Stella Benson*, 14 November 1910, Reel 3; Grant, *Stella Benson*, p. 54.

37. *Diaries of Stella Benson*, 4 July 1908, 5 July 1908, Reel 2.

38. Manuscript in private archive.

39. *Diaries of Stella Benson*, 6 July 1908, Reel 2.

40. Diary, 31 August 1908.

41. Ibid.

42. Diary, 30 December 1908.

43. Diary, 21 November 1909; Mary Cholmondeley to Charles Maude, 6 May 1909, NPC.

44. Diary, 21 November 1909.

45. Mary Cholmondeley to Charles Maude, 6 July 1909, NPC; Mary Cholmondeley to Charles Maude, 6 May 1909, NPC.

46. Mary Cholmondeley to Charles Maude, 27 August 1909, NPC.

47. Mary Cholmondeley to Charles Maude, 6 July 1909, NPC.

48. Mary Cholmondeley to Charles Maude, 13 April 1910, NPC; *The Times*, 20 March 1911, p. 12.

49. M. Cholmondeley and C. Maude, *The Hand on the Latch* (play), unpaginated MS, Department of Manuscripts, LCP 1911/8, British Library.

50. M. Cholmondeley, 'Vicarious Charities', *Cornhill*, 100 (December 1909), pp. 34–43, on p. 36.

51. M. Cholmondeley, 'The Romance of His Life', *Scribner's Magazine*, 46 (August 1909), pp. 172–83.

52. Diary, 21 November 1909.

53. Article not traced. Cholmondeley, 'Scrapbook', 98/46, Canterbury Museum, New Zealand.

54. Printed page stuck in Diary.

55. *Diaries and Letters of Marie Belloc Lowndes 1911–1947*, ed. S. Lowndes (London: Chatto & Windus, 1971), p. 42.

56. See, for instance, 'Votes for Men'. On Lady Ridley, see Pamphlet: Second Annual Report, Women's Municipal Party, 1915, Members of Council 1916, S. AND P. 16/5, Women at Work Collection, Department of Printed Books, Imperial War Museum, London.

57. Sutherland, *Mrs Humphry Ward*, p. 416.

58. 'Votes for Men', p. 200.

59. Ibid., p. 211.

60. Mary Cholmondeley to Matthew Nathan, 14 March [1911], MSN.

61. *Diaries of Stella Benson*, 12 January 1909, Reel 2; Diary, 15 March 1911.

62. Diary, 15 March 1911.

63. Mary Cholmondeley to Anne Thackeray Ritchie, 22 July [1896], ATRP.

64. Diary, 15 March 1911.

65. Mary Cholmondeley to Matthew Nathan, 29 January 1911, MSN.

66. Her first known reference is in a letter of about 1909, Mary Cholmondeley to Charles Maude, 2 April [no year], NPC.

67. Ibid.

68. Diary, 15 March 1911.

69. *The Times*, 20 March 1911, p. 12.

70. 'Money Received for Books by Mary Cholmondeley', private archive.

71. *Diaries of Stella Benson*, 28 August 1911, 20 July 1911, Reel 3.

72. Diary, 15 March 1911.

73. Mary Cholmondeley to Matthew Nathan, 14 March [1911], MSN.

74. Mary Cholmondeley to *The Times*, 4 April 1911, p. 3.

75. See Mary Cholmondeley to Henry Newbolt, 4 April 1911, Wolff uncat., HRHRC.

76. Death index, Elham, December 1911, vol. 21, p. 246.

77. Diary, 2 December 1911.

78. Diary, 24 December 1911.

79. Prior, 'Lyall, Sir Alfred Comyn (1835–1911)', *ODNB*.

80. Death index, Market Drayton, vol. 6a, p. 457.

81. Lawrence mentions the encounter briefly. See D. H. Lawrence to Louise Burrows, 20 November 1909, in *The Letters of D. H. Lawrence*, ed. J. T. Boulton, 8 vols (Cambridge: Cambridge University Press, 1979–2000), vol. 1, p. 144.

82. Mary Cholmondeley to Hugh Walpole, 3 April 1912, Wolff uncat., HRHRC.

83. Ibid.

84. Mary Cholmondeley to Hugh Walpole, 4 April 1913, Wolff uncat., HRHRC.

85. Mary Cholmondeley to Hugh Walpole, 10 April 1913, Wolff uncat., HRHRC.

86. Mary Cholmondeley to Hugh Walpole, 10 April 1912, Wolff uncat., HRHRC.

87. *Diaries of Stella Benson*, 4 October 1913, Reel 4.

88. Review of *Notwithstanding*, *Bookman*, 45 (November 1913), p. 124.

89. *Diaries of Stella Benson*, 22 July 1911, Reel 3; Mary Cholmondeley to Matthew Nathan, 14 April 1913, MSN.

90. Mary Cholmondeley to Matthew Nathan, 30 December 1912, MSN.

91. Mary Cholmondeley to Matthew Nathan, 31 October 1912, MSN.

92. Mary Cholmondeley to Matthew Nathan, 31 July 1915, MSN.

93. 'Money Received for Books by Mary Cholmondeley', private archive.

94. Mary Cholmondeley to Rhoda Broughton, 29 July 1913, DDB/M/C/2/2, DBC.

95. Reginald moved to Dorton in either 1912 or 1913. He does not appear as a resident there in Kelly's Post Office Directory (published every four years) for 1911, but he is listed in 1915. With thanks to Chris Low, Centre for Buckinghamshire Studies. Cholmondeley's first known letter from Dorton was written in 1913. See Mary Cholmondeley to Rhoda Broughton, 29 July 1913, DDB/M/C/2/2, DBC.

96. Mary Cholmondeley to Rhoda Broughton, 29 July 1913, DDB/M/C/2/2, DBC.

97. The Official Lists, *The Times*, 22 March 1915, p. 4.

8 War

1. Despite her comment to Matthew Nathan that she would not write another book, on 3 March 1915 she signed a contract with the French publisher Conard for her next novel, a contract which was never fulfilled. Contract in private archive.
2. Mary Cholmondeley to Rhoda Broughton, 13 June 1914, DDB/M/C/2/3, DBC.
3. Mary Cholmondeley to Matthew Nathan, 9 June 1914, MSN.
4. 'The Soldier', written in 1914, presents death in battle as both glorious and patriotic. Another famous piece of propaganda is the 1914 poster of Kitchener pointing towards viewers, with the caption 'Your country needs you!'
5. N. Ferguson, *The Pity of War* (London: Penguin, 1998), p. 205.
6. See Mary Cholmondeley to Matthew Nathan, 14 April 1919, MSN; Mary Cholmondeley to Rhoda Broughton, 16 August 1917, DDB/M/C/2/7, DBC.
7. M. Cholmondeley, 'Polydore in England', in H. Caine (ed.), *King Albert's Book: A Tribute to the Belgian People from Representative Men and Women throughout the World* (London: Daily Telegraph 1914), pp. 62–4, on p. 62.
8. I am grateful to Hazel Basford for pointing out that no refugees could stay on the Kent coast either, for this reason.
9. She mentions in an undated letter to Matthew Nathan that she is working for the Red Cross 'for at least half an hour a day'. See MSN. As the letter is addressed from Kensington this more probably refers to her later work at Carlton House Terrace.
10. Both would work at Lady Ridley's hospital in Carlton House Terrace, and Victoria would later work with disabled soldiers.
11. 'Polydore in England', p. 64.
12. Ferguson, *The Pity of War*, p. 229.
13. The Right Hon. David Lloyd George, in Caine (ed.), *King Albert's Book*, p. 32.
14. Ibid., p. 32.
15. Mary Cholmondeley to Rhoda Broughton, 21 November 1917, DDB/M/C/2/9, DBC.
16. Mary Cholmondeley to Rhoda Broughton, 12 November 1919, DDB/M/C/2/201, DBC.
17. *Ufford Monthly Magazine* (August 1914), SU.
18. *Ufford Monthly Magazine* (September 1914), SU.
19. *Ufford Monthly Magazine* (November 1917), SU.
20. Preface to *The Romance of His Life*, p. 22.
21. *Ufford Monthly Magazine* (December 1914), SU.
22. *Ufford Monthly Magazine* (January 1915), SU.
23. *Ufford Monthly Magazine* (November 1917), SU, puts the figure at twelve. Cholmondeley records twenty-two as the final total in the Preface to *The Romance of His Life*, p. 22.
24. The Official Lists, *The Times*, 22 March 1915, p. 4.
25. Mary Cholmondeley to Matthew Nathan, 31 December 1914, MSN.
26. Mary Cholmondeley to Matthew Nathan, 31 July 1915, MSN.
27. Mary Cholmondeley to Matthew Nathan, 31 December 1914, MSN.
28. Mary Cholmondeley to Matthew Nathan, 31 July 1915, MSN.
29. Records of the Queen Alexandra Field Force Fund, 1916, B.O.2–6/6, Women at Work Collection, Department of Printed Books, Imperial War Museum.
30. Mary Cholmondeley to Rhoda Broughton, 21 November 1917, DDB/M/C/2/9, DBC.

31. B.O.8. 32/3, Women at Work Collection, Department of Printed Books, Imperial War Museum.
32. Ibid.
33. *Diaries of Stella Benson*, 30 January 1915, Reel 4, 6 July 1917, Reel 5.
34. See Grant, *Stella Benson*, pp. 60–3, 74.
35. Mary Cholmondeley to Matthew Nathan, 31 December 1914, MSN.
36. K. Mullin, 'Braddon, Mary Elizabeth (1835–1915)', *ODNB*.
37. A. Marwick, *A History of the Modern British Isles, 1914–1999* (Oxford: Blackwell, 2000), p. 36.
38. See A. F. Winnington Ingram, *The Church in Time of War: Addresses and Sermons* (London: Wells, Gardner and Co., 1915).
39. Marwick, *A History of the Modern British Isles*, pp. 7–8, 810, 131.
40. 'Notes on Recent Books by Their Writers', p. 73.
41. Ibid.
42. *Fortnightly Review* (15 February 1915), supp. 43/7, Women at Work Collection, Department of Printed Books, Imperial War Museum.
43. The Official Lists, *The Times*, 22 March 1915, p. 4.
44. *Diaries of Stella Benson*, 19 March 1915, Reel 4.
45. *Ufford Monthly Magazine* (April 1915), SU.
46. *Diaries of Stella Benson*, 21 May 1915, Reel 4.
47. Mary Cholmondeley to Matthew Nathan, 31 July 1915, MSN.
48. Magazine *YM* (16 April 1915), B.0.3.10/109, Women at Work Collection, Department of Printed Books, Imperial War Museum.
49. Mary Cholmondeley to Matthew Nathan, 31 July 1917, MSN.
50. *Diaries of Stella Benson*, 24 May 1915, Reel 4.
51. Lubbock, *Mary Cholmondeley*, p. 30.
52. *Diaries of Stella Benson*, 14 July 1915, Reel 4.
53. Ibid., 19 September 1915, Reel 4.
54. Benson, *I Pose* (1915; London: Macmillan, 1930), p. 198.
55. Ibid., pp. 158–9.
56. *Diaries of Stella Benson*, 23 September 1915, Reel 4.
57. Ibid., 29 December 1916, Reel 5.
58. Ibid., 7 March 1916, Reel 5. See, for instance, 'The End of the Dream', in *The Romance of His Life*, pp. 216–52, on p. 231.
59. Mary Cholmondeley to Rhoda Broughton, 2 November [1915?], DDB/M/C/2/4, DBC. With thanks to the Costume Museum, Bath, for provisionally dating this letter.
60. Mary Cholmondeley to Matthew Nathan, 19 October 1915, MSN.
61. Mary Cholmondeley to Rhoda Broughton, 2 November [1915?], DDB/M/C/2/4, DBC.
62. *Ufford Monthly Magazine* (January 1916), SU.
63. Mary Cholmondeley to Rhoda Broughton, 21 November 1917, DDB/M/C/2/9, DBC; *Diaries of Stella Benson*, 5 and 8 July 1916, Reel 5.
64. See, for instance, Mary Cholmondeley to Rhoda Broughton, 21 November 1917, DDB/M/C/2/9, DBC.
65. A. D. Hall, *English Farming Past and Present* (n.p.: Read Books, 2007), p. 397.
66. *Ufford Monthly Magazine* (August 1916), SU.
67. *Ufford Monthly Magazine* (September 1916), SU.

68. H. Joseph, 93rd Field Ambulance, to Mary Cholmondeley, 26 November 1916, private archive.

69. M. Cholmondeley, 'Warp and Woof', *Englishwoman*, 96 (December 1916), pp. 227–35, on p. 232.

70. Ibid., p. 232.

71. S. Hynes, *A War Imagined: The First World War and English Culture* (London: Bodley Head, 1990), p. 100.

72. Mary Cholmondeley to Rhoda Broughton, 17 June [1817], DDB/M/C/2/5, DBC.

73. Preface to *The Romance of His Life*, p. 24.

74. Mary Cholmondeley to Rhoda Broughton, 14 July 1917, DDB/M/C/2/6, DBC.

75. Mary Cholmondeley to Rhoda Broughton, 16 August 1917, DDB/M/C/2/7, DBC.

76. Ibid.

77. LDBRC: 0060A, British Red Cross Museum and Archives.

78. *Diaries of Stella Benson*, 11 September 1916, Reel 5.

79. Ibid., 23 February 1917, 29 September 1917, Reel 5.

80. See note 95 to Chapter 7.

81. Mary Cholmondeley to Rhoda Broughton, 20 September 1917, DDB/M/C/2/8, DBC.

82. Ibid.

83. Mary Cholmondeley to Rhoda Broughton, 21 November 1917, DDB/M/C/2/9, DBC.

84. P. Fussell, *The Great War and Modern Memory* (Oxford: Oxford University Press, 1975), p. 175.

85. Mary Cholmondeley to Rhoda Broughton, 21 November 1917, DDB/M/C/2/9, DBC.

86. M. Corbett, 'Literary Domesticity and Women Writers' Subjectivities', in Smith and Watson (eds), *Women, Autobiography, Theory*, pp. 255–61, on p. 257.

87. *Under One Roof*, pp. 33, 30, 66–7.

88. Ibid., pp. 44, 47.

89. Mary Cholmondeley to Richard Bentley, 20 April 1895, 140, Add. MSS 46623–45, BL.

90. *Under One Roof*, p. 48.

91. Diary, 16 May 1877.

92. Diary, 24 December 1875 and subsequent days under same entry.

93. *Under One Roof*, p. 47.

94. Mary Cholmondeley to George Bentley, 14 December 1894, L51, BA.

95. *Under One Roof*, p. 45.

96. Ibid., pp. 50, 51.

97. Ibid., p. xii.

98. Ibid., p. 72.

99. Ibid., p. xiv.

100. *Diaries of Stella Benson*, 14 April 1918, Reel 5.

101. Mary Cholmondeley to Hugh Walpole, 10 February 1918, Wolff uncat., HRHRC.

102. See Mary Cholmondeley to Rhoda Broughton, 8 August 1918, DDB/M/C/2/11, DBC.

103. 'How to be Happy on Railway Journeys', *Eton Red Cross Magazine* (1 December 1917), p. 100.

104. Diary, 25 June 1900; Mary Cholmondeley to Rhoda Broughton, 17 June [1918], DDB/M/C/2/5, DBC. This phrase was widely used from 1914, after the publication of H. G. Wells, *The War that Will End War* (Leeds: Duffield and Company, 1914).

105. Mary Cholmondeley to Rhoda Broughton, 17 June [1918], DDB/M/C/2/5, DBC.

106. Mary Cholmondeley to Rhoda Broughton, 22 July 1918, DDB/M/C/2/10, DBC.

107. Mary Cholmondeley to Rhoda Broughton, 8 August 1918, DDB/M/C/2/11, DBC.

108. Ibid.

109. Mary Cholmondeley to Rhoda Broughton, 18 November 1918, DDB/M/C/2/13, DBC.

110. Mary Cholmondeley to Rhoda Broughton, 5 October 1918, DDB/M/C/2/13, DBC.

111. Mary Cholmondeley to Rhoda Broughton, 18 November 1918, DDB/M/C/2/13, DBC.

112. Ibid.

113. Ibid.

9 'I Dont Think I was Ever Brave'

1. Mary Cholmondeley to Rhoda Broughton, 18 November 1918, DDB/M/C/2/13, DBC.

2. Preface to *The Romance of His Life*, p. 22.

3. Mary Cholmondeley to Rhoda Broughton, 5 October 1918, DDB/M/C/2/12, DBC.

4. Mary Cholmondeley to Rhoda Broughton, 18 February 1918, DDB/M/C/2/14, DBC.

5. Mary Cholmondeley to Rhoda Broughton, 27 January 1919, DDB/M/C/2/18, DBC.

6. E. M. Delafield, *The War Workers* (London: William Heinemann, 1918), p. 59.

7. Mary Cholmondeley to Rhoda Broughton, 18 February 1919, DDB/M/C/2/14, DBC.

8. Mary Cholmondeley to Rhoda Broughton, 18 February 1919, DDB/M/C/2/18, DBC.

9. See Sutherland, *Mrs Humphry Ward*, p. 194.

10. Lubbock, *Mary Cholmondeley*, p. 87.

11. Mary Cholmondeley to Rhoda Broughton, 18 February 1919, DDB/M/C/2/14, DBC.

12. Mary Cholmondeley to Rhoda Broughton, 1 April 1919, DDB/M/C/2/15, DBC; Death index, Kensington, June 1919, vol. 1a, p. 71.

13. Death index, Isle of Wight, March 1919, vol. 2b, p. 1179.

14. Mary Cholmondeley to Rhoda Broughton, 1 April 1919, DDB/M/C/2/15, DBC; E. MacLeod Walls, 'Lubbock, Percy (1879–1965)', *ODNB*.

15. Mary Cholmondeley to Rhoda Broughton, 1 April 1919, DDB/M/C/2/15, DBC.

16. *Diaries of Stella Benson*, 23 September 1915, Reel 4.

17. Mary Cholmondeley to Rhoda Broughton, 20 May 1919, DDB/M/C/2/17, DBC.

18. K. Flint, 'Broughton, Rhoda (1840–1920)', *ODNB*.

19. 'Money Received for Books by Mary Cholmondeley', private archive.

20. 'The Dark Cottage', *Pears Christmas Annual*, 29 (December 1919), pp. 8–11, reprinted in *The Romance of His Life*, pp. 55–82, see pp. 55, 57.

21. Mary Cholmondeley to Rhoda Broughton, 20 May 1919, DDB/M/C/2/17, DBC.

22. Ibid.

23. Mary Cholmondeley to Rhoda Broughton, 20 June 1919, DB/M/C/2/19, DBC.

24. Mary Cholmondeley to Rhoda Broughton, 20 May 1919, DDB/M/C/2/17, DBC.

25. Mary Cholmondeley to Rhoda Broughton, 21 September 1919, DDB/M/C/2/20, DBC.

26. 'Her Murderer', in *The Romance of His Life*, pp. 173–99, on 176.

27. 'The Dark Cottage', p. 79.

28. Mary Cholmondeley to Rhoda Broughton, 12 November 1919, DDB/M/C/2/21, DBC.

29. Mary Cholmondeley to Rhoda Broughton, 5 December 1919, DDB/M/C/2/22, DBC.

30. Mary Cholmondeley to Rhoda Broughton, 20 February [1920], DDB/M/C/2/25, DBC.

31. Ibid.

32. Mary Cholmondeley to Rhoda Broughton, [9] February [1920], DDB/M/C/2/24, DBC.

33. Article on Mary Cholmondeley, *New York Press*, 11 February 1900, p. 15.

34. Death index, Headington, vol. 3a, p. 985.

35. Address to the Friday Club, undated, private archive. Tennyson's quote is untraced.

36. Address to the Friday Club, undated, private archive.

37. Grant, *Stella Benson*, p. 301.

38. 'The Goldfish', in *The Romance of His Life*, pp. 109–45, on p. 138.

39. Lubbock, *Mary Cholmondeley*, p. 95.

40. Mary Cholmondeley to Matthew Nathan, 1 November 1920, MSN.

41. Mary Cholmondeley to Matthew Nathan, 22 May 1921, MSN.

42. Ibid.

43. Lubbock, *Mary Cholmondeley*, p. 96.

44. Death Certificate, 16 July 1925, DYB 610614, National Archives, Kew; Mary Cholmondeley to Matthew Nathan, 28 September 1922, MSN.

45. Mary Cholmondeley to Matthew Nathan, [spring/summer 1922], MSN.

46. Mary Cholmondeley to Matthew Nathan, 23 November 1923, MSN.

47. Mary Cholmondeley to Matthew Nathan, 6 July 1924, MSN. See W. Maxwell, *Time Gathered: Autobiography* (London: Hutchinson, 1937), p. 286.

48. Mary Cholmondeley to Matthew Nathan, 2 November 1924, MSN.

49. Ibid.

50. Brown, *Contacts*, p. 111.

51. Obituary of Mary Cholmondeley, *The Times*, 17 July 1925, p. 19.

52. *The Times*, 17 July 1925, p. 19.

53. Jane Lindsay to Matthew Nathan, 25 January 1934, MSN.

WORKS CITED

Cholmondeley's Published Works (various editions, in order of first publication)

'Lisle's Courtship', *Household Words*, 36 (May 1884), pp. 501–7.

The Danvers Jewels (London: Richard Bentley and Son, [1887]).

Sir Charles Danvers, 2 vols (London: Richard Bentley and Son, 1889).

'The Cottager at Home', *Murray's Magazine*, 6 (July–December 1889), pp. 238–50.

Diana Tempest, 3 vols (London: Richard Bentley & Son, 1893).

Diana Tempest (1893; New York: Appleton, 1900).

Diana Tempest (1893; London: Macmillan, 1909).

'A Latter-Day Prophet', *Temple Bar*, 103 (1894), pp. 479–91.

'Waste', *Monthly Packet*, 527 (1 January 1895), pp. 81–90.

'A Day in Teneriffe', *Monthly Packet*, 92 (November 1896), pp. 492–501.

'A Second Day in Teneriffe', *Monthly Packet*, 92 (December 1896), pp. 615–23.

A Devotee: An Episode in the Life of a Butterfly (London: Edward Arnold, 1897).

Red Pottage (1899; London: Virago, 1986).

'Dick's Ordeal', in L. B. Walford et al., *Life's Possibilities* (London: Mowbray, 1899), pp. 61–81.

The Danvers Jewels and Sir Charles Danvers (London and New York: Harper Bros, [1900]).

'A Day in Teneriffe', *Chatauquan*, 33 (April–September 1901), pp. 591–7.

'An Art in its Infancy', *Monthly Review*, 3 (June 1901), pp. 79–90.

Moth and Rust together with 'Geoffrey's Wife and 'The Pitfall' (London: Murray, 1902).

'We Twain', in Mrs F. H. Williamson (comp.), *The Book of Beauty – Era King Edward VII* (London: Hutchinson 1902); reprinted in *Pearsons Magazine*, 15 (January–June 1903), p. 236.

Les Vers et la Rouille, trans. L. Pezet (Paris: Librairie Universelle, 1906).

'In the Small Hours', *Lady's Realm*, 23 (December 1907), pp. 129–33.

Prisoners: Fast Bound in Misery and Iron (London: Hutchinson, 1908).

'The Motive-Hunting Reader and the Theory of Malicious Origins', *Bookman*, 28:4 (1908), pp. 313–17.

'The Skeleton in a Novelist's Cupboard', *Pall Mall Magazine*, 42 (July–December 1908). pp. 413–17.

'The Lowest Rung', *Windsor Magazine*, 28 (August 1908), pp. 264–74.

'Votes for Men', *Cornhill*, 100 (July 1909), pp. 34–43, reprinted in *The Romance of His Life and Other Romances* (London: John Murray, 1921), pp. 200–15.

'The Romance of His Life', *Scribner's Magazine*, 46 (August 1909), pp. 172–83.

The Hand on the Latch (New York: Dodd Mead & Co., 1909).

'Vicarious Charities', *Cornhill*, 100 (December 1909), pp. 34–43.

Moth and Rust (London, New York and Toronto: Hodder and Stoughton, 1912).

After All [American title of *Nothwithstanding*] (New York: Appleton, 1913).

'Notes on Recent Books by Their Writers', *Dublin Review*, 4th series, 154:308 (January 1914), pp. 71–3.

'Polydore in England', in H. Caine (ed.), *King Albert's Book: A Tribute to the Belgian People from Representative Men and Women throughout the World* (London: Daily Telegraph 1914), pp. 62–4.

'Warp and Woof', *Englishwoman*, 96 (December 1916), pp. 227–35.

'How to be Happy on Railway Journeys', *Eton Red Cross Magazine* (1 December 1917), p. 100.

Under One Roof: A Family Record (London: John Murray, 1918).

'The Dark Cottage', *Pears Christmas Annual*, 29 (December 1919), pp. 8–11.

'Personalities and Powers: The Late Miss Rhoda Broughton', *Time and Tide* (27 August 1920), pp. 323–5.

'The Refuge' [American title of 'The Goldfish'], *Pictorial Review* (October 1920), pp. 18–19, 132, 133, 160, 162.

The Romance of His Life and Other Romances (London: Murray, 1921).

Reviews

The Danvers Jewels

    'Our Booking Office', *Punch* (22 October 1887), p. 192a.

    'Some Recent Novels of Manners', *Edinburgh Review*, 192:393 (July 1900), pp. 208–28.

Sir Charles Danvers

    'Novels of the Week', *Athenaeum* (9 November 1889), p. 632.

    Graphic (30 November 1889), p. 658.

    'Novels', *Saturday Review* (7 December 1889), p. 651.

    Murray's Magazine, 1 (1890), p. 287.

    'Some Recent Novels of Manners', *Edinburgh Review*, 192:393 (July 1900), pp. 208–28.

Diana Tempest

'New Novels', *Academy*, 44 (July–December 1893), pp. 563–4.

'Novel Notes', *Bookman* (December 1893), p. 87.

'Novels', *Saturday Review*, 76 (9 December 1893), pp. 653–4.

Dial (1 January 1894), p. 19.

'Recent Novels', *The Times*, 12 January 1894, p. 15.

Lang, A., 'At the Sign of the Ship', *Longmans*, 23 (January 1894), pp. 322–30.

'Two Clever Novels – Very Unlike', *Monthly Packet* (1 February 1894), p. 246.

'News Notes', *Bookman*, 32:6 (May 1894), pp. 37–8.

'Some Recent Novels of Manners', *Edinburgh Review*, 192:393 (July 1900), pp. 208–28.

A Devotee

Bookman (New York) (September 1897), p. 76.

Red Pottage

Spectator (28 October 1899), pp. 612–13.

'*Red Pottage* and Other Stories', *Saturday Review*, 88 (11 November 1899), pp. 622–3.

'New Novels', *Athenaeum*, 114 (18 November 1899), p. 683.

Review of *Red Pottage*, *Dial* (Chicago, IL), 27 (16 December 1899), pp. 492–3.

'Fiction', *Literature*, 5 (1899), p. 495.

'*Red Pottage*', *Literary World* (Boston, MA), 30:26 (23 December 1899), p. 450.

'Recent Novels', *The Times*, 25 December 1899, p. 13.

Henley, W. E., 'Some Novels of 1899', *North American Review*, 170:2 (February 1900), p. 253.

'New Novels', *Nation* (New York), 70 (March 1900), p. 245.

The Guardian, 11 April 1900, p. 528.

'Some Notes on "Red Pottage"', *Critic*, 37 (July 1900), pp. 30–1.

'Some Recent Novels of Manners', *Edinburgh Review*, 192:393 (July 1900), pp. 208–28.

'The Literary Week', *Academy*, 59 (July–December 1900), p.43.

'The English Clergy in Fiction', *Edinburgh Review*, 212:434 (October 1910), pp. 477–500.

'Dick's Ordeal'

Literature, December Supplement 5 (9 December 1899), p. 12.

Moth and Rust

'Fiction', *Academy and Literature*, 63 (June–December 1902), pp. 577–63.

'New Novels', *Athenaeum*, 2 (6 December 1902), p. 753.

Monthly Review (New York; 10 January 1903), pp. 15–16.

Prisoners: Fast Bound in Misery and Iron

'Literature: The Bonds of Fate', *Academy*, 71 (July–December 1906), p. 243.

Bookman, 31 (October 1906), pp. 41–2.

'Insular Fiction', *Edinburgh Review*, 205:419 (January 1907), p. 192.

The Hand on the Latch (dramatic version)

The Times, 20 March 1911, p. 12. [see 6 March 1911, p. 10; 13 March 1911, p. 10, for advance notice of play]

Stage (23 March 1911), p. 18.

Notwithstanding

Bookman, 45 (November 1913), p. 124.

Under One Roof

'The Bookman's Table', *Bookman*, 54 (May 1918), p. 76.

Archives and Manuscripts

Abbott, M., *Preserve their Memory – Shrewsbury Diocesan Priests (Deceased) 1850–2001*, unpaginated in-house publication of the Diocese of Shrewsbury.

Bodleian Library, University of Oxford

MS Autogr.b.11, no. 1012.

MS Nathan 132.

Bolton Archives and Local Studies, ZBEN/4/1/33.

British Library

Bentley Archive, Mic.B.53/177.

M. Cholmondeley, *Red Pottage* (play), unpaginated MS, Department of Manuscripts, LCP 1900/16.

M. Cholmondeley and C. Maude, *The Hand on the Latch* (play), unpaginated MS, Department of Manuscripts, LCP 1911/8.

Macmillan Archive, 364 F.

British Red Cross Museum and Archives, LDBRC: 0060A.

Brotherton Library, University of Leeds, Gosse Corrrespondence.

Cambridge University Library, Add. 8367/5.

Canterbury Museum, New Zealand

'G. R. Macdonald Dictionary of Canterbury Biographies', c294.

Mary Cholmondely, 'Scrapbook, relating to Family 1864–1920, 1936, 1940', Manuscripts Collection, 98/46.

Cheshire Records Office, Delves Broughton Collection.

Eton College Library, Anne Thackeray Ritchie Papers.

Guildhall Library, London, MS 16368.

Harry Ransom Humanities Research Center, University of Texas at Austin, Wolff Collection.

Imperial War Museum, London, Women at Work Collection, Department of Printed Books.

London Metropolitan University, Women's Library, Autograph Letter Collection: Letters of Rosa May Billinghurst and Dr Alice Ker.

National Archives, Kew

Census 1851, 1861.

DYB 622811.

National Art Library, London, 'Water-colour sketches of Rome, Bruges, Scotland, Hertfordshire, etc: by Miss Victoria Cholmondeley and Sir William Baillie-Hamilton', Catalogue, Modern Gallery.

National Library of Ireland, MS 8600(3).

National Library of Scotland, Murray Archive.

National Library of Wales, Aberystwyth, Pitchford MSS.

National Railway Museum, York, *Bradshaw's General Railway and Steam Navigation Guide for Great Britain and Ireland* (November 1890).

Princeton University Library, Manuscripts Division, Department of Rare Books and Special Collections, Nancy Price Correspondence (C0642).

Private Archives

Curtis Brown agency, Correspondence with various members of the Cholmondeley family.

Diaries and miscellaneous papers of Mary Cholmondeley.

Rugby School Archives, Rugby School Registers 1675–1842 (1901) and 1842–74 (1903).

Shropshire Archives, SA 1536: Condover Hall and its successive owners.

Southport General Records Office, registers of birth, marriage and death.

Suffolk Record Office, *Ufford Monthly Magazine* (1908–17), S Ufford 283.

Primary Sources

Anderson, J. K, 'On the Treatment of Spasmodic Asthma by the Subcutaneous Injection of Morphia', *Practioner*, 15:89 (November 1875), pp. 321–2.

Anon., 'Some Younger Reputations', *Academy*, 57 (July–December 1899), p. 689.

—, 'An Authoress's Childhood', *Woman's Weekly* (16 June 1900), p. 2.

—, 'Plays and Players', *New York Times*, 13 July 1902, p. 11.

—, Obituary of Charles Cholmondeley, *The Times*, 26 January 1897, p. 5.

—, Obituary of Richard Hugh Cholmondeley, *The Times*, 12 August 1910, p. 9e.

—, Obituary of Mary Cholmondeley, *The Times*, 17 July 1925, p. 19.

Arnold, E., 'Rhoda Broughton as I Knew Her', *Fortnightly Review*, 108:644 (August 1920), pp. 262–278.

Bagshaw's Gazeteer of Shropshire (n.p., 1851).

Barrett Browning, E., *Last Poems* (London: Chapman and Hall, 1862).

Barrie, J. M., *Echoes of the War* (London: Hodder and Stoughton, 1918).

Benson, A. C., *The Diary of Arthur Christopher Benson*, ed. P. Lubbock (London: Hutchinson & Co., 1926).

Benson, E. F., *Final Edition: An Informal Autobiography* (London: Longman's, 1940).

Benson, S., *I Pose* (1915; London: Macmillan, 1930).

—, *Living Alone* (1919; London: Macmillan, 1920).

—, *Women, Writing and Travel: Diaries of Stella Benson, 1902–1933 from Cambridge University Library*, 10 microfilm reels (Marlborough: Adam Matthew Publications, 2005).

Brown, C., *Contacts: Autobiographical Reminiscences* (London: Cassell and Co., 1935).

—, 'Bargaining with Writers', *Harper's Magazine*, 171 (June–November 1935), pp. 26–35.

Burke's Genealogical and Heraldic History of the Landed Gentry, ed. P. Townend, 18th edn, 3 vols (London: Burke's Peerage, 1965–72).

Caine, H. (ed.), *King Albert's Book: A Tribute to the Belgian People from Representative Men and Women throughout the World* (London: Daily Telegraph, 1914).

Cholmondeley, E., 'A Day of my Life in Chambers. By a Briefless Barrister', *Cornhill Magazine*, 58:11 (July 1888), pp. 1–12.

Cholmondeley, T., *Ultima Thule; or Thoughts Suggested by a Residence in New Zealand* (London: Chapman, 1854).

Crockford's Clerical Directory (London: Horace Cox, 1876–96).

Delafield, E. M., *The War Workers* (London: William Heinemann, 1918).

Dickens, C., *The Letters of Charles Dickens: The Pilgrim Edition, 1820–1839*, ed. M. House, G. Storey, K. M. Tillotson and W. J. Carlton (Oxford: Oxford University Press, 1982).

Draznin, Y., 'Did Victorian Medicine Crush Olive Schreiner's Creativity?', *Historian*, 47:2 (February 1985), pp. 195–207.

Gardner, S., 'To Her Own Hurt', *Sunday Stories*, 413 (19 March 1904), pp. 1–14.

—, in *Sunday Stories*, 434 (13 August 1904), p. 16.

Gilman, C. P., 'Why I Wrote the Yellow Wallpaper', in A. Richardson (ed.), *Women Who Did: Stories by Men and Women, 1890–1914* (London: Penguin, 2002), pp. 398–9.

Grand, S., 'The New Aspect of the Woman Question', *North American Review*, 158 (March 1894), pp. 270–6.

Heber, R., et al., *The Heber Letters 1783–1832*, ed. R. H. Cholmondeley (London: Batchworth Press, 1950).

Hodder Williams, E., 'The Reader: Mary Cholmondeley', *Bookman*, 18 (May 1900), pp. 40–7.

Kent, M., 'A Novelist of Yesterday', *Cornhill*, 151 (February 1935), pp. 194–200.

Klauber, A., 'Plays and Players', *New York Times*, 13 July 1902, p. 11.

Lang, A., 'At the Sign of the Ship', *Longman's Magazine*, 35:208 (February 1900), pp. 371–84.

La Rochefoucauld, F. de, *Réflexions ou Sentences et Maximes morales* (Paris: Garnier Frères, 1961).

Lawrence, D. H., *The Letters of D. H. Lawrence*, ed. J. T. Boulton, 8 vols (Cambridge: Cambridge University Press, 1979–2000).

Linton, E. L., 'The Girl of the Period', originally published in the *Saturday Review* (14 March 1868), pp. 339–40.

Lowndes, M. B., *Diaries and Letters of Marie Belloc Lowndes 1911–1947*, ed. S. Lowndes (London: Chatto & Windus, 1971).

Lubbock, P., *Mary Cholmondeley: A Sketch from Memory* (London: Jonathan Cape, 1928).

Maxwell, W., *Time Gathered: Autobiography* (London: Hutchinson, 1937).

Miller, Mrs F., 'How I Made my First Speech', *Woman's Signal* (4 January 1894), p. 5.

Mitchell, S. W., *Fat and Blood* (Philadelphia, PA: J. B. Lippincott and Co., 1885).

Park, R., 'Some Cases in which Morphia has been Administered in Large Doses Hypodermically; with Remarks', *Practitioner*, 24 (1880), pp. 424–33.

Playfair, W. S., *An Introduction to a Discussion on the Systematic Treatment of Aggravated Hysteria and Certain Allied Forms of Neurasthenic Disease* (London: Smith Elder & Co., 1883).

Ritchie, A., *Letters of Anne Thackeray Ritchie with Forty-Two Additional Letters from her Father William Makepeace Thackeray*, ed H. Ritchie (London: John Murray, 1924).

Salter, H. H., *On Asthma: Its Pathology and Treatment*, 2nd edn (London: John Churchill and Sons, 1868).

Somerville, H., 'Primum Vivere, Deine Philosophari', *Punch* (25 January 1904), p. 69.

Tennyson, A., *The Poetical Works of Alfred Tennyson, Poet Laureate, Etc: Complete in One Volume* (Boston, MA: Ticknor and Fields, 1857).

Thom, J. H., *Laws After the Mind of Christ* (London: Kegan Paul, Trench & Co., 1883).

Wells, H. G., *The War that Will End War* (Leeds: Duffield and Company, 1914).

Wharton, E., *A Backward Glance: An Autobiography* (1934; London: Everyman, 1993).

Winnington Ingram, A. F., *The Church in Time of War: Addresses and Sermons* (London: Wells, Gardner and Co., 1915).

Secondary Sources

Barry, D., *The St James's Theatre: Its Strange and Complete History 1835–1957* (London: Barrie and Rockliff, 1964).

Bassuk, E. L., 'The Rest Cure: Repetition or Resolution of Victorian Women's Conflicts?', *Poetics Today*, 6:1/2 (1985), pp. 245–57.

Cannadine, D., *Aspects of Aristocracy: Grandeur and Decline in Modern Britain* (New Haven, CT, and London: Yale University Press, 1994).

Colby, V., '"Devoted Amateur": Mary Cholmondeley and *Red Pottage*', *Essays in Criticism*, 20:2 (1970) pp. 213–28.

Corbett, M., 'Literary Domesticity and Women Writers' Subjectivities', in S. Smith and J. Watson (eds), *Women, Autobiography, Theory: A Reader* (Madison, WI: University of Wisconsin Press, 1998), pp. 255–61.

Crisp, J., *Mary Cholmondeley 1859–1925: A Bibliography*, Victorian Fiction Research Guides 6 (St Lucia, Queensland: Department of English, University of Queensland, 1981).

Culley, M., 'Introduction to *A Day at a Time: The Diary Literature of American Women, From 1764 to 1985*', in S. Smith and J. Watson (eds), *Women, Autobiography, Theory: A Reader* (Madison, WI: University of Wisconsin Press, 1998), pp. 217–21.

Edwards, E., *A History of Bournemouth: Growth of a Victorian Town* (Sussex: Phillimore, 1981).

Feltes, N. N., *Modes of Production of Victorian Novels* (Chicago, IL: University of Chicago Press, 1989).

Ferguson, N, *The Pity of War* (London: Penguin, 1998).

Fussell, P., *The Great War and Modern Memory* (Oxford: Oxford University Press, 1975).

Grant, J. *Stella Benson: A Biography* (London: Macmillan, 1987).

Hall, A. D., *English Farming Past and Present* (n.p.: Read Books, 2007).

Harris, J., *Private Lives, Public Spirit: Britain 1870–1914* (London: Penguin, 1993).

Hoppen, T. H., *The Mid-Victorian Generation* (Oxford: Clarendon Press, 1998).

Hynes, S., *A War Imagined: The First World War and English Culture* (London: Bodley Head, 1990).

Jordison, S., 'Bestseller versus Groundbreaker', *Guardian*, 21 April 2007, Supplement: 'Time Lines: 50 Books that Defined their Era', p. 3.

Judd, D., K. T. Surridge and K. Surridge, *The Boer War* (Basingstoke: Palgrave Macmillan, 2003).

Marwick, A., *A History of the Modern British Isles, 1914–1999* (Oxford: Blackwell, 2000).

Mason, A. E. W., *Sir George Alexander and the St James' Theatre* (London: Macmillan, 1935).

Mothershaw, G., *St Luke's Church, Hodnet: A Brief History* (n.p., 2005).

Nelson, C. C. (ed.), *A New Woman Reader: Fiction, Articles and Drama of the 1890s* (Plymouth: Broadview Press, 2001).

Oppenheim, J., *Shattered Nerves: Doctors, Patients, and Depression in Victorian England* (New York and Oxford: Oxford University Press, 1991).

Oulton, C. W. de la L., *Romantic Friendship in Victorian Literature* (Aldershot: Ashgate, 2007).

Oxford Dictionary of National Biography, ed. H. C. G. Matthew and B. Harrison (Oxford: Oxford University Press, 2004).

Peterson, L. H., 'The Role of Periodicals in the (Re)Making of Mary Cholmondeley as New Woman Writer', *Media History*, 7 (2001), pp. 37–44.

Schaffer, T., '"Nothing but Foolscap and Ink": Inventing the New Woman', in A. Richardson and C. Willis (eds), *The New Woman in Fiction and Fact, Fin-de-Siècle Feminisms* (Basingstoke: Palgrave 2001), pp. 39–52.

Shone, R., 'The Friday Club', *Burlington Magazine*, 117:866 (May 1975), pp. 278–84.

Showalter, E., *Sexual Anarchy: Gender and Culture at the Fin de Siècle* (London: Virago, 1992).

Sutherland, J., *Mrs Humphry Ward: Eminent Victorian, Pre-Eminent Edwardian* (Oxford: Oxford University Press, 1990).

Torquay: Queen of the Watering Places, Local Studies Education Series (Torbay: Torbay Library Services, n.d.).

Wachter, P., *Introduction to Platonics* (Bristol: Thoemmes Press, 1995).

Watt, M., *The History of the Parson's Wife* (London: Faber, 1943).

Wearing, J. P., *The London Stage 1900–1909: A Calendar of Plays and Players*, 2 vols (Meuchen, NJ: Scarecrow Press, 1981).

Ziegler, S., '"How Far am I Responsible?" Women and Morphimania in Late-Nineteenth-Century Britain', *Victorian Studies*, 8:1 (Autumn 2005), pp. 59–81.

Figure 1. Mary Heber. By permission of Charles Plowden.

Figure 2. Hodnet Rectory. Watercolour by Hester Cholmondeley. Private archive.

Figure 3. Mary Cholmondeley as a child. Private archive.

Figure 4. Mary Cholmondeley as a young girl. Private archive.

Figure 5. Miniature of Mary Cholmondeley. Private archive.

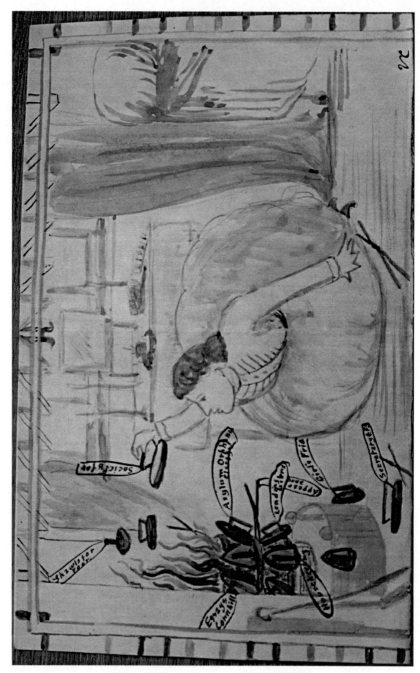

Figure 6. 'Too many irons in the fire, Mary'.
Watercolour by Victoria Cholmondeley (1885). Private archive.

Figure 7. Signed photograph of Mary Cholmondeley. Private archive.

Figure 8. Unattributed photograph of Mary Cholmondeley. Private archive.

Figure 9. Mary Cholmondeley. Publicity photo, used in the Appleton edition of *Diana Tempest* (1900). By permisson of Linda Peterson.

Figure 10. 'Mary Cholmondeley as she really is'. Used as frontispiece in Lubbock, *Mary Cholmondeley* (1928). Courtesy of Yale University Library.

Figure 11. Poster for Disabled Servicemen's Exhibition (1919). By permission of
Liverpool Records Office.

INDEX